C000165817

NEWCASTLE'S
50 GREATEST GAMES

NEWCASTLE'S
50 GREATEST GAMES

DAVID POTTER

First published in Great Britain in 2010 by The Derby Books Publishing Company Limited, 3 The Parker Centre, Derby, DE21 4SZ.

ISBN 978-1-85983-864-8

Printed and bound in Rzeszowskie Zakłady Graficzne S.A., Poland.

CONTENTS

ACKNOWLEDGEMENTS

This book owes a great deal to the extensive writings of Paul Joannou, whose works on Newcastle United are astounding in their depth, analysis and readability. To a lesser extent, the works of Dylan Younger and John Gibson must also be acknowledged.

On a personal level, I must thank my friends Richard Grant, John McCue and Phil Jones for their constant backing and encouragement, as indeed I must thank my wife for her tolerance and understanding. Various other people helped me out at different points – Mick Edmondson of The Back Page (a truly excellent bookshop), Hannah Wood of Leeds, who looked up a point of detail for me, and the professional and helpful staff of Newcastle Central Library and the National Library of Scotland in Edinburgh. Special thanks are due to Marjorie Smith of Cleadon village, a lady who knows nothing about football but who is a good friend of my wife and allowed us to stay in her house during my countless visits to see the Magpies. I must also thank my late father, Angus Potter, who, once he had finished talking about Celtic and Jimmy McGrory, would immediately start on about Newcastle United and Hughie Gallacher.

To these people I owe a great deal and I hope I have done something to tell the world what a massive thing Newcastle United has been and will continue to be in so many people's lives.

INTRODUCTION

The history of Newcastle United needs to be constantly told. It has already been done so on many occasions by better writers than I, but it is still a fascinating and ultimately very sad story. No one needs reminding that it is now well over half a century since any English honour was brought to Tyneside, and that although a European honour was landed in 1969, it was very much the second-rate European trophy called the Inter-Cities Fairs Cup, a trophy which has since suffered major restructuring and has twice been renamed.

This compendium of Newcastle's 50 greatest games is heavily weighted towards the early years, with the great Edwardian team of 100 years ago earning its justified place, and with several mentions of the truly great Magpies of the past, like Hughie Gallacher of the 1920s and Jackie Milburn and Bobby Mitchell of the 1950s. The reader may, of course, disagree with the choice of the 50 games, and some are not very great at all – the one in 1915, for example, was chosen simply to give readers a feel for what life was like on Tyneside in wartime; another, in 1953 against Aberdeen, saw the club in competition for a trophy that was important at the time, but which is now in danger of slipping into oblivion.

The reader may believe there is overemphasis on the old days. The reason is the mammoth one that no set of supporters has been so betrayed over such a long period of time as the ever-loyal Geordies. There can be little excuse for a city the size of Newcastle and its sometimes all-embracing obsession with football and the fortunes of its one and only club not to be in a position to share the riches and success of Manchester, Merseyside and London. Directors, managers and players have all come and gone, with the word 'messiah' being used with less and less conviction every time there is a change of regime. The faults lie deep, but there are two factors that can be identified in Newcastle's continuing failure to reach the place where they should be.

One factor is a chronic inability to read the transfer market. Far too many players have been allowed to go when they had a great deal to offer and, on the other side of the coin, a great deal of rubbish has been brought in from exotic places at ruinously expensive cost. Such players have often found it hard to adapt to the Geordie mentality, with its passionate and exclusive commitment to the club. Frankly, they have seldom experienced such things elsewhere, no matter where in the world they have plied their trade. And is the author imagining things when he wonders if there have not been rather too many players of dubious character and murky pasts? Tantrums, walk-outs, fights on training grounds and even on the field of play itself do happen in every football club, but are they not somewhat more common at Newcastle, and more spectacular? The author has long contended that more effort should be made to find players of good character from the local catchment area of Tyneside, and indeed from nearby Scotland, from where so many great players in the past sprung.

The other factor has been a traditional failure to perform well in London. One hundred years ago, it was widely believed that there was a 'hoodoo' connected with Crystal Palace. Wembley now sadly seems to be taking on that aura. In 1974, 1976, 1998 and 1999 teams left Tyneside convinced that the trophy famine was coming to an end – the local press told them that – but whenever they reached the hallowed ground the players felt that there was some sort of divine law that the stronger forces of Liverpool, Manchester City, Arsenal and Manchester United must be obeyed, and the team succumbed to them. It is what is commonly referred to as 'freezing on the day'. They were shattering disappointments to the broken Geordie army.

That there exists a massive cohort of well over 50,000 willing to support the team through thick and thin (should that be thin and thinner?) is in little doubt. There also exists in the wider world a far greater force of those who are well disposed to the Toon and its army, some of whom, like your author, are occasionally reluctant to commit their support to the team for fear of disappointment, such has been the cumulative effect of decades and generations of heartbreak. Yet my family has loved the Toon for over a century and why is that? My grandfather's youth coincided with the prime of Peter McWilliam and Colin Veitch, my father knew all about Hughie Gallacher and Stanley Seymour, and in the 1950s Jackie Milburn and Bobby Mitchell featured large in my own boyhood.

This book is an attempt to cheer up all Geordies, particularly now that, in 2010, the team is back in the top tier. Some games are obscure ones – all the more reason for bringing them to light, perhaps. Some are spectacularly awful for reasons unconnected with football; the writer has made no attempt to hide the violence of the 1970s, for example. Some are disappointing – Cup Final failures are included – but there are also the great days. Unusual things are featured. There was the time in a Cup Final when a player had committed such a bad tackle on an opponent, thereby injuring him, that he was shunned by the rest of his team. And most know that one of the greatest heroes of the club committed suicide by throwing himself under a train. Another of the talented champions almost missed his greatest moment due to a combination of internal politics and an attack of laryngitis.

This book is an attempt to try to understand the massive unrequited love affair that goes on between supporters and this mighty but unhappy club. There are good moments but, as in all love affairs, there is a lot of sadness, bitterness and misery as well. Nevertheless, the only answer is to keep loving. The future looks bright.

David Potter
Kirkcaldy
May 2010

Date: 15 April 1905

1

ASTON VILLA

Match: FA Cup Final   **Venue: Crystal Palace**

Score: 0–2   **Attendance: 101,117**

Newcastle United:	Aston Villa:
Lawrence	George
McCombie	Spencer
Carr	Miles
Gardner	Pearson
Aitken	Leake
McWilliam	Windmill
Rutherford	Brawn
Howie	Garratty
Appleyard	Hampton
Veitch	Bache
Gosnell	Hall

Referee: P.R. Harrower

The 1905 FA Cup Final at Crystal Palace saw the astonishing crowd of 101,117. It was not a record, because 1901 had seen a larger crowd, but that Final had involved Londoners Tottenham Hotspur. This was certainly the largest crowd ever to see two out of town teams and was further proof, if any was needed, of the phenomenal hold that football had over the population. Trains had been rolling into London all morning from both Newcastle and Birmingham, the home of the Villains, as they were called – a none too complimentary name, but accepted in the same spirit as Newton Heath in Manchester were willing to be called the 'Heathens', although they were now about to change their name to Manchester United instead.

Britain in 1905 was a land of contrasts. Edward VII was on the throne, an ageing, dissolute roue of a man, but one who retained a surprising amount of popularity, not least among the ladies. It was an age of elegance, of Empire, of Christianity – at least on the surface. Poverty was a dreadful scourge on society, with conditions in large cities like Newcastle little short of appalling. The government under A.J. Balfour was complacent and frankly not really too interested in the problems of the lower orders, although bodies like trade unions, the Liberal Party and a few of the more evangelical wings of the Church, like the Methodists, tried to tell the establishment that something would have to be done – and soon. A new political party with possibly subversive tendencies, the Labour Party, was fast appearing over the horizon.

Balfour was particularly unpopular. He was the nephew of Lord Salisbury, the previous Prime Minister, and it was widely believed that he had gained the job through nothing other than nepotism.

The great Newcastle side of the Edwardian era.

Lord Salisbury's Christian name was Robert, and therefore a new phrase entered the English language and has stayed there. If something happened quickly and as if by magic, in the same way as Balfour earned his uncle's job, one just said 'Bob's your uncle!'

Abroad, the Empire was at peace. The Boer War had now finished, with an astonishingly high casualty list for what was essentially a localised conflict, and Britain had done well to avoid the Russo-Japanese war that was going on in the Far East. Rumours and stories abounded, however, of Chinese slave labour in British colonies, and the feeling was beginning to grow that changes were required – changes which the rejuvenated Liberal Party, now that Gladstone and his obsession with Ireland had gone, pledged to bring.

This was the backdrop to the events of 1905. On Tyneside the performance of Newcastle United was stirring emotions. They were doing well in the League but, more importantly, had reached the Final of the FA Cup. They had not done this the easy way, needing three games to dispose of Plymouth Argyle and two to get the better of Tottenham Hotspur before beating Bolton Wanderers 2–0 and Sheffield Wednesday 1–0 to set up a Final against the greatest Cup fighters of them all – Aston Villa.

What well-dressed football players looked like in their civvies.

A fine view of the Crystal Palace. Observe that there is no penalty area.

Aston Villa had won the trophy in 1887, 1895 and 1897, but this was Newcastle's first Final. It would also be the first-ever trip to London for many of their supporters. Railway companies offered 'excursions' for a reasonable price, leaving Newcastle late on the Friday night or even very early on the Saturday morning and getting everyone back by Sunday afternoon. The prices (about 12 shillings and sixpence, normally) were just about within the means of most workers if they were prepared to make a few economies in other areas of their lives. This was considered to be important enough for everyone to make the effort – hence the huge crowds that left both Newcastle and Birmingham.

The Crystal Palace stadium had hosted the FA Cup Final every year since 1895 and was a superb huge ground on the site where the Crystal Palace Sports Centre now stands. It owes its name to *Punch* magazine, which first styled the building created for the Great Exhibition in 1851. It would very soon be a name that would send a shiver down the spine of all Newcastle supporters.

Newcastle's team contained six Scotsmen in Lawrence, McCombie, Gardner, Aitken, McWilliam and Howie; four local lads in Carr, Rutherford, Appleyard and Veitch; and one southerner in Albert Gosnell, a man originally looked upon with a little suspicion by the locals because he came from Colchester in Essex, yet it had been Albert who had twice kept them in the FA Cup with his goals in the two drawn games against Plymouth Argyle.

The strength of the team lay in the Scottish half-back line of Gardner, Aitken and McWilliam. Peter 'the Great' McWilliam was arguably the best of the three of them, with his visionary passing ability and ability to dribble and swerve his way past opponents. He had already won the first of his eight caps for Scotland. Alec Gardner, on the other hand, was never given a Scottish cap and was generally regarded as the best player never to have been capped for his country, and Andy 'The Daddler' Aitken was equally at home at right-half as at centre-half.

For some of the players there had been a previous encounter at Crystal Palace a fortnight before. Seven – Spencer, Leake and Bache of Aston Villa and McCombie, Aitken, McWilliam and Howie of Newcastle – had played in the England versus Scotland international of 1 April. As it turned out, all the Villa men played for England and all the Newcastle men for Scotland, doing nothing to silence the jeers that Newcastle was really part of Scotland, jeers that intensified when England won 1–0 with a goal from Villa's Joe Bache.

The international fixture had been a poor game in front of a disappointing crowd of 32,000. This was indeed a feature of Edwardian football – in England the FA Cup attracted bigger crowds than international matches, whereas in Scotland international football, particularly the game against England, dwarfed any parochial domestic concerns. It meant, however, that although Newcastle's Scotsmen would be burning for revenge, Aston Villa would have the psychological edge as far as the Crystal Palace was concerned, even though only 10 days previously, at St James' Park, in the midweek immediately after the international, Newcastle had beaten Villa 2–0. They had also beaten them 1–0 at Villa Park at the end of November.

The huge crowd might have caused a little concern to the authorities (the disaster at Ibrox in Glasgow in 1902 was never far from anyone's mind for the next decade or so), but the police (still called the 'peelers' or the 'bobbies' after their founder more than 70 years earlier, Robert Peel) did a good job in packing the supporters in. Some of those who didn't achieve admission watched the game from trees and even rooftops outside the ground, and the crowd of 101,117 remains probably the largest that Newcastle have ever played in front of.

There was much evidence that both the Geordies and the Brummies had visited an alehouse or two en route from the station, but the atmosphere was basically good-humoured, with Newcastle fans in particular clearly overawed at the huge number of supporters present. It was long before the days of segregation of supporters, but judging by the rosettes bought from the various stalls outside the ground, it would appear that the crowd could have been split into three: the Newcastle faction, the Aston Villa support and the Londoners who had just come along to see a good game of football.

Newcastle started badly. Their defence seemed to be badly affected by nerves after the introduction to Lord Kinnaird, the old Etonian who had done so much to promote the game, and were nowhere in sight as Harry Hampton opened the scoring in less than three minutes. It was a fine move starting from the left, with Hall passing to Hampton, who laid it off to Bache and then ran into position to pick up a return, bamboozling Aitken and McWilliam and being in the clear to shoot past Lawrence. This was a grim blow for the Magpies, and the defence were seen to argue furiously with each other.

It is very easy to blame other people for one's own shortcomings, but Newcastle did rally and slowly set about trying to repair the damage. They found it difficult to compose themselves in front of the huge crowd, however. Newcastle's style of play that year had involved accurate passing to each other, with phrases like 'pattern weaving' being used to describe their play. This unfortunately presupposes calmness and thought, neither of which was available to the Geordies at that moment in time.

More action from the 1905 Cup Final.

Villa, on the other hand, played fast, aggressive football with lots of dash and verve. Half-time came with no further score and the prospects looked grim for Newcastle, even though their supporters entered with gusto into the community singing, which included old favourites like *Goodbye, Dolly Gray* and *Clementine*.

Then, early in the second half, came Newcastle's big moment, of which there are only a few in each game, but which determine the outcome. It happened when Bill Appleyard, Newcastle's massive centre-forward, managed for once to elude the attentions of the Villa defenders and beat goalkeeper George, only for the ball to hit the post. Appleyard put his hands to his head in despair. It was almost as if he knew that Villa were going to score again.

This they did when goalkeeper Jimmy Lawrence stopped but failed to hold a shot from Hall, and the ball rebounded to the predatory Harry Hampton, who scored his and Villa's second. Newcastle now redoubled their efforts, but there was an assurance about Villa, as if they were a team who knew that this was going to be their day. Newcastle had one or two half-chances, but goalkeeper George was in fine form for the Villains and time ran out with the score still at 2–0.

Thus ended the Magpies' first FA Cup Final. They had not played badly; it was simply that Aston Villa had played better. The Cup was presented by Lord Kinnaird's daughter-in-law, and Villa's captain Howard Spencer paid tribute to a gallant Newcastle side, wishing them well in future Finals, 'providing they were not playing Aston Villa!' The game was summed up in a somewhat offensive way by a bigwig in English football who said that 'the Villa are an English team with nine Brumagen (sic) lads in the side and Englishmen are always steadier under excitement than Scots. The Newcastle lads had never played in a Final before and lost their heads.'

But, for Newcastle, the season was not yet over…

Date: 29 April 1905

MIDDLESBROUGH

Match: League Division One

Venue: Ayresome Park

Score: 3–0

Attendance: 15,000

Middlesbrough:	Newcastle United:
Williamson	Lawrence
McCallum	McCracken
Agnew	Carr
Aitken	Veitch
Jones	Aitken
Davidson	McIntyre
Hewitt	Rutherford
Common	Howie
Green	Appleyard
Atherton	Orr
Thackeray	Gosnell

Referee: T. Robertson, Glasgow

The crowds lining Grainger Street all the way from the Central Station to the Earl Grey monument on the fine spring night of 29 April would be in for a disappointment. They had been waiting for a couple of hours since news had reached the town that the team would be catching the 7pm train from Middlesbrough and would arrive at 8.08pm. This was 'the normal route for royal processions', according to the *Evening Chronicle*, thereby implying that this far more significant procession would go this way as well. In fact, it had been decided that the team would go to the Palace Theatre via Clayton Street, and thus the many thousands would not get the opportunity to see their heroes.

It should have happened two weeks before, but Newcastle went down to Aston Villa at the Crystal Palace in the FA Cup Final. This was a colossal disappointment, but there was now ample recompense in the winning of the League instead. It had been widely believed that the team were good enough to do both, as Preston North End and Aston Villa had done in the past, but the Magpies had let themselves and their huge support down badly at the Crystal Palace. However, their fans told each other that although the Cup was more prestigious, the League actually said who the best team in the country was.

The *Evening Chronicle* was able to state categorically that 1,639 Geordies were at Ayresome Park that day supporting Newcastle. That had certainly been the number of excursionists who had bought tickets for the 'football specials' that had left Newcastle all morning in the spring sunshine, conveying supporters wearing all sorts of strange 'Magpie headgear' and even one or two supporters in black and white 'kickerbockers' (sic) as well with all sorts of rosettes and rattles. Some of the supporters who caught the later trains were still wearing their working clothes because they had been doing a shift in the mines or the shipyards that morning and had been paid, as was the normal practice, on Saturday at noon. This Saturday, instead of going to the alehouse, they had bought themselves a ticket to see their 'pets' playing at Middlesbrough and possibly 'bringing home the bacon'.

Like Newcastle, Middlesbrough had been a growth area of football. They had been promoted to Division One in 1902, and in 1903 they had opened Ayresome Park, an impressive ground with a fine stand, which would stay in situ for the next 90 years. Their average gates were about 12,000, but with the influx of Geordies that day and the general interest in this particular game, the crowd rose to well over 15,000. There had grown a healthy rivalry between the three north-east clubs, and both Newcastle and Boro supporters were uncomfortably aware that Sunderland had already won the English League three times.

In view of the intense local rivalry and the importance of the fixture, a Scottish referee was engaged. This was Tom Robertson of Queen's Park, a man well respected north of the border, having already officiated at Scottish Cup Finals and international matches. He had also handled the Newcastle versus Stoke City game on Good Friday. The position was that Everton had 47 points while Newcastle and Manchester City had 46. Everton had, however, played all their games, while Newcastle played Middlesbrough, and Manchester City took on Aston Villa. Newcastle's goal average (goals scored divided by goals conceded) was far superior to that of Manchester City, so it followed that a win for Newcastle would win them the title.

The season had been all about consistency, because Newcastle had won the games that they ought to have won, even though they had also lost nine times. They had gone through a difficult spell on tricky pitches in January, but had come through it and had steadily improved throughout the season, visibly playing with great teamwork and understanding. There were very many fine players at St James' Park, as a glance at those who were chosen for England and Scotland would indicate, but all the superstars were men who could relate to other members of the team. There was a distinct lack of dressing-room tension because all the players got on.

Much of this was due to the influence of secretary-manager Frank Watt, a Scotsman, like so many of the team and the back-room staff. Technically, the team was chosen by the directors, but Watt was invaluable for his know-how and determination to make everything work. Said to be irascible and difficult to live with, he nevertheless had a soft side to him as well, and as he was not officially in charge of things he could be the players' friend and confidant as well as their boss. He preferred to stay in the background but his influence was huge. He had taken time to build up the side, but it had been well worth it.

Frank Watt, the legendary 'manager', is on the right of this picture.

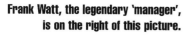

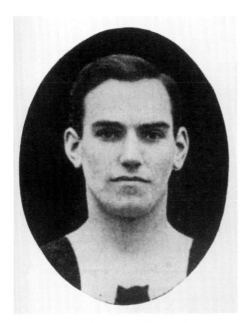

Colin Veitch, opera singer, left-wing politician and great Geordie footballer.

April had been difficult for the Geordie supporters. Apart from the Cup Final disappointment to Villa, there had been two League defeats. The Newcastle supporters had been subdued when the team had gone down 2–0 to Blackburn Rovers on 1 April. Colin Veitch was out anyway, and the Board then allowed no fewer than four of the best players – McCombie, Aitken, Howie and McWilliam – to play for Scotland in the international against England. Scotland lost, and so did Newcastle, so it was a far from happy day. Then, the week after the Cup Final defeat, on Easter Saturday, the team went down to Sunderland at St James' Park after having beaten Stoke City convincingly on Good Friday.

There remained two away games at Sheffield Wednesday and Middlesbrough. A good win at Owlerton (as Hillsborough was then called) on the Wednesday night meant that another win on Saturday would do the trick. It was the end of a long hard season, but as Newcastle had already beaten the Owls twice that season (including once in the FA Cup semi-final) the *Evening Chronicle* could see no reason why the Geordies would not beat them again without the aid of Sheffield Wednesday 'taking it easy', and the paper rightly poured scorn on the suggestions emanating from Lancashire that Sheffield Wednesday were not trying against Newcastle. The team got a good 3–1 win, with goals from Orr, Howie and McWilliam.

The long, gruelling season had, however, taken its toll with injuries, and Newcastle were without McCombie, Gardner and McWilliam for the short trip to Middlesbrough, and one or two of the others were only half-fit. The wing-halves, Gardner and McWilliam, had been the driving forces of the side all season and they would be sadly missed. Veitch, who had played in the forward line most of the season and particularly in the Cup Final, was brought back to midfield to cover for McWilliam, thereby allowing a welcome return for Ronnie Orr, but the other wing-half position went to a young local lad called Teddy McIntyre. It would be Teddy's big moment. It was only his second game for the club, his previous being the infamous one when the weakened team went down to Blackburn Rovers on 1 April.

The weather was beautiful, although there were rain showers around, as befitted the day that the cricket season began. The newspapers were as interested in the imminent arrival of the 1905 Australians as they were in who was to win the League Championship. The crowd at Ayresome Park was a good one and 'almost filled the small enclosure', as the *Evening Chronicle* put it.

It did not take Newcastle long to go ahead. In the sixth minute Jimmy Howie embarked on a great run, tore through the Boro defence and centred, trying to find Bill Appleyard. The burly Appleyard did not quite get there in time, but Ronnie Orr arrived to do the needful and scored a goal that was greeted with wild enthusiasm by the Newcastle travelling support as 'bonnets, handkerchiefs and sticks' went up in the air in wild Geordie enthusiasm. Newcastle now remained very much on top. They were clearly determined that they would not to allow the League Championship to slip away from them in the same way as the FA Cup had done, and young Teddy McIntyre was conspicuous in his hard work for Newcastle.

Half-time came with Newcastle still on top but in a very precarious position. Everyone was aware that all it needed was a goal for Middlesbrough to put everything back into the melting pot once again. But any anxiety did not last long. After eight minutes of the second half Jackie Rutherford was on hand to notch a second, and scarcely had the cheering for this one died down when Appleyard was there to put the matter beyond any reasonable doubt. Almost as a sign, the rain which had been intermittent in the middle part of the game totally disappeared and the game finished in glorious sunlight.

It was the first time that Newcastle had won a major honour, and the *Sunday Pictorial* was delighted because it said that Newcastle were the best football team throughout the season. Manchester City lost in any case, something that hardly mattered, but it meant that Everton would be second, and again the *Sunday Pictorial* was happy because Manchester City were 'not as good as the other two'.

The team's transport to the station was escorted by fans singing their praises and enjoying the conversation of their heroes as men like Colin Veitch, Jimmy Howie and Ronnie Orr chatted amiably with them. The train left Middlesbrough Station at 7pm and in those days it took an hour and eight minutes to get to Newcastle. The wonders of telegraph had alerted the fans back home to the joyous result, and thus it was that Newcastle Station saw its first-ever return of conquering champions. It was even better than winning the FA Cup, in that it would have taken the team longer to get back from London, whereas on this occasion the Geordies could celebrate on the actual night of the game, and those who had been there to see it could recall with pleasure every kick of the ball. Drink flowed that night, but on this occasion excess was justified. The team had planned a tour of central Europe in May. It would be fitting to visit places like Vienna and Prague as champions of England.

Led by the chairman, Mr John Cameron, they were greeted by the Mayor and Mayoress, Mr and Mrs Baxter Ellis, at the Palace Theatre, and then they were royally entertained by the variety performance, with many jokes made by the comedians about famous guests in the audience met by loud cheering. Nor did the festivities stop there – on the following Wednesday they were all invited by the Mayor to his residence at Mansion House in Ellison Place for a celebration banquet.

As for the fans, to whom this meant so much, they celebrated for weeks and talked about their team endlessly.

Date: 31 March 1906

3

WOOLWICH ARSENAL

Match: FA Cup semi-final **Venue: Victoria Ground, Stoke**

Score: 2–0 **Attendance: 19,964**

Newcastle United:	Woolwich Arsenal:
Lawrence	Ashcroft
McCombie	Cross
Carr	Sharp
Gardner	Bigden
Aitken	Sands
McWilliam	McEachrane
Rutherford	Garbutt
Howie	Coleman
Veitch	Freeman
Orr	Fitchie
Gosnell	Templeton

Referee: Cannot be traced

Everyone had been highly impressed by the progress made by Woolwich Arsenal. Newcastle fans recalled that the Gunners had played their first-ever Division One match little more than 18 months ago at St James' Park in September 1904. They had been little match for the mighty Newcastle United that day, but that was no disgrace because few teams could live with the great Geordie team of that year, and Arsenal had gone on to finish 10th in Division One. Their other game that season against Newcastle at Arsenal's home ground, the Manor Ground, Plumstead, had been on the last day of 1904, and they had once again played honourably but lost 2–0.

This season, 1905–06, they had excelled themselves. On Christmas Day 20,000 had seen a thrilling game at Plumstead in which Arsenal just edged it over Newcastle 4–3, and then in the New Year of 1906 the Gunners had reached the semi-final of the FA Cup in a campaign which had included some fine games, including one which really raised the eyebrows in the North East when they beat Sunderland 4–0. The strong Manchester United (or Newton Heath as some still called them) were then beaten in the quarter-final at Old Trafford to set up a game against last season's Championship winners and defeated FA Cup finalists, Newcastle United.

Newcastle had stuttered of late and did not look as if they were going to win the League Championship this year. There had been an excellent autumn with six victories in a row, including an 8–0 beating of Wolverhampton Wanderers, but then, as winter gave way reluctantly to spring, form had faltered with three defeats in a row, including a painful one at local rivals, Middlesbrough.

In addition, the Cup campaign had been a struggle, with draws at Derby and Birmingham before Newcastle eventually got the better of them in replays at St James' Park.

Their fans were often at a loss to explain their eccentric form. There seemed to be little doubt that they had the best players in the land. They had men like Rutherford, Veitch, McWilliam and Howie, second to none in any comparison, but crucially Veitch had struggled a little with injury this season, and it was no coincidence that this was the time when the team were not doing particularly well. He had also suffered from a change of position as he had now been moved up to centre-forward, allowing Andy 'the Daddler' Aitken to come in as centre-half.

To a certain extent, this was a change forced on secretary-manager Frank Watt by an injury to the normal centre-forward, the burly Bill Appleyard, but it was not as radical a change as it sounds. Victorian and Edwardian football had often relied on the centre-forward and the centre-half exchanging places and being referred to as the centre-halves, with one concentrating on attacking and the other on defending. Great emphasis was placed on 'leading the line', which meant the distribution of balls to both wings, then charging forward parallel to the winger and being in the right position for a cross. That would be the forward centre-half's job. The defensive centre-half, on the other hand, would have to be able to run backwards when the opposition wingers had the ball.

Optimism was in the air in Britain in the early months of 1906. There was increasing competition economically from the two 'new' countries of Germany and the United States of America, but the British Empire was still a mighty power. The huge country (which Britain herself had done so much to create) called the United States of America was distant and did not really interfere too much in Europe and Africa. Although occasionally prickly about the American continent, President Teddy Roosevelt was quite happy to let things go on as they always had in other parts of the world. Germany was more of a problem. Clearly a far stronger and more robust power than France had ever been, she was building up her naval and military strength just in case France wanted a war of revenge for her defeat in 1871 and the loss of Alsace and Lorraine, which the Germans had taken from her. On the other hand, the Kaiser, despite being a bit temperamental and unstable, was the nephew of King Edward VII, so it was felt that there would not really be any huge problems.

A Liberal government had recently been returned to power with a huge majority, and they pledged to improve living conditions, which in some areas of the country, not least Tyneside, were looked upon as a disgrace for a country that was undeniably still the richest on earth. The Prime Minister was a little-known but benign and gentle Glaswegian character called Sir Henry Campbell-Bannerman, but there were other dynamic characters around in the urbane Herbert Asquith, the Welsh wizard called Lloyd-George and the man who claimed to be a hero of the Boer War and talked about it endlessly, one Winston Churchill.

The FA Cup semi-finals were played on the last day of March. The other semi-final was between the two Merseyside teams of Liverpool and Everton. It might have made more sense to keep the game there and toss a coin for the venue, but it was decided to play the game at Villa Park, Birmingham. Newcastle's semi-final was to be played at the Victoria Ground, Stoke, judged to be more or less equidistant between London and Newcastle. It attracted a slightly disappointing 19,964 fans. One suspects that there may have been more if the game had been held slightly further north.

The crowd was estimated as containing about half 'Novocastrians whose trains had pulled in about an hour before the start' and half dressed in the red favours of Woolwich Arsenal, with a few locals 'intent on seeing how good the northerners really were'. In fact, the northerners turned out to be very good; this was one of Newcastle's better games of the season.

The real attraction was the interchanging and the accurate passing of the three inside men, Jimmy Howie, Colin Veitch and Ronnie Orr. Picking up passes from the wing-halves, Gardner and McWilliam, Newcastle's inside trio dazzled the Woolwich defenders, and it was a wonder that the score was restricted to 2–0. The first goal came about halfway through the first half when a ball came from Andy 'the Daddler' Aitken (no one seemed to know why he was so called) to Jimmy Howie, who, with two opponents converging upon him, sent the ball across to Ronnie Orr. Orr immediately lobbed the ball forward ahead of Veitch, who, having read the situation brilliantly, charged forward and cracked the ball home on the half-volley from the edge of the penalty box. This was football at its best, and the cheers of the northern fans rent the air as the neutrals clapped politely. Newcastle then pressed for the rest of the first half, but Arsenal's goalkeeper, Jimmy Ashcroft, showed everyone why he was England's 'keeper with a remarkable series of saves from Veitch and Howie. The other goalkeeper, Jimmy Lawrence, much loved by the Geordie fans, and grossly undervalued by the Scotland selectors, had little to do because his team were so well on top, but what he was asked to do, he did well.

Another goal then came in the second half. Once again it was the result of neat inter-passing, but this time it was Jimmy Howie who applied the final touch. This was early in the second half, and although the Londoners tried, they made little impression on a Geordie defence which was 'niggardly and parsimonious' throughout. At the other end Newcastle's forwards were described as being 'prodigal of chances' and 'a 5–0 scoreline would not have been an unfair reflection on proceedings'. The game finished with Newcastle well on top, and with their supporters wondering which of the Merseyside duo, Liverpool or Everton, would face them in the Final. It would turn out to be Everton.

With such a fine Newcastle side, it was little surprise that four of them played the following week at Hampden Park in the Scotland versus England international. It was played before a six-figure crowd, thus putting the new Glasgow stadium, opened in 1903, in the same bracket as the Crystal Palace for holding large crowds. All of Scotland could rejoice in the talents of McWilliam, Howie and Aitken, while Veitch performed gallantly for England in Scotland's 2–1 victory. Jimmy Ashcroft, who had played so well for Woolwich Arsenal, was in goal for England, sadly overstepping the line with the ball in his hands to concede Scotland's first goal and having no chance with a drive from Jimmy Howie for the second.

It was all the more disappointing, therefore, that Newcastle's FA Cup triumph ended in anti-climax. The Final took place at Crystal Palace on 21 April, some three days after the great San Francisco earthquake, news of which was now beginning to filter through to the rest of the world. There had been earthquakes before, but few on this scale in such a densely populated area had been experienced, and it may be that some of the players were upset by it all; poverty on Tyneside throughout the whole of the 19th century had forced many Novocastrians to try their luck in the New World, and it was still not clear how bad the casualties had been. Relatives may have been involved.

This was, however, a weak excuse, even though some of the Newcastle newspapers tried to use it. It was far more likely that Newcastle were already beginning to believe that the Crystal Palace was an unlucky ground for them (they had lost there the previous year). For whatever reason, they definitely underperformed and conceded the only goal of the game in the last quarter of an hour to Sandy Young of Everton, who could thus claim to have won the FA Cup before Newcastle did.

Another possibility is that Newcastle simply took the game too easily, believing that if they played the way they had in the semi-final then no power on earth would stop them. The trains northwards that night of the semi-final, full of joyful fans, simply would not countenance the fact that anyone else could live with the great Newcastle United.

4

BRISTOL CITY

Match: League Division One **Venue: St James' Park**

Score: 3–0 **Attendance: 35,000**

Newcastle United:	Bristol City:
Sinclair	Demmery
McCracken	Cottle
Carr	Annan
Gardner	Hanlon
Speedie	Wedlock
McWilliam	Spear
Rutherford	Smith
Howie	Burton
Appleyard	Gilligan
Orr	Maxwell
Duffy	Staniforth

Referee: T. Kirkham, Burslem

Easter 1907 saw the city in a fervent state as the club closed in on their second League Championship. By a quirk of fixture arranging Newcastle had games at home on Good Friday, Black Saturday (as it was then called because it was the only day in the year when Christ was dead, according to the Church calendar) and Easter Monday. The games were against Stoke City (a 1–0 win), Bristol City and Blackburn Rovers. The game against Stoke had been tight, with only a Jackie Rutherford goal separating the teams, but Newcastle had held on to their proud 100 per cent home League record, something that clearly put them in contention for their second League Championship in three years.

If proof was required that football was beginning to centre on Newcastle in the Edwardian era, it was in the choice of St James' Park as the venue for the international match the following week between England and Scotland, then looked upon as the showpiece of the season and the game which defined the happiness of both countries, Scotland in particular. In some ways, Newcastle was the logical choice for this game because it was the closest ground for Scottish fans to travel to and the Newcastle area contained lots of Scottish people, but the real reason was that Newcastle had taken over as the leading team in the country.

There was an Achilles heel, however, and it was the FA Cup. Newcastle were beginning to wonder whether there was a curse preventing them winning the Cup. If there was such a curse it would seem to be called 'Crystal Palace', because in 1905 and then 1906 they had lost in the Final, first to Aston Villa and then to Everton, at that ground. During this particular season they had managed to lose on their own St James' Park to the team called Crystal Palace in the very first round. It was their only home defeat of the season and, amazingly, Crystal Palace were not even a Football League team at that time. The result was so astounding that rumours spread through Tyneside not so much about 'hexes' and 'curses', as about bribes and collusion with bookmakers.

These rumours were just that and could not be substantiated. They were probably not taken seriously, as high attendances in subsequent games would seem to indicate, but fans were certainly puzzled by the poor performance and felt that the winning of the League Championship was the very least that Frank Watt and his team could do to make it up to them.

Form since that dire January day against Crystal Palace had been acceptable, with only three away defeats to the two Liverpool teams and a sore one at Roker Park one Wednesday afternoon after the original game had been postponed, but there had been good performances too, notably a 5–0 win over Manchester United, an always-welcome win over Middlesbrough and a tight victory over the mighty Aston Villa.

The visitors for this day, Bristol City, were an attractive side, and the Edwardian era had seen a growth in football in the south-west of the country as well. The Citizens, as they were called, were much awaited in Newcastle because it was their first-ever visit to the Toon. Bristol City had only been founded in 1897 and had played their first Football League game in 1901 in Division Two. They had won Division Two in 1906 and were this year in contention, along with Everton, Newcastle and Sheffield United, for Division One. A win today would really put a marker down; they would then be only four points behind but with a game in hand. They had some fine players, like the small left-back Joe Cottle, the huge centre-half Billy Wedlock (both of them England internationals), and at centre-forward a prolific Scottish goalscorer called Sam Gilligan, who only left Celtic because he could not displace the mighty Jimmy Quinn. Gilligan also had the distinction of being the first player to kick a ball at the new Hampden Park, Glasgow, because he had taken the kick-off at the first game on 31 October 1903.

A few Bristol supporters arrived to see their team. They were cheerful and friendly as they made themselves known to the locals, being very noticeable with their distinctive accents as they talked about 'Brissol' and asked their way to 'St Jamel Park'. They ordered cider in the local hostelries and sang songs advising Geordies to

'Drink oop thy cider

Or else tha' won't live very lang!'

Newcastle's victory against Stoke the day before had been bought at a price. The left-wing pair of Brown and Gosnell were injured and had to be replaced by Ronnie Orr and Chris Duffy. That was bad enough, but there was also no Colin Veitch, who was replaced by Finlay Speedie, normally an inside-forward. Veitch had not apparently been injured and rumours spread that he had been dropped by secretary-manager Frank Watt. This would have been astonishing, but what was more likely was that he was simply given a rest. Watt, like modern managers, did occasionally rotate his squad.

Veitch was deservedly called the pivot of the team. He was an old fashioned centre-half who could do anything, including attack. A centre-half in those days was often expected to be a double centre-forward as well. This was a technique perfected at the same time in Scotland by Jimmy Quinn and Willie Loney of Celtic, and Veitch was the sort of man who was prepared to go and watch football when he was not playing in order to perfect his technique. He was 100 per cent reliable and appreciated the value of teamwork because he was also involved off the field in activities like drama and opera, where the importance of teamwork cannot be undervalued. In the same way that every actor relies on someone else for his cue, so too does every footballer rely on a pass from a colleague.

What further endeared him to the hearts of Geordies (and he was very definitely a Geordie himself) was his involvement in left-wing politics. He was an intelligent, articulate and compassionate man, distressed by the poverty and deprivation around him, and he realised that, as in a football team, no man can exist as an island. Teamwork is of the essence. Veitch is deservedly one of the iconic figures of Newcastle history.

Then there was Peter 'the Great' McWilliam. Wing-halves were and perhaps still are (although they are called something else now) the key men in a team. They have to be able to win the ball, to carry it forward, to distribute and spray passes, to take a grip on a game and dominate it. In all these things Peter was absolutely superb, combining all these qualities with a touch of the arrogance that Jim Baxter, for example, would show some 60 years later.

Goalkeeper Jimmy Lawrence was injured and in goal was the remarkable character called Tommy Sinclair. Tommy had joined the club from Rangers in March of that year after he had won a Glasgow Cup medal for Celtic. Celtic's regular goalkeeper, Davie Adams, had been injured while playing in a benefit match for a Rangers player, and Rangers had felt duty bound to lend their reserve goalkeeper to Celtic. They would have cause to regret their generosity when Sinclair returned to Ibrox without losing a Scottish League goal. He could claim to have played for the League Champions of both Scotland and England in 1907 (six games for Celtic and three for Newcastle) but sadly hadn't won a League medal for either team.

The game started with 35,000 Geordies (a few thousand up on the previous day's game) in rare good humour, cheering and applauding the good play of their heroes and even appreciating the occasional good move of their West Country opponents. The *Evening Chronicle*, well aware that this game was as close to a League decider as one was ever likely to get, commented on the tension and excitement in the air, but was clear that the game went 'steadily in Newcastle's favour' as the home side, tentative at first but later more confident once Speedie settled down in his unfamiliar role of centre-half, took command.

They had gone ahead after five minutes when Jimmy Howie, commonly known as 'Gentleman Jim', scored with a 'long, fine shot' and from then on took command, with Appleyard, Howie and Orr all coming close before half-time. The second half, however, belonged to Jackie Rutherford, who rampaged down the right wing as if the Bristol defence didn't exist and scored the two goals which more or less eliminated the gallant Bristolians from the Championship.

Rutherford's first came after about quarter of an hour of the second half, when a drive from Ronnie Orr was only half-cleared by the Bristol defence and Rutherford was on the spot to 'make the net bulge'. His second and Newcastle's third came with only five minutes remaining when a clearance from Speedie found him just inside the Bristol half and he 'went racing clean away from the field' to make it 3–0 for Newcastle United.

Newcastle's supporters were 'high as kites' as they made their way down to the city centre after the game. It would now be difficult to imagine them not winning the title, because even if Everton were to win their two games in hand, Newcastle would still be two points clear. Newcastle now had Blackburn Rovers on Easter Monday. They would win that game 3–1 to make it a very happy Easter indeed on Tyneside.

The following Saturday, while the international between England and Scotland was going on at St James' Park, the weakened Newcastle side, with several men playing for their country, went down 1–0 at Notts County. The League was eventually clinched anticlimactically on 13 April with a goalless draw at St James' Park against Sheffield United. Some Newcastle fans were even disappointed at that because they had now lost their 100 per cent home League record.

A few days before that last match in the League, in something that is hard to imagine being replicated a century later, the Newcastle players were taken to a Brotherhood Meeting in the Wesleyan Chapel, Gateshead, to hear a talk by Harry Walker of the English FA about 'Football and the National Life', reminding them of their duties as citizens and as players. Perhaps modern-day players could do with a similar reminder.

5

Date: 28 March 1908

FULHAM

Match: FA Cup semi-final

Venue: Anfield, Liverpool

Score: 6–0

Attendance: 45,571

Newcastle United:	Fulham:
Lawrence	Skene
McCracken	Ross
Pudan	Lindsay
Gardner	Collins
Veitch	Morrison
Willis	Goldie
Rutherford	Hogan
Howie	Dalrymple
Appleyard	Harrison
Speedie	Millington
Wilson	Moucher

Referee: J.T. Howcroft, Bolton

1908 was an exciting year. On Tyneside there was talk of a League and Cup double, which would have been the first in the 20th century. Newcastle had won the League in 1905 and 1907 and were well placed by the end of March, not having lost a game since Boxing Day 1907, and their progress to the FA Cup was spectacular and confident, with the form of centre-forward Bill Appleyard in particular giving cause for optimism.

The opponents for this match, however, would be interesting. This was a team called Fulham, a new star in the London firmament. They had a ground with the unlikely name of Craven Cottage on the banks of the Thames, past which the annual Boat Race between Oxford and Cambridge Universities was rowed. They were playing in their first season of Division Two of the Football League, having won the Southern League in 1906 and 1907 and, therefore, had been deemed good enough, by the mysterious and arcane authorities who decided such things, to enter the Football League.

Fulham were doing very well in Division Two, beating teams like Derby County, Lincoln City, Bradford City and Barnsley, but it was their form in the FA Cup that really made everyone sit up and take notice. With an enthusiastic and shrewd manager called Harry Bradshaw at the helm, they raised eyebrows with an 8–3 defeat of Luton Town away from home on a mudbath of a pitch in early January, then dispatched Norwich City, before being confronted by the might of Manchester City, winners of the FA Cup in 1904.

A draw in the first game at Hyde Park, Manchester, had been impressive enough. Fulham might have won had the game not been played in a gale which deceived goalkeeper Skene and allowed City an undeserved late equaliser. But then, at Craven Cottage on the Wednesday afternoon, before an astonishing crowd of nearly 40,000, Fulham came from behind to win 3–1 against their illustrious opponents.

It was now the other Manchester team, Manchester United, who faced them in the quarter-final. United in 1908 were not the global name they are a century later, but they were still a force to be reckoned with as they included 'the Welsh wizard' (a nickname he shared with the up-and-coming politician and then-president of the Board of Trade, David Lloyd-George) Billy Meredith in their team. Like Newcastle United, they were going strong in their bid for a double. However, on this occasion Fulham won through and beat them 2–1, even though most honest Londoners would concede that the provincials were the better team.

Newcastle were delighted with Fulham's success. They would not have fancied either of the Manchester teams, and Fulham, no matter how impressive in the Second Division or the Cup run, were still virtual unknowns outside their own area of London. None of their players had ever been considered for international honours, other than their goalkeeper, Leslie Skene, who had played once for Scotland in 1904 against Wales at Dens Park, Dundee, whereas Newcastle's XI was packed full of men who represented England and Scotland.

One of the Newcastle stars was injured, however. This was Peter McWilliam, the mighty left-half and arguably the best player in the Newcastle team. He had been playing brilliantly all season, but had missed the previous week's game against Birmingham and would be out for a considerable time. This gave an opportunity to Dave Willis, a man who would in later years make a curious contribution to football folklore in that he was responsible for Alec James's baggy pants. Willis became trainer with Raith Rovers, and when the young James suffered from rheumatism in his thighs Willis encouraged him to wear several layers of pants on cold days, so the outer layer had to be exceptionally huge. James was a small man and looked curious in those baggy pants, but Willis's idea worked and James showed his gratitude by marrying Willis's daughter.

Willis was a good player in his own right, but not as good as McWilliam, and the Geordies feared that McWilliam would be badly missed. At right-half was Alec 'Punky' Gardner, a solid and reliable performer who was somehow or other always overlooked by the Scotland selectors, to the mystification of all Tyneside and men like McWilliam and Howie who played with him. It can only be explained away in terms of Scotland feeling that they were already over-dependent on Newcastle players and had to assuage the large 'Home Scot' lobby that felt, in a typically insular way, that Scotland should look first at those who played in the Scottish game. There was some compensation for Gardner, however, in his sustained popularity at St James' Park, where he was deservedly made captain.

The semi-final was played at Anfield, home of Liverpool. This was not a wise choice. Although the facilities and the ground were more than adequate, 28 March 1908 was also the day of the Grand National horse race at nearby Aintree. Two huge sporting events in the same city on the same day led to a huge influx of people from all over England, not only Newcastle and London. Trying to cash in on the situation, the rascally railway companies raised their fares – in some cases without telling customers in advance – and this may have had an adverse effect on the crowd. But 45,571 seemed to be about what would have been expected for a semi-final, and it was a considerably larger audience than Newcastle's previous semi-final two years previously. It was by some distance the biggest group that Fulham had ever played in front of, although Newcastle were more used to such attention.

The Grand National that year was won by a horse called Rubio at 66/1. Rubio was, quite literally, a cart horse and had on one occasion (allegedly) pulled a London bus. His victory was a major surprise for all who followed horse racing and staked money with the then technically illegal (but transparently tolerated and unpersecuted) bookmakers. The football that day would not yield such a surprise.

Newcastle's great side of this era.

Conditions were wet, something that might have made the game more of a contest, but by half-time, Newcastle were 2–0 up and it should have been more. The goals had been scored by Bill Appleyard, with a great diving header from a free-kick, and Jimmy Howie after the ball was crossed to Appleyard and he dummied for Howie to score. It was often said that Newcastle played their best football in the wet, and they clearly revelled in these conditions.

Fulham's honest journeymen could only stand and gape at all this. There was everything that a football connoisseur would have wished – accurate passing, fast running, good wing play and two lovely goals – and there was more to come in the second half. First Alec Gardner scored a soft goal when he picked up a loose ball and ran forward with no one tackling him to score, then Jack Rutherford delighted his many admirers by running in from the right with a couple of defenders in his wake to make it four. There were those who felt that Rutherford was the best player in the team and this gave grist to their mill.

The game was now all but over. It was then that the game's one unsavoury incident occurred, all the more offensive (to modern eyes at least) because it was so unnecessary. It concerned 'shoulder-charging', the ethics of which are, 100 years later, indefensible. It was allowable for a forward to 'shoulder-charge' the goalkeeper and try to bundle him into the back of the net as long as the ball was in the goalkeeper's hands, the goalkeeper's feet were on the ground and the shoulder (not the arm and not the elbow) was used. It was also allowed for defenders to shoulder-charge forwards in order to protect their goalkeeper. This piece of thuggery was allowed in the British game until European influence gradually took over and made it illegal, but as late as 1958 one of Nat Lofthouse's goals (allowed by the referee) in the FA Cup Final remained an appalling sight.

Bill Appleyard was one of the great shoulder-chargers, using his weight on many occasions and rivalled only by Jimmy Quinn of Celtic and Scotland in this art. On this occasion the Fulham goalkeeper, Leslie Skene, who had had a fine game up to this point and had been responsible for keeping the Newcastle score to respectable proportions, was badly injured. (Skene, incidentally, had played for Scotland in 1904 when an amateur with Queen's Park, and in later years he went on to win the Military Cross for gallantry in World War One and to become a distinguished doctor, specialising in mental health.) No goal resulted from Appleyard's charge and Skene was able to continue, but his injury hampered his ability to stop the fifth and sixth goals.

The fifth goal was scored by Jimmy Howie. It was executed with what seemed to be a cross and would have been gathered without any bother by a fit Skene. Then Jack Rutherford added a sixth with a great individual dribble and solo goal. The game finished with the gallant Fulham well beaten and, according to the *Daily Mirror* 'painfully effete, their combination ragged, their attacks came with snatches'. The *Sunday Pictorial* is even more direct: 'They lacked pace, dash and skill…and were really outclassed.'

For Newcastle and their supporters, however, this was a truly great day, much remembered in future years as a magnificent example of attacking football and looked upon often as the apogee of Frank Watt's great Newcastle side. The 6–0 scoreline remains a record for an FA Cup semi-final; indeed, it is rare for the later stages of any Cup competition to see such a comprehensive beating.

The very size of the victory contained the seeds of the downfall of Newcastle United, however. There would have been little doubt that if the team continued to play like this they would have won both the League and the Cup in 1908, but complacency set in as everyone forgot that Fulham were a Second Division team – a good Second Division team, but still a small outfit with no real experience of big occasions like semi-finals. Newcastle, still without the crucial influence of Peter McWilliam, now pressed the self-destruct button and lost their next three League games, thereby throwing away their chance of winning the League. They then lost the FA Cup Final as well.

6

Date: 25 April 1908

WOLVERHAMPTON WANDERERS

Match: FA Cup Final

Venue: Crystal Palace

Score: 1–3

Attendance: 74,967

Newcastle United:	Wolverhampton Wanderers:
Lawrence	Lunn
McCracken	Jones
Pudan	Collins
Gardner	Hunt
Veitch	Wooldridge
McWilliam	Bishop
Rutherford	Harrison
Howie	Shelton
Appleyard	Hedley
Speedie	Radford
Wilson	Pedley

Referee: T.P. Campbell

Newcastle's League season had been disappointing following their winning of the Championship in the previous campaign, but there was a certain amount of optimism that things could be made good in the FA Cup Final. The winning of the Cup was long overdue. They had been unlucky against Aston Villa in 1905, then in 1906 had played dreadfully in one of the worst Cup Finals of them all against Everton, but here they were, back at the Palace, for what would appear to be a 'third time lucky' encounter. Their opponents were Second Division Wolverhampton Wanderers, who had actually won the Cup back in 1893, but although the Wolves had impressed everyone with their progress this year the Cup Final of 1908 looked like a mismatch. The previous week the Scottish Cup Final had been played between Celtic and St Mirren – a similar mismatch – and Celtic had won 5–0. It seemed inevitable that the same would happen here.

Yet was it as simple as all that? Newcastle fans had been appalled at the team's form in early April when three games in a row had been lost to Bolton, Everton and Aston Villa. There had been no narrow, unlucky defeats; they had all been by more than the one goal. There had been injuries and Jimmy Howie had been away playing for Scotland on 4 April as the team went down 2–0 to Everton, but it had still been a disappointing run of form, ruining what little chance they might have had of winning the Championship. And then, after seeming to stabilise, the Toon's Easter had been ruined by defeats to Sunderland at home on what was called, not without cause, Black Saturday, followed by a defeat to other local rivals, Middlesbrough.

This was hardly the best preparation for the Cup Final at Crystal Palace, already being called an unlucky ground for the Magpies, but on the other hand the form in the FA Cup had been very impressive, with centre-forward Bill Appleyard having scored eight goals so far with a hat-trick against his home town team, Grimsby Town, and two against West Ham United. He was a huge, burly man and was not afraid to use the shoulder-charging tactic so common in Edwardian football.

Injury worries surrounded at least two of Newcastle's team. One was left-back Albert 'Dick' Pudan, suffering from a 'bout of boils'. This seems a bizarre complaint to modern ears but was common enough in the early years of the 20th century. Often it was a euphemism for a more embarrassing complaint like a venereal infection, but it also happened that the skin would suddenly erupt in painful pustules, explained away by the lack of variety in diet with not enough fish, vegetables and fruit.

A more serious complaint concerned Peter McWilliam. An ankle injury sustained in March had kept him out of the side for about a month and cost him a place for Scotland against England. Quite a few Newcastle fans were convinced that if Peter had been available in early April the Geordies would have won the League, but the ankle complaint looked to be so serious that even when he returned to play a couple of League games he did not look to be as fit as he might have been. But he was such a great player that secretary-manager Frank Watt felt that he was worth persevering with. It did seem to quite a few observers, however, that Newcastle were sometimes dangerously over-reliant on McWilliam.

Wolves had finished halfway up the Second Division, some 17 points behind winners Bradford City, whom they had beaten in the first round of the FA Cup in January. Thereafter, their progress had been steady but not spectacular, disposing of Bury, Swindon, Stoke and Southampton. They had some good players, but no great household names.

There was one great character among them, however, a man who even in 1908 sounded like a relic from a bygone age of innocence. This was Kenneth Hunt, who would be ordained as a cleric in 1909, but who in 1908 was still pursuing his studies at Oxford University and played for Wolves as an amateur. He was a fine right-half, so far resisting the siren calls from his friends and colleagues to turn professional and to train full-time as a footballer. As his counterpart on the left was called Alf Bishop, there was a certain ecclesiastical ring to the half-back line.

Billy Harrison on the Wolverhampton right wing would have been forgiven for not having his mind entirely on the game, because something momentous had happened in his life that very morning: he had been informed by telegram that his wife had given birth to triplets. Amidst all the congratulations and joking, he must have wondered how he was going to be able to feed and look after another three children, however much he enjoyed the glory of this highly unusual event.

There had been speculation that the game might have been postponed. Fans arrived in London for the game to find the city in mourning, with many public buildings draped in black. This was because the ex-Prime Minister Sir Henry Campbell-Bannerman had died on the Wednesday before the game and the funeral in Westminster Abbey would not be held until the Monday, before the coffin was taken to his last resting place in Meigle, Perthshire. He had actually died in 10 Downing Street, although he had resigned from office a couple of weeks earlier. He was much respected and loved, not least on Tyneside, where his reforms were seen as some sort of attempt to alleviate the poverty that had enveloped the place for the past 100 years and more.

The crowd was a slightly disappointing 74,967, but there were reasons for that. In the first place it was two out-of-town teams (as was made obvious by the plethora of rosettes in black and white, and in black and gold) and the weather was none too good. The rain was very heavy early in the morning (there had been some snow the night before, but it had turned to sleet at nightfall and rain by dawn), although it had eased off a little by the time the game kicked off. The recent death of the ex-Prime Minister meant that it was not possible for any member of the royal family to be there, so it was Sir John Bell, the Lord Mayor of London, who would present the trophy and the medals to the winning team after the game.

Newcastle began the game with a flourish, knocking the ball about well to each other and relying on runs from Rutherford and Wilson on the wing to make space and then cross the ball for Appleyard to do the needful. But Finlay Speedie was also in good form, showing the crowd why he had won two Scottish League medals with Rangers at the turn of the century and on one occasion releasing Rutherford but to no great effect. Newcastle fans began to question the wisdom of playing Peter McWilliam, however, particularly on such heavy ground, when he was manifestly only half-fit. He was slowed down even further after receiving a knock in the early stages.

Wolves, with goalkeeper Lunn in impressive form, settled and gradually their wing-halves, Hunt and Bishop, took a grip of the game, nullifying the influence of the ever-dangerous Jimmy Howie and cutting off the source of supply to the wingers. It was Hunt who scored the opening goal for Wolves. There was a touch of luck about it because the wet ball slipped through the goalkeeper's hands, but it was a good 25-yard shot from Billy Harrison. Then, just before half-time, Wolves scored again when Hedley collected the ball in midfield, fended off a challenge from the normally reliable Billy McCracken and crashed a ball from about 20 yards past Lawrence.

When this half-time score of 2–0 was telegraphed to Newcastle, those waiting outside the Post Office or the various newspaper offices gasped with disbelief. It was hard to imagine such a disastrous score against a mediocre Second Division team, but it was true enough. Back at the Crystal Palace the incredulity was shared by the Newcastle players. Had they taken the opposition too lightly? They were now up against it, but there was still time to get back into the game.

However, it was still the Wolves 'who were howling and playing with their tails up', as the metaphor went in the newspapers, with Lawrence, still upset by his earlier blunder, being the busier goalkeeper. Newcastle were clearly suffering through having McWilliam half-fit, but it was also true that Appleyard was failing to live up to his early season form, having this time run up against a man of similar bulk and determination, Billy Wooldridge, the centre-half and captain of Wolves, who was playing the game of his life and asserting total mastery of Appleyard, particularly in the air.

It was Wooldridge's one and only bad header of the game that led to Newcastle's goal. A corner-kick was taken and not headed clear, and the ball came fortuitously to the feet of Jimmy Howie, by some distance Newcastle's best man on the field. This came in the 75th minute and raised the spirits of the wet, black and white bedecked Geordie supporters on the mainly uncovered terracing of the Crystal Palace. It was now surely a matter of Newcastle asserting themselves and scoring the equaliser for a replay in midweek at a venue other than the unlucky Crystal Palace.

Unfortunately the goal came at the other end, and it was new father Billy Harrison who scored it. He beat McWilliam then was tackled clumsily by Pudan. Both men went down, but it was Harrison who got up first and charged on goal, with the two half-fit Newcastle players behind him. Lawrence came out to narrow the angle but Harrison hit the ball fast and low into the corner of the net. This was within the last five minutes and there was now no way back for Newcastle.

It was a hard defeat for Newcastle to take. The *Daily Mirror's* 'Citizen' describes it as 'hard Cheddar' for the Newcastle fans to have now travelled three times in four years to the Crystal Palace and not to have seen a victory. Newcastle should have won. Several players were out of touch and McWilliam and Pudan should not have been played. There were reasons for the defeat, but no rational analysis did much to dispel the impression that Crystal Palace was indeed an unlucky and hoodoo ground for Newcastle and that, for some reason, Newcastle were fated never to win the FA Cup.

7

Date: 28 April 1910

BARNSLEY

Match: FA Cup Final replay **Venue: Goodison Park, Everton**

Score: 2–0 **Attendance: 60,000**

Newcastle United:	Barnsley:
Lawrence	Mearns
McCracken	Downs
Carr	Ness
Veitch	Glendinning
Low	Boyle
McWilliam	Utley
Rutherford	Bartrop
Howie	Tufnell
Shepherd	Lillycrop
Higgins	Gadsby
Wilson	Forman

Referee: J. Ibbotson

There could be little doubt about who were the best team in Edwardian England. Newcastle United had won the League Championship in 1905, 1907 and 1909. They had a fine stadium, a large and passionate crowd and a team that simply oozed talent and was able regularly to supply players for both the England and Scotland international sides. But there seemed to be a problem with the FA Cup. Newcastle had yet to win that trophy, in 1910 considered to be the most prestigious of the lot. Cup Final defeats in 1905, 1906 and 1908 had been severe disappointments to the city and to the thousands of 'trippers' who would travel south to see them on big occasions. In these days, Cup Finals were played at the unlucky venue of Crystal Palace. Already it was commonly referred to as the 'Palace of Doom'.

In 1910 Newcastle's League challenge faltered and they finished a respectable fourth, the League being won by Aston Villa, and there is a certain indication that some League games were sacrificed by secretary-manager Frank Watt for the Cup run. No team in the North East had ever yet won the trophy – even the great Sunderland 'All the Talents' side of a decade previously had failed to do so – and 1910 saw little else talked about on Tyneside. The political crisis caused by the House of Lords having turned awkward about Lloyd George's budget, the General Election in January, which produced a hung parliament, the continuing reports of the ill health of King Edward VII: all these things were important. But the destination of the FA Cup was vital.

The road to the Final had been fairly uneventful. A struggle against Stoke in the Potteries had needed a St James' Park replay, but after that it had been home ties all the way and comfortable

Arguably Newcastle's best-ever player – Peter McWilliam – not without cause called 'Peter the Great'.

victories over Fulham, Blackburn Rovers and Leicester City. The semi-final was at White Hart Lane and a sizeable Geordie crowd travelled down on the train to see a 2–0 win over unfancied Swindon Town, with goals coming from Jack Rutherford and Jimmy 'Tadger' Stewart.

Thus it was the Crystal Palace yet again for the FA Cup Final, and this year's opponents were to be Barnsley. The Tykes, as all Yorkshiremen were called, were a Second Division team, but their path to the FA Cup Final had raised a few eyebrows because they had beaten Blackpool 6–0 in January, had got past Bristol Rovers, West Bromwich Albion and Queen's Park Rangers, and then had amazed all Lancashire by beating Everton 3–0 in the semi-final replay at the end of March. As there were two northern sides in the Final it was felt by some Newcastle supporters that a ground like Old Trafford or Goodison might have been more acceptable, but others looked forward to their trip to London – something that was fast becoming an annual, if melancholy, occasion. It certainly was time to lift the Crystal Palace curse.

Those who felt that 23 April was the day that the Cup would be coming to Tyneside for the first time were given a certain amount of encouragement by the news on the previous Wednesday that the Scottish Cup had been won this year by Dundee for the first time. Was it then a year for 'new' teams to win the trophy? A colder, more realistic assessment was based on the consideration that Newcastle simply had better players (Peter McWilliam and Sandy Higgins had both starred for Scotland in the 2–0 defeat of England three weeks previously) and that the run of bad luck at Crystal Palace had to come to an end sooner or later.

A crowd of 77,747 were there to see a disappointing game in which it had looked for a long time as if supernatural forces were once again at work. The teams were well within the last 10 minutes before Rutherford equalised Barnsley's first-half goal. Barnsley supporters felt that Rutherford was offside and some newspapers sympathised. Newspaper reports also mention the lack of animation in London that night among the trippers, because there was little to celebrate by either set of fans. The Geordies had two causes for relief, though. One was that the team were still in the FA Cup, and the other was the venue for the replay, which would be held not at Crystal Palace but at Goodison Park, Liverpool, on Thursday 28 April with a 3.30pm kick-off.

Incredible as it may seem to modern eyes, Newcastle had to play two League games before the replay. On the Monday night they travelled to Bristol City and then, on the night before the replay, they were expected to play League winners Aston Villa. Unashamedly, Newcastle put out a reserve team for both these now irrelevant fixtures, keeping the star men for the big occasion.

'Citizen', the writer in the *Daily Mirror*, was impressed by the crowd that turned up on that Thursday afternoon at Goodison. The receipts were £4,166, and Citizen states that 'if the ground holds 60,000, then that number were present.' Certainly there was a great deal of overcrowding and mounted police were required to clear the playing area as spectators were redirected to less crowded parts of the terracing.

The crowd would have contained a sizeable number from both Newcastle and Barnsley, but many would also have been from the local area, well disposed towards Newcastle not only for the traditional, primeval 'Roses' rivalry between Yorkshire and Lancashire, but also because Barnsley had beaten Everton in the semi-final in somewhat contentious circumstances. During the game, however, loyalties of the neutrals might change.

It had rained heavily in Liverpool all morning, but by kick-off time the sun had come out and a wind had sprung up. The pitch was still heavy, though, something that seemed to favour the burlier Newcastle side. Barnsley won the toss and chose to play against the wind in the first half, hoping to keep Newcastle quiet by defensive play initially and then to strike in the second half. Newcastle, however, desperate for that trophy which meant so much to them, were not prepared to be kept quiet. They were well-motivated; indeed, some of what happened in the game might indicate a degree of over-motivation.

The game was notorious for two controversial and violent incidents. The first one concerned the somewhat contentious 'shoulder-charging' of the goalkeeper. This was technically legal, but could be guaranteed to cause a great deal of argument. It was Sandy Higgins who went in hard on Barnsley goalkeeper Freddie Mearns, a man from Sunderland. Mearns was knocked to the ground and a free-

The English Cup triumph of 1910 meant a great deal to the club and their supporters, as can be seen in these mementoes. Observe the 'old' English Cup in the top picture and the dog in the lower one.

kick was awarded, but Mearns needed attention, and after he had recovered he rushed at Higgins with fists raised and would have meted out some revenge had referee Mr Ibbotson and teammate Dickie Downs not stood in his way and persuaded him of the error of his ways.

Before half-time, in one of Barnsley's rare attacks, a little revenge was dished out. The victim, however, was not Newcastle's goalkeeper but left-back Jack Carr, who was laid out by a charge that referee Ibbotson thought was fair – an opinion not shared by the Geordies and which looked for all the world like retaliation. Happily, Carr recovered, and the ball had gone past in any case, so there was no harm done except to the relations between the two sets of players, 'which were not at all cordial'.

It was after half-time that Newcastle went ahead. Seven minutes had been played when a fine move involving Veitch and Higgins put Albert Shepherd through. He outstripped Downs and Boyle, even against the strong wind, and when Mearns came out to narrow the angle, Shepherd slipped the ball past him with a fast, low shot. It was a goal worthy of winning an FA Cup and was much celebrated by the Newcastle players and fans, and it was all the sweeter for Shepherd himself, who had been dropped for the semi-final against Swindon Town after allegations of involvement with bookmakers.

Newcastle were now well on top as Barnsley clearly tired. It was what followed soon after the goal that cast a black shadow over Newcastle's performance. It centred on Dickie Downs of Barnsley, who seemed to receive a deliberate kick in the 'abdomen', as it was coyly put by the press. The miscreant was not named (one imagines that it was Downs's direct opponent, the mercurial and enigmatic Scotsman, George Wilson, although it may have been Sandy Higgins) but the *Daily Mirror* is in little doubt about the severity of the offence: 'He should without a moment's hesitation have been ordered off the field'. Downs struggled to his feet but then collapsed again and had to be helped off by other players, including some Newcastle ones.

During the stoppage other members of the Newcastle team 'walked away or turned their backs on the offender as he spoke to them', and cries of 'Dirty Newcastle' were heard from all around the ground, with the neutral fans, now preferring Barnsley after the shoulder-charging incident in the first half and what they saw as violent conduct by Newcastle, something which had never really been associated with them in the past. Newcastle's *Evening Chronicle*, which generally blames everything on the 'wretched nature of the pitch' eschews the whole Downs incident and says laconically 'Downes (sic) was injured, but resumed.'

Downs did come back but was clearly struggling, and Newcastle were now even more in command. Soon after Downs's reappearance Glendinning fouled Higgins in the penalty box and Mr Ibbotson had the honour of awarding the first-ever penalty-kick in an FA Cup Final. Bill McCracken, the normal penalty-taker, lumbered up to take the kick but captain Colin Veitch, on a whim, suddenly told Albert Shepherd to step up, on the grounds presumably that Shepherd had already scored a goal and would be feeling confident. Shepherd slotted the kick away without any bother.

The game now fizzled out, with Barnsley looking a beaten team. They would, however, nurse a sense of grievance about this game for a long time, but that would be of little concern to the Geordie supporters who arrived back late that night at Newcastle railway station with the trophy that they had striven for for so long, the FA Cup. They arrived from the west, having come via Carlisle. Scarcely could the Emperor Hadrian ever have imagined such scenes of triumph all along his wall as were seen that night.

Date: 26 April 1911

8

BRADFORD CITY

Match: FA Cup Final replay **Venue: Old Trafford**

Score: 0–1 **Attendance: 66,646**

Newcastle United:	Bradford City:
Lawrence	Mellors
McCracken	Campbell
Whitson	Taylor
Veitch	Robinson
Low	Torrance
Willis	McDonald
Rutherford	Logan
Jobey	Speirs
Stewart	O'Rourke
Higgins	Devine
Wilson	Thompson

Referee: J.H. Pearson

When Mr Pearson blew his full-time whistle at Crystal Palace to end the first game of the 1911 FA Cup Final, the Newcastle supporters all heaved a sigh of relief. It had been a terrible game of football against Bradford City, ending in a goalless draw, but at least Newcastle had not lost. This was quite vital to the Newcastle psyche because their previous visits to Crystal Palace had become a music hall joke. They had lost there three times, their best performance being a draw in the previous year. They had won the replay in 1910, but only because it was played at Goodison, not the 'Palace of Doom'. They now had the opportunity to become the first team for 20 years to win the FA Cup two years in a row.

On the other hand, the Crystal Palace was a missed opportunity to lay the curse to rest. If anything, Newcastle had been the better team, but for one reason or another had been unable to finish off the plucky Bradford side. It may have been that the thought of the curse affected them and they lacked the courage or the confidence to go for the jugular. As a result, the forward line, which had been producing the goods earlier in the season, failed to function and the game, universally described as a 'bore' and a 'non-happening', finished tamely.

There is, of course, no such thing as a curse. Rational analysis will indicate that there is no supernatural deity or power which prevents a team from winning a trophy. But in the heat of the battle – a far from rational place – players will believe that there is a jinx, especially when the ball hits the post and rebounds out rather than in, a key player is off form, a refereeing decision goes the wrong way and so on. The feeling that one is not allowed to win something is a strong one and generations of players can be affected by it – Hibernian have not won the Scottish Cup since 1902, Liverpool have not won the English League since 1990 and Newcastle have not won any major English trophy since 1955. There is the feeling of a curse about each of these records.

There were also rational and more tangible reasons for Newcastle's inability to escape the Crystal Palace hex. Two key players were out of action, one being Peter McWilliam, the left-half. He was called 'Peter the Great', not after a resemblance to any tsar of Russia, but more because of his consistently great and powerful play. He came from the unlikely provenance of a small village called Inveravon in Banffshire in the north of Scotland, and he had been with the club since 1902 and was associated with all the success of that era. He was generally regarded as the best half-back in the business with his famous body swerve and ability to change defence into attack with one kick. On 6 March 1911, however, while captaining Scotland against Wales at Ninian Park, Cardiff, he sustained a nasty knee ligament injury which ruled him out for the rest of the season and effectively curtailed his career, although he would later become a successful manager with Tottenham Hotspur.

This was bad enough, but then a further blow was dealt with an injury to prolific goal scorer Albert Shepherd. Shepherd had been the hero of the previous season's Cup Final and it was a serious blow when he collided with the Blackburn Rovers goalkeeper the week before the Crystal Palace game and was ruled out of the Final. These two blows were bad ones for Newcastle, but they were still expected to win. They were, after all, the current holders of the trophy and had experienced little bother in reaching the Final.

There had been a slight blip with Northampton, and Hull City had put up a fine show, but Bury, Derby County and Chelsea had been put to the sword. League form had been respectable, if a trifle disappointing. The team finished eighth, well behind winners Manchester United, and even several points behind north-east rivals Sunderland, who seemed to be reviving. The idea that the really great

A fine shot of the 'Palace of Doom', as Crystal Palace became known.

days of a few years earlier, when the League Championship had been won in 1905, 1907 and 1909, had now gone did not sit well with the Magpies.

There had been several very good performances, however, with arguably the best being the 6–1 defeat of Bradford City in early December 1910. To a certain extent, this result had been reversed a couple of weeks before the Final when Bradford had won 1–0 in Yorkshire, but few people took that game seriously because Newcastle had rested a few players. It was generally believed that Newcastle had better players in Wilf Low, Sandy Higgins, Jimmy 'Tadger' Stewart and the still-mighty Colin Veitch, who had been the backbone of all Newcastle's success in the past decade. In Frank Watt, nominally the secretary, but in all but name the manager, Newcastle also had the best man to lead the club.

Bradford City had not yet been in existence for a decade, but their progress had been remarkable. They had reached Division One in 1908, and in the 1910–11 season they had finished fifth, bringing a great deal of kudos to Valley Parade. This was their first FA Cup Final, and although they had done well at Crystal Palace it was believed that their hour had passed. Surely the might of Newcastle, even without their star men in McWilliam and Shepherd, would be too much for the Bantams? It would surely be Newcastle who would bring home the FA Cup for the second year running? Not that they would do that in the literal sense, though, because this would be the first year of the new and current FA Cup, the previous one having been presented to Lord Kinnaird. Ironically, Bradford had not a single Yorkshireman in the team, which consisted of two men from Nottingham, an Irishman, and no fewer than eight Scotsmen.

The crowd was officially given as 66,646, with receipts of £4,478. This was a record for a Cup Final played in the provinces, but it was widely believed by all who were there that there was a far bigger attendance than that. It was in the financial interests of the authorities sometimes to understate the attendance so that taxes could be avoided or pockets could be lined, and there was also a large number of young men who managed to climb the wall and gain entrance for nothing. One newspaper estimates the attendance at 75,000.

It was a fine spring day in Manchester with a stiff breeze. Newcastle won the toss and chose to play with the wind, and they were soon on the attack, pegging the Bradford defence back and making it very difficult for them to get the ball out of their own half, let alone mount any sort of attack on the Newcastle goal. Newcastle came close on several occasions, not least when Colin Veitch shot past the post or when Bradford goalkeeper Mark Mellors saved from Sandy Higgins.

As often happens after a sustained period of pressure, a goal came at the other end. It was a funny goal, and one that would haunt Newcastle's goalkeeper Jimmy Lawrence for the rest of his life. It was not his first-ever mistake in an FA Cup Final but it was a costly one and a blot on the career of a man who made a staggering 496 appearances for the club from 1904 until after World War One. He had played for Scotland against England at Goodison in a 1–1 draw a few weeks before and had the misfortune to lose Scotland's only goal to his Newcastle teammate Jimmy Stewart. This high-profile error in the FA Cup Final was probably the reason why he never played for Scotland again.

It was a long ball from Robinson, which Lawrence could have and should have come for and clutched. For some reason he stayed on his goal line and allowed Speirs to get a touch. It was not a clean header, though, because Speirs was distracted by Newcastle defenders and his own man, Thompson (whose head collided with that of Speirs), and the ball was headed downwards. Ridiculously, Lawrence allowed the ball to bounce over his shoulder and into the net. It was an odd goal and reports are vague – the *Daily Mirror*, for example, claims that it was O'Rourke who scored – and the only explanation for Lawrence's indecisiveness was presumably because he expected the whistle to go for a foul.

While the Bradford fans celebrated, Newcastle fans were not too disheartened. There was well over an hour of the game to go, and the team were playing well and creating many chances. Albert Shepherd, had he been playing, would surely have put one or two of them away, but the luckless George Jobey missed a few and 'Tadger' Stewart was also having an off day. Bradford's goalkeeper, Mark Mellors, on the other hand, was having a great match. He was always in the game and he punched, grasped and dived magnificently to ensure that half-time was reached with Bradford still 1–0 in the lead and now with the advantage of the wind.

Newcastle came out battling in the second half. Jobey, who was a better midfielder than a forward, changed places with the determined Veitch, and Newcastle renewed their assault on the Bradford goal. The *Daily Mirror* reported that Newcastle had worked hard in the first half, and they continued to do so in the second, but Bradford's defence was solid. Confidence now grew in the Bradford ranks as they passed the ball about to each other sensibly on the ground, not risking the long clearance which would, in the wind, take the ball out of play and cause them to lose possession.

Newcastle gradually lost heart, their only threat really being George Wilson on the left wing, whose forays caused more than a little consternation, but Mellors continued to be inspired and he was well supported by full-backs Campbell and Taylor as well as centre-half Torrance. Towards the end, as Newcastle tired, Bradford came more and more into the game and Logan hit the bar within the last few minutes.

The referee's whistle brought despair to the Geordies. They would have loved to have said they were the last team to win the old FA Cup and the first to win the new one, but it was Bradford City who collected the trophy (made, funnily enough, by a Bradford silversmith firm called Fattorini's) and Newcastle returned to the city with at least their reputation intact after a gallant performance. But to supporters who were now reared on success, this was a hard pill to swallow.

9

Date: 16 January 1915

WEST HAM UNITED

Match: FA Cup first-round replay **Venue: St James' Park**

Score: 3–2 **Attendance: 28,130**

Newcastle United:	West Ham United:
Mellor	Hughes
McCracken	Burton
Hudspeth	Cope
Spink	Whiteman
Low	Askew
Hay	Woodards
Douglas	Ashton
Hibbert	Leafe
Pailor	Puddefoot
King	Fenwick
Goodwill	Casey

Referee: Mr Warner, Nottingham

The war had come on everyone so suddenly. The 1914 season had ended with Newcastle in mid-table mediocrity, and everyone enjoyed the beautiful weather that summer, although it would have been a fair bet that Geordies talked about little other than their beloved but now disappointing football team. There had been political struggles with Ireland and with the Suffragettes, but no one could have foreseen what was to happen in Europe.

The assassination of the Austrian heir at the end of June was bad, but it was a local affair. Then the big powers began to back themselves into corners, leaving themselves no room for manoeuvre and invoking arcane alliances to justify their posturing. The Kaiser and the Tsar seemed hell bent on war, and duly got it, the Kaiser making the fatal error of invading Belgium, thereby obliging the British Empire to join in. Britain thus found herself fighting against Germany and on the same side as France and even Russia – the two countries against whom she had fought wars in the 19th century.

The next four years would be madness, but it is fair to say that in August 1914 no one realised just how long and crazy it was going to be. Phrases like 'over by Christmas' and even 'before the leaves fall' were commonplace as everyone wanted to enjoy the excitement, a relief from the drudgery of the Tyneside shipyards and hideous coal mines. Football grounds were used as recruiting areas and young men began to be shamed into joining up in the headlong rush to slaughter, when more sober voices (including Lloyd-George himself in his later years) realised that it might have been better to deploy men with certain professions, like shipwrights for example, on the home front rather than allowing them to go and get killed. It was all done under the guise of patriotism, summed up so aptly by Samuel Johnson all those years ago as being 'the last refuge of the scoundrel'.

By late 1914, as news of casualties came back to Newcastle, there was a strong body of opinion that felt that football should stop. A team of fit young men were setting a very bad example if they played football instead of being at the front. 'Khaki is preferable to a black and white jersey for a respectable Magpie' shrieked one letter in the newspaper, and playing football was 'unpatriotic'.

The counter-argument was a very potent one, in that some light relief was required from the horrors of war. Soldiers home on leave would enjoy watching their favourite team and even when at the front or at sea would like to hear in letters how their men were getting on. Football was played in the army. Sometimes there were organised games between regiments of battalions with strips and referees; more often there were impromptu games a few hundred yards from the front line of Newcastle versus Sunderland, Scotland versus England, North versus South and so on. There is even the famous story of a game against the Germans on Christmas Day.

Newcastle fans, both at home and abroad, would have been far more interested in the games at St James' Park on Christmas Day and Roker Park on Boxing Day, in which the away team won on both occasions. Professional football was continuing but with restrictions. Players were only given a one-year contract for a team and could only play part-time. The rest of the week they had to have a war-related or otherwise essential job. No midweek games were allowed lest it interfere with necessary war work, and international games between Scotland, England, Ireland and Wales were stopped, although, perversely, a game between the Scottish League and the English League took place. 'Guest' players, on leave from the forces or who were living in a different part of the country because they were involved in essential war work, were allowed.

Scotland suspended the Scottish Cup, but the FA Cup continued for one year, at least in England. Newcastle were glad of this because it allowed them to continue their love-hate relationship with the trophy. They had won the Cup only once in 1910, but had now had the pain of losing four Cup Finals, in 1905, 1906, 1908 and 1911. The club had seen more pain in 1913, losing to Sunderland in the third game of the quarter-final after two contentious draws.

It was generally agreed that Newcastle in 1914–15 were a pale shadow of the side who had won three League Championships in 1905, 1907 and 1909. This was not surprising; no team can stay at the top for ever and there had been changes of personnel. War, of course, brought its own problems. A player staying out of town could not guarantee being there on time, such were the travails of war transport, and it was not unknown for a player to run out onto the field with his legs all black. This would have been a coal miner, obliged to do a shift on Saturday morning before he was allowed to play for Newcastle United in the afternoon.

Attendances were naturally down on the pre-war years because so many potential spectators were elsewhere, but it would be wrong to assume that football was not taken seriously. If anything, it became even more important to the Geordie psyche, as something was needed to take one's mind off the horrors that were already happening in Europe. Thus when Newcastle were drawn against Southern League team West Ham United (once called the Thames Iron Works Football Club), hopes were high that progress could be made even though the game was in London at the Boleyn Ground, so called because of a tenuous connection with the unfortunate spouse of Henry VIII.

Before a small but enthusiastic crowd of about 15,000, Newcastle started well, scoring twice through Tommy Goodwill, but they tired in the second half after a particularly tedious overnight train journey, allowing Dick Leafe to level the game for West Ham. The case of Tommy Goodwill is a classic example of what war can do. A good football player who played all of season 1914–15, he volunteered to join the army of Lord Kitchener in 1915 when Newcastle gave up for the duration. Goodwill was cut down, like so many other young men, on that horrible morning of 1 July 1916 on the River Somme. He was only 22.

Newcastle's best player in 1915 was, by some distance, their captain, James Hay. He had been with them since 1911 as a direct replacement for Peter McWilliam, and it is fair to say that Newcastle's decline would have been more steep but for the passing, ball-winning and leadership skills of James 'Dun' Hay. His greatest days had been with the all-conquering Celtic, when the half-back line of Young, Loney and Hay had been the mainstay of what is generally regarded as the greatest team ever in Celtic's illustrious history. Now aged 35, he felt he still had a few years left in him.

In the replay the following Saturday West Ham won the toss and chose to play with the wind towards the Gallowgate End, and in three minutes they went ahead when Askew won a header and headed on to Casey, who hammered home from eight yards. Newcastle were a little put out by this but when they did get back into the game it was from a great piece of play involving Goodwill, who played a one-two with King then sent the ball to Bob Pailor to do his duty. This was on the half-hour mark and immediately after this Pailor was tripped in the penalty box as he walked up the field, but referee Mr Warner was on hand to prevent things getting out of hand. A minute later Pailor headed home in a goalmouth scramble.

At half-time the 28,130 crowd ('the sixpenny parts of the ground were well filled' says the *Evening Chronicle*) were invited to join the Northumberland Fusiliers. A variety of dignitaries, starting with the Lord Mayor, Alderman T. Fitzgerald, took the microphone to deliver the message, but unfortunately the message did not get through because the speakers, which had been rigged up in the four corners of the ground, were drowned out by the strong wind. Leaflets were also handed out to 'likely looking young men' as the *Evening Chronicle* put it. A few members of the crowd expressed their willingness to join the colours and were cheered and clapped as they came out on to the pitch.

Both teams scored in the second half, and Newcastle had to survive a late onslaught to hold out for a narrow and just-deserved victory after Dick Leafe scored for the Hammers and Billy Hibbert for the Geordies. A long ball from McCracken was not cleared by Cope and Hibbert was on the spot to fire home 'with tremendous power' from 15 yards. Hibbert was a fine player, bought from Bury in 1911 after he had won his one and only cap for England, but he had not yet scored as many goals for the club in the way that Appleyard had used to do a few years previously.

Newcastle eventually lost to Chelsea in the quarter-final of the FA Cup and finished 15th out of 20 in Division One in this unusual season. Perhaps the biggest talking point of the season belongs, however, to John King, the talented Scottish inside-forward. On Good Friday Newcastle travelled to Tottenham Hotspur. White Hart Lane was buzzing with 18,000 fans, including a fair number of soldiers about to embark for overseas, wishing to see Spurs, now managed by Peter McWilliam, playing against the team that McWilliam had played for with such distinction for so long.

The only problem was that Newcastle did not have a goalkeeper. Bill Mellor, the only goalkeeper in the party, injured himself in the warm up and such were wartime necessities that they did not have another one with them. McWilliam nobly offered a reserve and even to make a loudspeaker appeal for some young goalkeeper in the crowd, but John King offered to step up – and then kept a clean sheet!

For whatever reason, Newcastle United decided not to continue after the summer of 1915. Many felt that this was the wrong choice and it did lead indirectly to several men joining up, including the tragic case of Tommy Goodwill, but things were becoming prohibitively difficult on a practical level and the moral and emotional blackmail was becoming harder and harder to resist.

10
ARSENAL

Date: 30 August 1919

Match: League Division One　　　　　　**Venue: Highbury**

Score: 1–0　　　　　　　　　　**Attendance: 55,000**

Arsenal:	Newcastle United:
Williamson	Lawrence
Shaw	McCracken
Bradshaw	Hudspeth
Graham	Curry
Voysey	Low
McKinnon	Finlay
Rutherford	Robinson
Groves	Henderson
White	Wilson
Blyth	Hall
Baker	Hibbert

Referee: W.O. Furness

'The braggart bully of Berlin,
The man of greed and lust,
Plunged in a gulf of dark despair
Lies bleeding in the dust.
He thowt he had an easy job
To conquer aal the world,
But he and aal his evil band
To ruin have been hurled.'

So writes 'G.J.B. of Gosforth' as Newcastle prepared to face their first post-war game against Arsenal at Highbury. World War One had now been over for nine months, and the 'limbo' season, in which the world was at peace but football had proved impossible to organise on any major level, was now over. This would be Newcastle's first serious game since 1915.

Newcastle had, to all intents and purposes, been in abeyance since that date. For reasons of distance and the problems involved in travelling during the war, Newcastle had not taken part in any League competition, although one might have thought that with a little imagination and determination, there could have been some sort of competition during the dark and desperate days of the war to lighten the gloom. There had been in other parts of the country, in London and

Scotland, for example, but the only football played by the Magpies at all since 1915 had been the Northern Victory League, hastily organised after the Armistice in November 1918 and which lasted from January 1919 until April of that year.

For this reason the start of the season was looked forward to even more than normal, and Newcastle's first game on 30 August 1919 was at a place called Highbury, in London, against a team once known as Woolwich Arsenal, but now more and more just known as Arsenal. It was a mystery to most people why Arsenal found themselves in Division One. A decision had been taken to expand Division One from 20 to 22 clubs, but there had been little to suggest that Arsenal, who had finished fifth in Division Two in 1915, deserved to be there. They had done well enough in the wartime London Combination, but had never won it, and quite a few teams, notably their North London rivals Tottenham Hotspur, felt that they deserved to be there before Arsenal. But Arsenal, even in 1919, had money and influence and could 'knock on doors'.

Newcastle had never before played at Highbury. When they had last met in season 1912–13 Arsenal played at a place called Plumstead, and they had been relegated that year. Enterprise secured them this ground that would be called Highbury, a better ground and more favourably situated, with good links to the town centre. The stadium was on land originally leased from the St John's College of Divinity, and the landowners were insistent that no home games would be played by Arsenal on either Christmas Day or Good Friday.

Ten years had now passed since Newcastle last won the League Championship. The years leading up to and including World War One had seen a slight decline in Newcastle's status as other teams took over, including Sunderland in 1913, to Newcastle's chagrin, but Newcastle were still a respectable outfit with a large support, increasingly consisting of a number of supporters affluent enough to travel by train to away games. The war had seen a rise in the number of buses on the roads of Great Britain, but London was just too far away to travel by that method. A few people sailed down the east coast, however.

In some ways football had prospered during the war, in that although organised football was makeshift, there had been a great deal of it played. In the fields behind the trenches there had always been games going on, and lots of footballs had been sent by well-meaning people, reckoning that fit young men would be better off playing football than frequenting the bars and whorehouses of northern France. There was thus no lack of interest in football in 1919.

Newcastle were lucky in that they still had several members of their great team of before the conflict still playing for them. This was possibly a mixed blessing as these men would now be getting on in years and inevitably would have lost some of their sharpness. There was, for example, Jimmy Lawrence, a well-known and much-loved goalkeeper who had been with the club since 1904 and who had played in all the great games of the Edwardian era, and had been desperately unlucky not to earn more than one Scottish cap. There was also Billy McCracken, that feisty, awkward Irishman, a great full-back who, along with Frank Hudspeth, perfected the offside trap, so much so that when opposition players arrived at Newcastle Station before a game and heard a whistle they would remark 'Oh no, I'm offside already and I haven't even seen the ground!'

Wilfred Low, commonly known as the Laughing Cavalier, largely because he did not laugh too often on the field, was still playing. He was a handsome, burly centre-half from Aberdeen, known for his ability to break up attacks. He was still very much in contention for Scotland caps (he would play in two of their games in the first post-war season) and his career had prospered during the war, in which he had served with the Royal Engineers and had on occasion made guest appearances for various London teams, mainly Fulham. He had been the bedrock of the defence before the war and remained very popular on Tyneside even though he had a brother, Harry, who played for Sunderland.

On the other hand there would be no Albert Shepherd. The charismatic hero of Tyneside had gone to Bradford City on the very eve of the war and injuries had brought a premature end to his career. Colin Veitch had now returned from the war, in which he had served as Second Lieutenant, but was now involved in the training side of the club rather than the playing side. In this role he would be a vital part in developing the team that would win the FA Cup in 1924.

The great Jackie, Jack or Jock Rutherford was now playing for the Gunners. The *Sunday Sun* has this marvellous quote from one of the Arsenal directors, who told the reporter that Rutherford 'is like holding up a glass of old port to the light before making a closer acquaintance with its liquid sunshine'. Clearly the Arsenal director was a poet in his spare time, but there can be little doubt that Rutherford was a star player for Arsenal in the same way as he had been for Newcastle before his transfer in 1913.

The very nature of the situation in 1919 meant that Newcastle had several debutants that day: Ray Robinson, Jimmy Henderson, Jack Wilson and one or two others whose experience was limited, to put it mildly. The crowd was given as 55,000 that sunny day and it was yet another sign that the war was now over. Football was back and everyone wanted to reassure themselves that there would be no more recruiting drives, no more army parades, no more guns, no more field dressing stations and no more red Post Office motor bicycles with telegrams of bad news.

Already though there were signs that the post-war world was going to be vastly different from the cosy world of before the war. The country had got used to the idea of female tram conductors on trams in London (they would still be needed there for some time, such was the shortage of men) and women now began to be more assertive. Labour unrest was already a feature of British life — there had even been a police strike in some parts of the country — and it was becoming obvious that the railways and the mines were going to cause trouble. War was still going on in Mesopotamia, Russia and closer to home in Ireland, but on this bright summer day in perfect weather London was at peace.

There had been several changes since 1914 — melancholy ones like the disabled enclosure, with men on crutches and wearing the 'hospital blue' uniform; lines of the blind, arm on the shoulder of the man in front of them, being led in to hear a commentary from several volunteers; women collecting for various hospitals and nursing homes; and beggars, not always disabled and sometimes with ill-clad children beside them to attract sympathy. Fortunately it was a warm day, and somehow this did not seem so bad in the sunlight. There were men with no obvious signs of disfigurement but who stared at the world with dull, uncomprehending eyes. They were the shell-shocked, men who attracted little sympathy from the authorities, who were often described as 'lacking in moral fibre' or simply 'cowards'. Their wounds would not heal very easily, any more than would the mental wounds of the women and children who had lost their breadwinners.

It was not all grim, though. There were others who were just glad to be alive and going to a football match. Cockney accents mingled with the occasional Geordie one, and everyone who had served knew someone who came from the other camp, as it were. Drink had been taken in great quantities and songs tore through the air — not so much *The Blaydon Races* or their London equivalents but the old war songs like *Tipperary* and the resigned, philosophical 'We're here because we're here because we're here…', the song that went on for ever.

One first-half goal would settle the game and it came in the 25th minute from Newcastle debutant Jimmy Henderson, who picked up a good ball from Jack Wilson to put it past Williamson with a 'finely judged, oblique shot to put the leather into the net'. The goal was greeted with loud cheers by the Newcastle supporters and even the partisan London crowd gave it a round of applause. The *Evening Chronicle* claims that there was 'no more popular team in the south than Newcastle'. It was the first goal the crowd had seen in 'real' football for some time. They were less happy when Newcastle spent most of the second half deploying their offside trap, where McCracken, Low and Hudspeth all moved forward at the same time to leave several forwards in an offside position. This struck Londoners and newspapermen as negative, and it would eventually lead to a change in the law.

As Newcastle boarded their train at King's Cross Station that night after a good evening meal, they had the satisfaction of knowing that a new era had begun and they were leaving the capital with two points. Wednesday afternoon would see the arrival of West Bromwich Albion at St James' Park. That was something to look forward to.

Date: 13 February 1924

11

DERBY COUNTY

Match: FA Cup second-round third replay   **Venue: St James' Park**

Score: 5–3   **Attendance: 32,496**

Newcastle United:	Derby County:
Mutch	Olney
Hampson	Chandler
Hudspeth	Crilly
Mooney	McIntyre
Spencer	Thoms
Gibson	Plackett
Low	Keetley
Cowan	Whitehouse
Harris	Galloway
McDonald	Storer
Seymour	Murphy

Referee: J.T. Howcroft, Bolton

The 32,496 who made their way to the Gallowgate on the afternoon of Wednesday 13 February 1924 would have been forgiven for a sense of *déjà vu*. After all, they had been there exactly a week previously to see the same two teams playing at the same stage of the same tournament. There had been some 18,000 more last week, the decrease in numbers this week possibly reflecting a certain amount of ennui, 'turnstile fatigue', or more mundanely, a lack of money or ability to get another afternoon off work.

In 1924 things had changed in the world. There was now a Labour Prime Minister in Ramsay MacDonald, although he was hardly secure in power, and he was heavily dependent on Liberal support in a very uneasy and brittle coalition that was not likely to last for long. Nevertheless, it was an indication of how life was never going to be the same again in the wake of World War One, and poor George V had to confess to his diary one night that he wondered what grandmama (Queen Victoria) would have thought of a Labour government.

The opposition was Derby County, a team currently doing well at the top of the Second Division but one that Newcastle would have been expected to deal with fairly easily and competently. As it turned out, there had now been three 2–2 draws between the two teams. The first had been at the Baseball Ground on Saturday 2 February, then at St James' Park on Wednesday 6 February, and another at Burnden Park, Bolton, on Monday 11 February. For a while it seemed that the deadlock was to be broken at Bolton, when Derby were 2–1 ahead in extra-time, but Stan Seymour scored a last-minute equaliser. The Bolton game had seen a low attendance and after it was drawn both teams had rejected the idea of another neutral venue and had opted to toss a coin for home grounds. Newcastle had won the toss and Derby were less than upset with this because they knew of the huge gates that the Magpies could attract. Even the 32,496 who appeared (although a trifle disappointing) was a far bigger gate than one would have reasonably expected anywhere else.

It is very common for supporters to be cynical about the number of drawn games in Cup ties and the resultant big gates in replays. The riot at the Scottish Cup Final of 1909 had been about this very point, but it does remain very difficult to explain how a 'draw' can be arranged. It would have to involve all the players, and it is hard to imagine this being done without someone leaking the story to the press. After all, if a player is prepared to go along with corruption in the first instance, he would probably also be inclined to accept a backhander from a newspaper for selling his story.

While it would be naïve to believe that match-fixing does not go on – it certainly did happen, for example, in Italy in the early 2000s – it would be over-suspicious to believe that it necessarily happened here. Apart from anything else, it was not succeeding in its aims, as we have already mentioned the law of diminishing returns in the lower attendances. It was, however, widely believed in the shipyards and coal mines of the area that the tie was being unnecessarily prolonged. The penalty shoot-out rule of modern times prevents this sort of thing happening now.

There is a hint of political machinations at work in the choice of referee for this fourth game. Sam Rothwell of St Anne's had refereed the first two games without any hint of controversy, but Derby were up in arms about the third game. They claimed that the penalty that Frank Hudspeth put away was a soft one and that the free-kick from which Seymour levelled the tie was no free-kick at all. This seems, nearly 90 years later, to have been a moan at a few decisions that they didn't like rather than any serious claim against the competence or integrity of Mr Rothwell, but Derby insisted on another referee. Newcastle agreed, and the cynics once more had a field day, suggesting that there was a pact between the two clubs whereby Newcastle could have a home tie but Derby could appoint the referee. For whatever reason, it was Mr Howcroft of Bolton who appeared with the whistle.

Arguments raged among the Geordie faithful about the usefulness or otherwise of Scottish striker Neil Harris. He was small and nippy, with the ability to get round a defender, but he had little in the way of heading ability and far too often his yield of goals had been less than expected. He is described on a cigarette card as being 'a player of the most aggressive type but apt to be impetuous through an excess of zeal; fast on the ball and free in distribution'. He was a Glaswegian who had played for Partick Thistle before World War One. The war had taken him to Ireland, where he played for Distillery, and then to London and to Fulham, with whom he won the Victory Cup in 1919. He had then joined the Magpies in 1920. His goalscoring record of 19, 23 and 14 in the three previous seasons had been acceptable without being outstanding, but it was noticeable that he was never able to displace Andy Wilson, the sitting tenant in the Scotland centre-forward position. The events of this day were to change that, however.

The very few Derby supporters in the ground (the paucity was hardly surprising as it was midweek and this would be the third time they had travelled north in 11 days) had scarcely arrived when their centre-forward, with the unlikely name of Randolph Galloway, put them ahead. Five minutes later, the same Galloway did it again, and the Newcastle supporters who had been on early shift and had rushed to the ground, piece bags and all, could scarcely believe it when they climbed up the steps to the terracing to be told that the team were 2–0 down.

This time it looked as if there was to be no comeback. The players were all exhausted after so many games (although 'exhaustion' was something that normally cut very little ice with supporters who had been down mines doing backbreaking work) and the Derby team were passing the ball around well. But left-half Willie Gibson, in his first season for Newcastle, began to take a grip on the game. Gibson had joined Newcastle from Ayr United, the club having been tipped off by Jimmy Hay, the great left-half of a decade previously. Hay was now manager of Clydebank, but had coached Gibson at Ayr a few seasons before that and had kept in touch with Newcastle's secretary, Frank Watt.

By half-time Newcastle were not only back in the game, they were actually ahead thanks to a hat-trick scored in 25 minutes by Neil Harris. It was one of those games when everything goes right for a striker – when the ball goes the right side of the post, when the defender makes a mistake, when the goalkeeper does not have a 'blinder' – and the score at half-time read Newcastle 3, Derby 2. The goals were all routine, unspectacular ones, scored due to Harris simply being in the right place at the right time to take advantage of all the good work men like Gibson, Seymour and McDonald were doing, particularly down the left-hand side of the field.

The teams left the field at half-time having scored five goals between them and the pace of the game gave the lie to any idea of players being tired. The key factor was adrenaline and the basic urge to play, no matter how many games had been played in recent days. It was all about attitude, and both teams deserved a great deal of credit for their desire to win this football match.

The goals did not stop there. About 10 minutes into the second half left-winger Stanley Seymour, already one of the darlings of the St James' Park crowd in spite of his Sunderland background, scored again to make Newcastle safe, or so it appeared. Soon after that the game was in the balance again when Harry Storer scored for Derby County to bring the game back to 4–3. This time adrenaline took hold of Derby County, and Newcastle's back three of Sandy Mutch, Billy Hampson and Frank Hudspeth were called on to save the day as wave after wave of Derby County attacks rained on them.

It was Newcastle who won through, though, this time with a goal scored by the much under-rated Willie Cowan, the least known of Newcastle's Scottish inside trio of Cowan, Harris and McDonald. He was a shy man by nature, but on the field he could be a mazy dribbler with a devastating shot from both feet, and this was Billy's moment of glory as he latched onto a loose ball on the edge of the box and hammered home.

This made it 5–3 and now Derby really were exhausted. They had been close to levelling the score and bringing the tie to extra-time and what would have been a scarcely believable fifth game, but Cowan's goal knocked the heart from them. They still received a sporting ovation from the Geordie crowd at the end, although one would have to say that there was a certain amount of relief that the tie was all over at last. The tie had lasted some 420 minutes and had yielded 20 goals.

There were long-term effects of this tie. One was that Newcastle got some momentum to go on and win the FA Cup, and another was that the tie was much talked about in newspapers and journals and did a great deal to create the long-standing belief that Newcastle were a great Cup-fighting team. They would indeed have more than their fair share of marathons in years to come. The third effect was on Cowan and Harris. Scotland selectors began to take an interest in them, and it was no surprise on Tyneside when they were chosen to play for Scotland in the nation's first-ever trip to Wembley on 12 April. (Poor Tommy McDonald, the inside-left, was left wondering why he wasn't invited as well.) They would also return to Wembley a couple of weeks later for the FA Cup Final.

12

Date: 26 April 1924

ASTON VILLA

Match: FA Cup Final   **Venue: Wembley**

Score: 2–0   **Attendance: 91,695**

Newcastle United:	Aston Villa:
Bradley	Jackson
Hampson	Smart
Hudspeth	Mort
Mooney	Moss
Spencer	Milne
Gibson	Blackburn
Low	York
Cowan	Kirton
Harris	Capewell
McDonald	Walker
Seymour	Dorrell

Referee: W.E. Russell

Wembley! The very name in the 1920s conjured up wealth and prosperity. It was something to aspire to, something to aim for, and when Newcastle reached the second Final of the FA Cup to be played there the whole of Tyneside was set alight with anticipation. Crystal Palace, on five occasions the cause of disappointment to the Magpies, in two draws and three defeats, had now had its day. Stamford Bridge had been used for 1920, 1921 and 1922 and Wembley had been opened in time for the 1923 Cup Final between Bolton and West Ham.

The opponents in 1924 were to be Aston Villa, the greatest FA Cup team of them all. They had already won the Cup on six occasions – three times in the 19th century; once in 1905 on the all-too-well-remembered occasion of Newcastle's first Cup Final; then in 1913 when they beat Sunderland 1–0 before an astonishing crowd of over 120,000; and finally in the first Cup Final after World War One, when they beat Huddersfield Town 1–0 in 1920 at Stamford Bridge. Against that, Newcastle had only 1910 to boast about.

Everyone knew about Wembley's first Cup Final in 1923, in particular about the heroics of Police Constable Scorey and his white horse in keeping the crowd at bay to allow the game to take place and to prevent serious injuries, but the long-term effect of that was that the 1924 Cup Final and all subsequent ones would have to be all-ticket, a revolutionary concept for the times. An estimated quarter of a million fans had endeavoured to see that 1923 Cup Final, but the 1924 Cup Final would be limited to 91,695. Two Newcastle players, Willie Cowan and Neil Harris, had had

A fine picture of Frank Hudspeth shaking hands with the opposing captain. Note the style of dress of the referee and the large centre spot with a diameter in the circle. This is before the semi-final and the opposition is Manchester City.

an opportunity to play on the ground before the Cup Final, as they had been fortunate enough to have been selected for Scotland to play against England in the 1–1 draw a fortnight earlier.

There had not been a great deal to shout about on Tyneside in the years since World War One, although League positions had been consistently good. Like the rest of the country, the Newcastle area had suffered terribly in World War One, but by 1924 there was a certain amount of optimism in the air. There was now, for example, a Labour government, albeit a minority one and one that was not destined to last long, and there were definite signs that life was changing, with the working man considerably less inclined to accept the leadership of the rich, the Church and the officer class than before. The early 1920s were hard times, but as the recurrent labour problems in the mines, the railways and the docks would indicate, the working men were now going to fight.

A trip to London to see a Cup Final was possible – even before the war Newcastle had never lacked supporters on their baleful trips to the Palace of Doom, as the Crystal Palace was nicknamed – but the cost was prohibitive. 53 shillings would give you an all-in trip, including meals, ticket and train fare, leaving on the Friday night and returning on the Sunday. That price, however, would represent considerably more than a week's wages, but the important factors were commitment and determination. Geordie supporters have never lacked these. The Toon Army was there in strength that day, some coming by train and others by steamer, choosing to brave the winds and rain of the North Sea to get to London.

Newcastle United would be fined £750 for their conduct in the run-up to the Cup Final. On several occasions they fielded a weakened team in League matches in order to protect their first-team players for the big match. They were neither the first nor the last to do that, but most teams were slightly more circumspect than Newcastle were in 1924. On the Monday before the Cup Final, by sheer chance, they had to play Aston Villa at Villa Park. There was nothing subtle about Newcastle's approach to this one. They fielded virtually their reserve team, with only two recognised first-teamers in goalkeeper Sandy Mutch and left-half Willie Gibson. Newcastle lost 6–1 and left the field to the jeers of the Villa fans. Goalkeeper Mutch injured his knee and was compelled to miss the Final.

Newcastle took their players south a few days before the Final to stay in a hotel at Harrow on the Hill. It would be fair to say that for quite a few of the Newcastle players this would be a different world, staying in this opulent hotel in a prosperous suburb of London. It was in stark contrast to the grim industrial areas of the north-east of England and the west of Scotland from where so many of their players sprung. Staying in a hotel like this would be regarded as one of the perks of a professional footballer's life in the 1920s.

On Cup Final morning the players woke up to rain – grim, relentless rain. Supporters of both teams arrived in the capital to find everything wet, even to the extent of a rumour spreading that the game had been postponed. This was not likely to happen, however, as the drainage at the new stadium was superb. The teams were presented to the Duke of York, the shy, stammering, younger son of King George V and Queen Mary. He was a genuine football fan and was frequently asked to make an appearance on such occasions. His elder brother, the Prince of Wales, had in any case broken his

Action from the 1924 Cup Final as Newcastle come close to saving.

collarbone while hunting a few weeks earlier, and his father had opened the Wembley Exhibition centre a few days before. He could not reasonably be asked to come back so soon, but fortunately 'Bertie' was more than happy to oblige.

The all-ticket crowd was comfortably housed in the stadium by the appointed time, many of them clearly overwhelmed by the size and magnificence of the ground and quite a few obviously

Frank Hudspeth with the Cup.

having enjoyed some liquid refreshment in London. But they were orderly and well behaved, with Villa supporters mixing freely and happily with the black and white visitors from the North East and exchanging greetings with each other in their distinctive regional dialects, which sometimes rendered communication difficult. A local paper carried a story of a Newcastle supporter's chance encounter with an Aston Villa fan with whom he had shared a trench in 1917.

The pitch was wet and greasy, and both teams put up a fine performance, although the consensus of opinion was that Villa were the better team in the first half. Both teams had had some chances, but Villa had rather more. Newcastle's stand-in goalkeeper, Bill Bradley, a local giant from Gateshead, saved his side on several occasions, but half-time came and went with no goals scored and the game seemed to be heading for extra-time.

Gradually through the second half, though, Newcastle began to take control. Crucially the half-back line of Mooney, Spencer and Gibson began to get a grip on the midfield. In the 1920s a good half-back line was what won games because they gathered balls and distributed them, the wing-halves working in a triangle with the inside and outside-forward on their side of the field and allowing the centre-half to move up the pitch to be a second centre-forward. Villa, possibly discouraged by their inability to score, and certainly exhausted by their supreme effort, began to lose the key area of the middle of the park.

The game was well within the last 10 minutes when Newcastle struck. Accounts of the build-up play vary, but it is certain that Glaswegian Neil Harris was the man who scored. Harris had struggled for a few years at St James' Park since he joined Newcastle at the end of the war, but in 1924 he had struck a rich vein of form, particularly in the Cup run, in which he had scored the two goals that beat Manchester City in the semi-final. On this occasion the *Sunday Pictorial* tells us that 'rapidly the ball was passed between all three inside-forwards. Then Spencer pushed it out to Stanley Seymour. The left-winger slipped the ball back and Cowan shot. It was repulsed by Jackson. Neil Harris had run behind Cowan and on the latter's right hand. The ball came to him a few inches from the ground and a first-time shot left Jackson hopelessly at sea.'

The Geordie fans went wild with delight, and the crowd was still in turmoil when Aston Villa rallied in desperation and inside-right Billy Kirton (a Geordie, ironically, who had scored the extra-

It's a pity no one was able to smile for the camera in this picture of the 1924 Cup-winning team.

time goal for Villa to beat Huddersfield in the 1920 Cup Final) had a clear header on the Newcastle goal, but he put it over the bar, to the visible and audible distress of the supporters from Birmingham.

A couple of minutes later the Cup was won, and it was a glorious goal. Once again Willie Cowan was involved, slipping the ball to Stanley Seymour, who made one of his many significant contributions to the history of Newcastle United by slamming the ball hard into the roof of the net and putting the issue beyond any doubt. Seymour, who had learned most of his football in Scotland at Greenock Morton during the war, had had a poor game up to this point, being well marked by right-back Smart, but this goal was his finest hour so far, and he would recall it with pleasure on many occasions over the next five decades of his life.

Mr Russell's whistle went soon after, with Geordie cheers ringing round the ground, and Villa fans either staying to cheer sportingly or going home to nurse the black feelings and emotions that only a Cup Final defeat can bring. It was Frank Hudspeth, a veteran of the Royal Navy in World War One and a veteran in the footballing sense as well, who picked up the Cup. Frank had been a fine servant for the club, the only club that he had ever wanted to play for. He had a few days previously celebrated his 34th birthday, and he had several years left in him yet.

By the time that Frank picked up the trophy the telegrams had been sent to the various Post Offices and newspaper offices in Tyneside, outside of which those Geordies who had not been able to afford the fare to London had gathered. The news was greeted with joy as impromptu renderings of *The Blaydon Races* resounded round the city. But even that was only a preparation for the great reception that would be given to the team when they returned to Newcastle.

13

Date: 30 April 1927

SHEFFIELD WEDNESDAY

Match: Division One

Venue: St James' Park

Score: 2–1

Attendance: 28,421

Newcastle United:	Sheffield Wednesday:
Wilson	Brown
Maitland	Felton
Hudspeth	Blenkinsop
McKenzie	Leach
Spencer	Kean
Curry	Marsden
Urwin	Hooper
Clark	Strange
Gallacher	Trotter
McDonald	Allen
Seymour	Wilkinson

Referee: Cannot be traced

It would be understandable if the Geordies had made their way to St James' Park on the afternoon of 30 April 1927 with a spring in their step. They were English League Champions in all but name. A draw against Sheffield Wednesday would secure it for them mathematically – even avoiding a heavy defeat would do the job – but it had been obvious for some time that they would win the title for the fourth time overall, thus breaking the stranglehold that Huddersfield had over English football. Huddersfield had won the title for the past three years and had been Newcastle's main rivals for it in 1927.

It had now been 18 years since Newcastle had last won the Championship in 1909, a year that seemed a long time ago, the intervening years made all the worse by the all-embracing effects of World War One. But this season Newcastle United had Hugh Kilpatrick Gallacher at his best. 'Hughie' is considered by some historians to have been the greatest centre-forward of all time. He was certainly the best that Newcastle had ever had, according to the song:

'Dae ye ken Hughie Gallacher, the wee Scots lad?
The best centre-forward the Geordies ever had.'

This season of 1926–27 was very definitely Gallacher's Newcastle peak. He was a prolific goalscorer with tremendous ability to do everything that was required to score a goal. He could head

Hughie Gallacher, Newcastle's wayward genius.

Hughie and his wife. Note the bowler hat, double-breasted suit and cigarette.

a ball, he could turn when his back was to the goal and fire home unstoppable shots, he could score with either foot, and he had the striker's instinct of being able to be in the right place at the right time. He was fortunate enough this season in particular to enjoy great service from Bob Clark, Tommy McDonald and Stanley Seymour, and the goals simply would not stop coming. He would score a phenomenal total of 39 goals in League and Cup, a remarkable total considering how many men he had on him, marking him closely and being none too particular, in some cases, about the way that they did it.

Men of genius, particularly on the football field, often have character defects and Hughie was no exception. He was simply a lad from the deprived and impoverished Lanarkshire coalfield who could play football, and he had no idea how to handle life off the field. He was not universally liked. Bob McPhail, who played with him for both Airdrie and Scotland, described him as 'a selfish wee fellow', and his first few months with Newcastle after he joined them in December 1925 were marked by arguments and quarrels with his teammates.

It was in summer 1926 that the Newcastle directors assessed the Gallacher situation and made the decision that he should be appointed captain. This decision was greeted with incredulity in Tyneside and in Gallacher's native Scotland, but it was based on the sound reasoning that as the club had laid out the colossal sum of £6,500 for Gallacher, everything must be done to make this idea work. He would have to take some responsibility, and he would perhaps get some kind of an inkling of what a big professional club was all about. Those who questioned the judgement of the Newcastle board of directors were eating their words by Christmas.

Whatever may have been said about him off the field, he was never less than totally fit on the field and totally dedicated to the cause. He was small and stocky but had very strong shoulders, so necessary in those days to see off the charges of the sometimes brutal defenders. He was no shrinking violet in the tackle himself, it must be said, and he had a long memory for those who had tried to injure him. He was also very obviously a man of the people, always willing to talk on the street, clearly enjoying the adulation. He had a good side to him as well. There was a story that one cold frosty night near Christmas he saw an old drunk shivering in a doorway near the railway station. He immediately took off his overcoat and wrapped it round the old man on the grounds that he could afford another one, whereas the man could not. Whether this story is true or not will never be determined, but the fact was that it was told about him – and believed.

In his first game as captain on 28 August 1926 Aston Villa were beaten 4–0 at St James' Park, and Hughie scored all four. On another four occasions that year he scored hat-tricks, and it was very seldom that he did not find the net. The team lost at Roker Park that year on 30 October, to the disappointment of the Geordies, but it was put down to 'Wor Hughie' being away playing for Scotland against Ireland that day, scoring Scotland's first goal in a 3–0 win.

There was more to this team than Hughie Gallacher, however. Mention has been made of the service provided by the other forwards, but the strength of a team in the 1920s often lay in its half-back line. Newcastle had Roddie MacKenzie, Charlie Spencer and Willie Gibson, although Gibson was out injured by the end of the season. Further back there was the incomparable Frank Hudspeth, to whom praise is due for his commitment to the club – he played 472 games for them – and his self-effacing loyalty, which allowed him to step down from the captaincy to make way for Gallacher without any tantrums. He may have had his own views about Gallacher as a character, but he carried on in his own inimitable way. Grossly undervalued by the England selectors, Hudspeth was one of the many Newcastle players about whom it was said that he must have wished he had been Scottish. That way he might have earned far more international recognition.

Life on Tyneside was far from easy in 1927 in the vindictive aftermath of the General Strike as unemployment rose and jobs were scarce. But football always was a huge thing for Newcastle and this year it was even more so. A crowd of 67,211 saw Gallacher score the only goal of the game to beat Sunderland on 19 March, and then another crowd of over 62,000 saw him doing likewise against Huddersfield on Good Friday, a result which put the League Championship within Newcastle's grasp. In those days they often played return fixtures over the Easter Weekend and Huddersfield won the return game at Leeds Road on the Tuesday to give themselves a slight chance, but that all but disappeared on the Saturday when Newcastle earned a draw at Upton Park against West Ham United. On that day, incidentally, all London was captivated by the idea that a team from Wales, Cardiff City, had lifted the English Cup by beating Arsenal with a goal scored by a Scotsman, Hughie Ferguson.

Gallacher felt that he had a point to prove. He had been upset on 2 April when he had played for Scotland at Hampden and Scotland had lost 2–1 to England in what was, incredibly, their first defeat at Hampden since it had opened in 1903. Gallacher had not scored that day and it had been Everton's Dixie Dean who had taken all the honours with his two late goals. Such things hurt Hughie. For all his bravado and aggression (made all the worse by alcohol), Hughie was a sensitive creature and the criticism of his performance in the Scottish press had hurt, as indeed had the jibes of the English crowds, who had revelled in what was a rare victory against Scotland.

There was also Wednesday's Jimmy Trotter, a Geordie from Byker, who was rivalling Gallacher's goalscoring. He would end up scoring one more League goal than Gallacher that season, but that day it was an interesting sideshow to what was the main attraction. Sheffield Wednesday themselves were no great shakes – they would finish up 16th in the League – but they had a great tradition to maintain and, like most Yorkshire institutions, had no great love of Newcastle United.

Spurred on a by a crowd of 28,421 (slightly disappointing, but the weather was by no means encouraging), who had been more than a little annoyed by a prolonged taking of photographs before the game began, Newcastle started strongly, but it was soon obvious that nerves were playing a part on this occasion, as was the fine form of Sheffield Wednesday's England goalkeeper, Jack Brown, who 'excelled with his punching' and impressed 'Hereward' of the *Evening Chronicle*.

The game was 'well advanced', as the *Sunday Pictorial* put it, before Newcastle went ahead, and inevitably it was Hughie Gallacher who scored from a Stan Seymour cross. Immediately afterwards,

Newcastle's squad which won the League in 1927, the last time they were champions of England.

however, Sheffield Wednesday equalised as the Newcastle defence paid far too much attention to Jimmy Trotter and did not notice Alf Strange, who popped up to shoot after goalkeeper Willie Wilson made one of his rare errors.

It was half-time and everyone's nerves were playing tricks on them, but as the players came out for the second half and before anyone kicked a ball the tension was eased. Such were the wonders of the modern telegraph system that the half-time scoreboard was able to tell everyone the news from Burnden Park, Bolton, where the home side were leading Huddersfield Town 2–0.

This made everyone breathe more easily, and Newcastle players and fans now began to enjoy themselves. Gallacher scored what proved to be the winner in the 75th minute. It was a classic of his kind. Local boy Tommy Urwin, widely believed to have been a Sunderland sympathiser in his youth but now as much a Geordie as anyone, charged up the wing and crossed a low-driven ball, which Hughie bent down to head home. The game finished with everyone in rare good humour, with even the good play of the Wednesday being applauded by the magnanimous Geordie crowd. They could afford to be so because their team were now assured of the Championship. With men like Hudspeth, Seymour and particularly Gallacher on board, the future looked bright, and surely there would be many more Championships coming to St James' Park.

The game finished and the Mayor appeared to shake all the players by the hand as a local colliery band played the tune *The Conquering Heroes*, a melody that had enjoyed a heyday in 1918 and was now used for triumphant sporting occasions like this one. It is unlikely, one fears, that anyone from the crowd of 28,421 that day of 83 years ago at St James' Park will still be with us, so it follows that no living person has seen Newcastle United become the Champions of England. This is sad, but it is perhaps all the more reason why we should recall the great days of that mighty side.

14

Date: 12 March 1932

CHELSEA

Match: FA Cup semi-final **Venue: Leeds Road, Huddersfield**

Score: 2–1 **Attendance: 36,709**

Newcastle United:	Chelsea:
McInroy	Millington
Nelson	Odell
Fairhurst	Law
McKenzie	Russell
Davidson	O'Dowd
Weaver	Ferguson
Boyd	Jackson
Richardson	Mills
Allen	Gallacher
McMenemy	Miller
Lang	Pearson

Referee: G.T. Davies, Bury

It would be a fair guess, as the trains sped towards Huddersfield from Newcastle on the fine morning of 12 March 1932, that conversation centred on one man, and that was Hughie Gallacher. Hughie was still the hero of the North East. In an area which absolutely craves a goalscoring hero, Hughie filled that role to perfection, famously bringing home the bacon to win the League Championship in 1927. The following year he played for Scotland in the 'Wembley Wizards' game between Scotland and England, a 5–1 Scottish victory still talked about to this day.

He was adored for his play and goalscoring, but there was another side to him as well that one would have had to have been blind to be unaware of. He was a drinker, a womaniser, a troublemaker and a fighter as well as being a great goalscorer. Rumour had it that he was involved in gambling and in shady business deals, but these things would have been tolerated by the fans as long as he was banging in the goals, which he could do with such versatility and verve – with his head, from the edge of the penalty box, from close in – and whatever was said about his private life, he was never less than totally fit and committed on the field of play. He did, however, come to a bad end in 1957 when, facing a charge of child neglect and still struggling with alcoholism, he threw himself in front of a train just outside Newcastle.

History has not always been kind to Hughie and it is noticeable that the 'Rangers' side of Scotland has few good things to say about him. Andy Cunningham, who joined Newcastle from Rangers, was clearly of that persuasion as he moved from player to player-manager then manager of the club.

Hughie's departure from Newcastle had been sudden and abrupt. It was late May 1930. Gallacher had literally just returned to his native Belshill in Lanarkshire after spearheading Scotland to a 2–0 win over France in which he had delighted the Parisian crowd so much that they chanted 'Vive L'Écosse' and 'Vive le Gallacher'. A Chelsea director appeared on his doorstep to tell him he would be playing in London next season rather than Newcastle. It was a secret deal which suited both teams – Newcastle wanted rid of him, and Chelsea, desperate to taste success and irked by London rivals Arsenal winning the FA Cup for the first time that year, would have the services of a truly great player.

Almost two years on, Newcastle fans had never really forgiven Cunningham and the directors for this clandestine piece of skulduggery and pocket-lining performed in the close season (to avoid demonstrations and riots, one presumes) while the main character was abroad in France. Being abroad in 1930 meant that the person was effectively incommunicado for several days, and thus Newcastle fans were suddenly deprived of their hero. Hughie himself would have had little say in the matter, as was often the case in those days. It was a far cry from the modern world, in which agents often have an undue and usually unhealthy influence on such matters.

The loss of Gallacher was all the more keenly felt in a support which had lost so many other things as well in the terrible economic catastrophe that hit the region and all other areas of heavy industry in the early 1930s. Deserted even by their own government, which they had worked hard to see elected in 1929 and which had now joined the Conservatives to talk about things like a 'doctor's remedy' to cure the country of its economic maladies, Newcastle supporters became more and more obsessed by the team that meant so much to them. How dare anyone take their beloved Hughie away from them?

Against that was the argument that Gallacher was trouble and that Chelsea would now have to deal with his wayward personality. The club had to be bigger than any one player, even if that one player was outstanding. His return to Newcastle early in the 1930–31 season has been well documented. That, however, was a League match. This 1932 clash was given more impetus by the fact that it was in the FA Cup and at the semi-final stage.

Chelsea had been late to arrive on the scene. Football had originally tended to be a north of England game, with strong teams in Blackburn, Liverpool and even Birmingham, with London generally lagging a little behind. Chelsea had been founded in 1905 and had never enjoyed any great success, lingering in the Second Division more often than the first. Their FA Cup history had not been great. The only time that they had reached the FA Cup Final had been the year in which many people believed that football should not have been played. This was 1915, the year of the 'Khaki Cup Final' as some people called it, because of all the soldiers on leave in the crowd, and they had lost 3–0 to Sheffield United at Old Trafford, the game not being played in London for fear of Zeppelin attacks.

Yet Chelsea had a good support in spite of their lack of success, representing their own geographical community, and they had a huge ground at Stamford Bridge, so big that the FA Cup Finals of 1920, 1921 and 1922 were held there until Wembley took over from 1923 onwards. The FA Cup was the big thing for Chelsea, as it was for most teams. Their supporters were uncomfortably aware that Tottenham Hotspur had won the trophy twice, and in 1930 Arsenal had joined the ranks of the winners, but Chelsea had still not done so. It was as well for their many supporters who travelled to see this semi-final that they did not know that another war, two coronations and many other things would happen to London before the FA Cup would come to Chelsea at last in 1970.

It was a bright spring day on 12 March 1932. The *Evening Chronicle* commented on the number of cars that travelled to the game and the thousands of fans who were locked out of Leeds Road. There were 36,701 inside to see a game that had all sorts of issues. In the first place it was Newcastle versus London, the North versus the South. This was a real and poignant concern, because there was the feeling that in the days of the depression, the south received preferential treatment over the north. But all these worries were minimal compared with the one that really mattered, and this was Hughie Gallacher.

Newcastle score against Chelsea in the semi-final of 1932.

Davie Davidson, Newcastle's centre-half from the unlikely provenance of Forfar, who had been a disappointment at Liverpool and had taken time to settle on Tyneside, was being asked to play the key role. He had to stop Gallacher scoring if Newcastle were to progress to the Final of the Cup, the eventuality craved by the thousands of Geordie fans. It was to be a severe trial for the young Scotsman, but the *Evening Chronicle* considered that it was a good omen that Davidson's address was in Wembley Avenue, Monkeaton.

Davidson knew that Gallacher, notorious for his indiscipline and volatile temper, could be easily riled. The way to do that was not to foul him, but to play him fairly by marking him completely out of the game. Andy Cunningham knew this as well, and Davidson was told to ignore everyone else and concentrate on Gallacher. This he did, and for a spell things worked well for Newcastle who, with the bulk of the crowd behind them, attacked in strength. Early goals from Jack Allen and Tommy Lang put them well in command. Allen scored when a free-kick had been only partially cleared and Lang's goal was a great header from a Boyd cross. But then, just before half-time, came a lapse of concentration from Scottish right-half Roddy McKenzie, and Gallacher escaped Davidson's close marking and pulled one back for the Londoners.

At half-time Newcastle, although 2–1 up, felt very vulnerable, but several players now answered the call of duty. One of them was Sam Weaver, the bustling left-half who had not enjoyed the best of seasons and had on occasion felt the wrath of the crowd. But manager Cunningham recognised the value of this man and retained him in the team, knowing that when he came good he would be really good. Cunningham also told Davidson to continue to stick with Gallacher and let the rest of the defence do what they must.

It was a long second half as Chelsea, with the boost of that goal late in the first half, pressed and laid siege to the Newcastle goal. Right-winger Alec Jackson, another 'Wembley Wizard' of 1928 (there were four on the field that day in Gallacher, Jackson, Chelsea left-back Tommy Law and Newcastle captain and right-back Jimmy Nelson), now came more and more into his own, causing all sorts of trouble down Newcastle's flank and sending cross after cross into the penalty area, trying to find the golden touch of Gallacher. But Davidson was immense at centre-half, getting to the ball before Gallacher did, clearing his lines brilliantly, heading out crisply to colleagues, never being afraid to concede a corner if necessary and radiating confidence as the Chelsea attacks became more and more desperate. 'No Road This Way' was the way the Monday papers would describe Davidson, and behind him Albert McInroy, once of Sunderland, was a marvellously effective goalkeeper.

Chelsea forced corner after corner and a penalty claim was denied, but Newcastle held out. The final whistle was greeted with a great shout of acclamation and relief. Newcastle accepted the reluctant congratulations of Gallacher (for whom an English Cup medal would have meant so much, to go with the Scottish medal he had won with Airdrieonians in 1924), still themselves groggy with the thought that they had made it to Wembley.

The *Sunday Sun* was worried about world affairs. On Sunday 13 March there was to be the election for the Chancellorship in Germany between von Hindenberg and the dangerous character called Adolf Hitler, but as far as football reporting went, it was jubilant. Colin Veitch, the great player of the Edwardian era, now writing for the paper, was jubilant and quotes Hughie Gallacher as expressing his disappointment, but wishing the Geordies all the best. Manager Andy Cunningham said, 'I am the happiest man in the British Isles.' Some Newcastle supporters would claim to be just as happy, but there was one sad postscript in that Harry McMenemy (whose father, the great Jimmy 'Napoleon' McMenemy of Celtic fame, was at the game to watch him) came off the field to be told that the family had suffered a double blow in that his brother-in-law had died and his sister was very ill. This was a shame; McMenemy had been one of the architects of Newcastle's victory.

Date: 23 April 1932

15

ARSENAL

Match: FA Cup Final   **Venue: Wembley**

Score: 2–1   **Attendance: 100,000**

Newcastle United:	Arsenal:
McInroy	Moss
Nelson	Parker
Fairhurst	Hapgood
MacKenzie	Jones
Davidson	Robertson
Weaver	Male
Boyd	Hulme
Richardson	Jack
Allen	Lambert
McMenemy	Bastin
Lang	John

Referee: P. Harper, Stourbridge

'Gannin along the Euston Road/To send the Gunners to blazes' was the ill-disguised parody of *The Blaydon Races* sung by Magpies in London on the day of the 1932 FA Cup Final. It seemed they had taken over London, having begun arriving in the early morning with their black and white rattles, striped trousers and rosettes. Some of them had clearly imbibed quite a lot, but they were well-behaved and orderly.

The early 1930s were grim times on Tyneside. The worldwide recession hit the area hard, and unemployment was rife with many families suffering grim poverty and deprivation. In this respect, the Newcastle area was possibly no worse hit than any other place, but as Newcastle had been at the forefront of the previous century's Industrial Revolution, with all its undesirable side effects of poor housing and living conditions, the recession seemed to be worse on the Tyne. The money required to do something about the shocking deprivation lay in the hands of those who simply did not wish to do anything.

However, football still remained. Since 1927, when they had won the League Championship, Newcastle had been disappointing. The fans, in spite of their straightened economic circumstances, had stayed loyal. In the dole queues there was talk of horse racing, dogs and politics, but above all else there was the constant love affair with Newcastle United. What would really lift the area would be the winning of another major trophy.

The manager was Andy Cunningham, a Scotsman who had made his name as a legend with Rangers. Cunningham and the directors remained very unpopular for the decision to sell Hughie

Gallacher two years previously and it was now even more incumbent upon Cunningham to produce a good team for the supporters and to once again win a trophy. The FA Cup, with which Newcastle had had a love-hate relationship in the Edwardian era, seemed to represent the better prospect because League form was patchy.

This season of 1931–32 saw the Magpies display another mediocre League performance, finishing 11th. It was, in all truth, an improvement on recent seasons, but still a good way short of what the Geordie fans felt that they were entitled to expect. There was a remarkably dull game, for example, in early December 1931, when Portsmouth came to St James' Park and, according to the bemused journalist who wrote about the game for the *Sunday Sun*, there was not a single corner-kick, let alone a goal in the 0–0 draw. There were some shockers: Everton beat them 8–1 at Goodison on 31 October, which was particularly distressing for the travelling supporters, and there was a rather bad run in the spring, but what made up for it all was the Cup campaign.

Even in the Cup ties, though, form was unpredictable and on occasion it would have to be said that Newcastle were lucky. The early rounds saw a struggle against Blackpool first, with a 1–1 draw then a 1–0 victory, before a remarkable three games against lowly Southport. After two 1–1 draws (the game at Haig Avenue, Southport, attracting a ground record 20,010 on a Tuesday afternoon) it was as if Newcastle said 'Enough of this nonsense', because they won the third game at neutral Hillsborough by the astonishing score of 9–0. Fairly comfortable home wins followed over Leicester City and Watford – the latter attracting over 57,000 – to set up a semi-final tie against Chelsea, now including Hughie Gallacher, at Leeds Road, Huddersfield.

Newcastle won through to meet Arsenal in the FA Cup Final at Wembley. It often distresses and saddens traditionalists to hear the FA Cup being demeaned by some of the larger clubs, who say they would rather be fourth in the Premiership, so that they can enter the Champions League, than win the English Cup. This is to be deplored, and in 1932 this attitude would have been laughed at, derided or simply not believed. The FA Cup Final was the biggest game of the season.

Newcastle's League form in the run-up towards the Cup Final was poor, including a defeat to Arsenal, but all this was of no concern at all in comparison to the big one. Tickets were difficult, if not impossible, to acquire, but many Geordies went down to London anyway, hoping to hang around outside the ground and possibly be lucky enough to obtain a ticket. There was, of course, no television as yet, but there would be a radio commentary for those lucky and wealthy enough to own a radio, the FA Cup Final having been broadcast on the radio for the first time in 1927. In 1932 Mr W. Pope of the Newcastle Radio Society invited all the blind people of Newcastle to come to the Chronicle Hall to hear the commentary of the game. One suspects that one or two people suddenly developed a problem with their sight that day.

Arsenal were the team of the establishment, the rich team of London, managed by Herbert Chapman, a brusque and determined Yorkshireman. They had won the Cup in 1930 and the League in 1931, and they would end up second in the League to Everton in 1932. They were by some distance the favourites for this year's trophy, but Newcastle were given a great boost a couple of days before the game by the news that Alec James, Arsenal's legendary Scottish wizard, had dislocated his 'ee and was out of the game. There was also the belief in Arsenal circles that Newcastle were some of bogey team for them in that they had seldom done well against them in the 1920s. In addition, on the only two occasions that they had met in the FA Cup, in 1902 and 1906, Newcastle had in both games beaten Woolwich Arsenal (as they were then called) 2–0.

There was no lack of Scotsmen in the Newcastle team – six in fact. There was Davie Davidson, who had tamed Gallacher in the semi-final; captain Jimmy Nelson, a 'Wembley Wizard' from the great game in 1928 when Scotland beat England 5–1; Roddy MacKenzie from Inverness; Jimmy Boyd from Glasgow; Harry McMenemy, the son of the great 'Napoleon' McMenemy of Celtic; and Tommy Lang from Larkhall. The others were local boys from the North East. This was the pattern of most of Newcastle's history when they had a good side – local, committed boys, spiced up with a few from Scotland. It is hardly accidental that Newcastle's decline dates precisely from the day that they abandoned this idea.

The triumphant Newcastle team with the Cup in 1932.

It is a shame that the game was dominated by one incident. This ignores the good football played for the rest of the time on what was a fine afternoon after heavy morning rain. Arsenal scored first when left-winger Bob John put them ahead. Newcastle piled on the pressure and then in the 38th minute came the major talking point, and one which was the most controversial goal in history until the Geoff Hurst goal in the 1966 World Cup Final, the Diego Maradona 'Hand of God' goal of 1986 or the Thierry Henry handball of 2009.

Davidson intercepted a Hapgood pass to Cliff Bastin and sent Jimmy Richardson up the wing. He reached the byline and crossed for Jack Allen to score an easy goal. There was a half-hearted appeal that the ball might have been over the line as Richardson crossed, but no great fuss was made at the time, although Colin Veitch conceded in the *Evening Chronicle* that there were 'grave doubts' about the legitimacy of the goal. Statements that appear in modern books to the effect that 'to a man the Arsenal defence stopped, awaiting the referee's whistle' are not backed up by contemporary newspaper reports, the photographs that appeared in the press or the newsreel film of the game that shows the Arsenal goalkeeper, Frank Moss, charging dementedly after the referee, Mr Percy Harper, but only after he and other defenders had made an effort to stop the goal.

Thus it was 1–1, and from then on Newcastle took command, particularly in the second half when the Arsenal attack made no headway whatsoever against Davidson and the well-organised Newcastle defence. There were 13 minutes remaining when Newcastle snatched what proved to be the winner as Jack Allen scored again. This time there was no doubt, because he beat two men before he scored a wonderful goal. Arsenal had little time to rally and looked for all the world a defeated team as Jimmy Richardson hit the post late in the game.

Mr Harper's whistle went, to the great joy of the Geordies. The Cup was presented by Queen Mary to captain Jimmy Nelson, the players were given their medals, the celebratory meal was held and everyone with the Newcastle party went to bed thoroughly satisfied with a great day's work. It was only the following morning and, more particularly, on the Monday morning, that the London-based press, with an Arsenal support to appease, started to claim that the ball from which

Newcastle's winner came was over the line. The pictures which appeared in the newspapers certainly did tend to suggest that an error had been made. Then came the British Movietone newsreel film, which in 1932 took an unconscionable time to develop, but it certainly seemed to give further indication that the ball was, in fact, over the line before Richardson crossed. But the decision had been made and there seemed little doubt that Newcastle had deserved their triumph. It was claimed that about a quarter of a million Geordies lined the streets of the Toon to welcome them back, such was the love of the community for its team.

It would certainly appear that an injustice was done to the Gunners in the over the line incident, but it remains a shame that 1932 is often defined by that one incident. It would hardly be the only time that a refereeing mistake has been made in a match, even an important one, and the stress laid on that error seems to do less than justice to the magnificent performance of the Newcastle team and the boost that they gave to their beleaguered and impoverished community. The Geordie supporters also suffered from a great deal of injustice, and it was far worse than a refereeing decision in a football match.

In particular, too little credit has been given to the courage of Jack Allen, who played in this game heavily strapped up because he was suffering from a double hernia – a condition that required immediate and urgent surgery at the end of the season. Newcastle had now won the FA Cup for the third time and another string had been added to the bow of Newcastle's FA Cup tradition.

16

Date: 5 October 1946

NEWPORT COUNTY

Match: League Division Two   **Venue: St James' Park**

Score: 13–0   **Attendance: 52,137**

Newcastle United:	Newport County:
Garbutt	Turner
Cowell	Hodge
Graham	Oldham
Harvey	Rawcliffe
Brennan	Low
Wright	Cabie
Milburn	Davis
Bentley	Wookey
Wayman	Craddock
Shackleton	McNab
Pearson	Bowen

Referee: H. Hartley, Bolton

Europe and the world had been at peace (more or less) for over a year. The fascists had been defeated, retribution was being dispensed at Nuremburg to the Nazis who had survived the war and the soldiers had now all returned. Football was back and attendances were high as unemployment was now a thing of the past, certainly on Tyneside, as every ounce of coal was now needed for the massive rebuilding of war-ravaged Britain and Europe. This season, 1946–47, would be the first official football season.

Newcastle had spent the war years in the Second Division. The 1930s had not been a great decade for the club, and soldiers from Newcastle were often met with quizzical looks from their friends from other parts of the country who simply could not understand why it was that a team with such a pedigree and such a support could not get themselves back into the top tier. Clearly one of the first tasks for Stan Seymour would be to get Newcastle back to where they felt they belonged, but almost 20 years had now passed since the great Hughie Gallacher era when Newcastle had won the Championship in 1927.

The first few games of the 1946–47 season probably shocked the directors of the club with the massive crowds that turned up. Attendances were high all over the country, just as they had been high in 1919 after the previous war, but Newcastle's fixtures often caused serious crowd congestion problems both inside the ground and outside. All three home games so far had exceeded 50,000, and the one against Burnley (which they had lost) had seen more than 60,000 inside and serious traffic problems in the streets of the city – somewhat remarkable when one considers the paucity of private cars in 1946. Football was clearly back in a big way, and on this October day 52,137 fans were there to see a team that was hardly the leading light of British football – Newport County.

Hailing from a part of the United Kingdom where rugby prevails, Newport is no longer a League club and teetered on the brink of extinction for a while, but in 1939, the Ironsides (as they were called, in a reference to the heavy industry that went on all around them) had won the Third Division South of the English League and were thus belatedly enjoying the fruits of that success by playing their first full season in the Second Division. For a team whose average attendance was about a tenth of that of Newcastle's the sheer size of the crowd must have been an intimidating factor. They had already been on the wrong end of a thumping this season, going down 7–0 to West Bromwich Albion, but they had one Newcastle connection in their captain Norman Low, son the great Wilfred Low of Newcastle and Scotland, 'the Laughing Cavalier', who had been tragically killed in a motor accident in 1933.

Newcastle had upset a few of their fans by not trying harder to retain the services of Albert Stubbins, who had expressed an understandable desire to play First Division football. Liverpool had paid £13,000 for him, and the money had almost immediately been used to buy from Bradford Park Avenue a fellow by the name of Len Shackleton. He had apparently done well in wartime football in Yorkshire, but was not very well known anywhere else, although it was said that he was also a more than useful cricketer. Those who had seen him had said he was a talented inside player, but no one could tell how he would do in the 'real' football of 1946. Certainly, at first glance, it seemed that an exchange for Stubbins would have to be really good if he were to be mentioned in the same breath as the man he had replaced. Little did anyone realise what would happen on his debut.

Newcastle did have other good players as well. They had talented wingers in Jackie Milburn, a local boy from Ashington, and a Scotsman by the name of Tommy Pearson. There was a fine wing-half in Joe Harvey and a tough centre-half in Frank Brennan, but no one as yet was really convinced about the centre-forward, Charlie Wayman (often unkindly called 'Jane' after the Hollywood actress, Jane Wyman), or the inside-forward, Roy Bentley. This match, however, would answer a few questions.

The Geordies' first glimpse of Shackleton, signed on the Thursday before, would reveal a man of about average height, a slight, lean figure with a cocky, jaunty way of walking, his gait hinting at his character because he was a born joker. The start of the game was electric, with Shackleton creating some fine play and winning a penalty kick. Unfortunately Charlie Wayman missed from the spot, and the more pessimistic of the Newcastle support began to mutter about the consequences of having an opportunity and not taking it. The other team then hit back.

How little the prophets of gloom knew about what was going on. Shackleton, clearly revelling in front of the biggest crowd he had ever seen, crossed for Wayman to head home. Two minutes after that Shackleton beat several men in a mazy run, played a one-two with Bentley and scored again. By the half-hour mark, the same Wayman-Shackleton combination struck again and Wayman had scored twice to complete his hat-trick.

It was astonishing enough for the Newcastle supporters to find themselves 4–0 up at such an early stage of the game, but by half-time it was 7–0, Shackleton having scored a hat-trick in record speed on top of the one goal that he had scored earlier. It is notoriously difficult to say how quickly something happened in the days before the games were recorded on video, but one source says that the hat-trick goals all happened within 155 seconds, which, if true, would be a serious challenge to the three scored by Jimmy McGrory of Celtic against Motherwell in 1936, hitherto believed to be the fastest hat-trick of all time.

Whatever happened, it was clear that Newport County's defence could not cope with this blistering football. They must have been relieved to hear Mr Hartley's half-time whistle and go in only 7–0 down. In those days half-time scores were put up on a primitive type of scoreboard with number plates of the kind one would find in the scorebox at a rural cricket ground. Several grounds could not give this result as they did not have a number seven. Others refused to believe the amazing

Len Shackleton was more associated with Sunderland, but he had his moments for Newcastle as well.

score, thinking that BBC Radio had been kidded on by a Newcastle supporter or someone from Wales who did not like Newport County, or even that someone had confused the score of the Newport rugby team with the football one.

The Geordies at St James' Park knew the truth, but they could not believe it. And it had not finished yet. The promising young Jack Milburn scored two, Roy Bentley struck another, Wayman got his fourth, Shackleton his fifth and then, with the crowd in serious danger of losing count and even afraid to go to the toilet lest they missed one, Wookey of Newport scored an own-goal, which Shackleton greedily claimed as his sixth.

The press were glad that they had lots of pencils and paper to record all this, but even then some newspapers disagreed on the tally for each player. At the end there was the rare phenomenon of a sympathising Newcastle crowd cheering on the luckless Welshmen and willing them to score at least one goal. Sadly they could not oblige, and they seldom managed to get over the halfway line, so astounded were they by the brilliant play of Shackleton, who sprayed passes all over the field and even had a few of his opponents running away from him lest they be made a fool of. He combined particularly well with Tommy Pearson and it was a shame that Tommy was the only forward not to get on the score sheet. It was a tremendous occasion and an outstanding performance, and it had the city of Newcastle talking about it for years afterwards, even after Shackleton did the unforgivable and went to Sunderland.

The *Sky Sports Football Yearbook* indicates that this score, although equalled by Stockport County in 1934, has never been bettered in a Football League match, although occasionally in a Cup game. Preston North End beat Hyde United 26–0 in 1887 and the world record is still Arbroath 36, Aberdeen Bon Accord 0 in 1885, and it is difficult to imagine this happening in the 21st century. It remains a phenomenal match. The opposition was poor, it would have to be admitted, but the standard of the Newcastle play was superb, particularly the form of the 'Clown Prince', as Shackleton was later known.

The match was long before TV cameras, and newsreel cameras were deployed only for big games like Cup Finals, so no visual record of the game exists. This is a shame, but at least 52,137 people saw it and had the opportunity to tell their grandchildren about it. The season unfortunately ended up as one of Newcastle's 'nearly' seasons, as they finished fifth in the Second Division and lost in the semi-final of the FA Cup, but there was at least one great game and one great player to savour.

Date: 17 April 1948

17 SHEFFIELD WEDNESDAY

Match: Division Two

Venue: St James' Park

Score: 4–2

Attendance: 66,483

Newcastle United:	Sheffield Wednesday:
Fairbrother	McIntosh
Cowell	Westlake
Craig	Swift
Harvey	Whitcomb
Brennan	Turton
Dodgin	Cockcroft
Houghton	Marriott
Stobbart	Quigley
Milburn	Jordan
Woodburn	Froggatt
Walker	Woodhead

Referee: H. Trentholm, Stockton

The word 'austere' is often used to describe the late 1940s. The picture is often painted of the Chancellor of the Exchequer, Sir Richard Stafford Cripps, grasping at people's taxes and warning them of the dangers of luxury and extravagance. This picture is only half true, if it is not total rubbish. World War Two had indeed wrecked the British economy, but on the other hand there was also a government in power that had pledged to create a better and more equal society. There was also full employment, with many opportunities for improvements in careers which involved the building of new houses and hospitals. The standard of living was immeasurably higher than it had been during the poverty and unemployment of the early 1930s.

One could certainly never have used the word austere to describe British football in that decade. The passion for the game had increased during the war years, and now that peace had been restored, crowds flocked to the game in huge numbers, with newspapers and radio feeding the passion of the masses. Newcastle's average home attendance was 56,299, and that was for the Second Division.

Newcastle had been in the Second Division since the black year of 1934. During the war the Magpies had played in the Football League North, and in the first official season of 1946–47 they had finished a respectable but still slightly disappointing fifth in the Second Division. There was a saying on Tyneside at the time that the war would not be completely over until such time as Newcastle were back in Division One, the place that was surely their natural habitat given the number of spectators that they could attract.

The ball was brown and heavy, there were no floodlights, players wore heavy shirts (sometimes rather faded ones as clothing, particularly football shirts, was still rationed), the goalkeepers always wore yellow and the referee and his linesmen always wore black. Boots were huge things that needed to be fed with a substance called 'dubbin', and there was always a pair of flags at the halfway line. The fans were intense and vocal, the tackling was fierce and there was no place for softies. In the winter months the games kicked off at 2pm so that they could finish before the light faded. The results were given out by BBC radio at 5pm on a programme called *Sports Report*, and evening papers appeared an hour or so later with an account of the game. Football was a great thing in the late 1940s for a population who were just glad that they were alive.

Season 1947–48 saw some good football and some great games, with home form being particularly impressive, but the supporters had suffered a serious and seemingly fatal blow in the events of February 1948 when Len Shackleton, the great entertainer and scorer of goals, had fallen out with the club and had been transferred. This was bad enough, although not unprecedented, as many fine players, like Hughie Gallacher of 20 years previously and Albert Stubbins of more recent times, had been unable to cope with the rigid demands and eccentricities of Newcastle's management, but Shackleton had been sold to Sunderland, of all clubs. Sunderland were a First Division club, and one of the reasons why promotion to the First Division became an obsession in the whole city of Newcastle in 1948 was that they would have a chance to play against Sunderland and 'Shack'.

Newcastle's chronic and melancholic inability to play in London had cost them dear in this season. League defeats at Fulham, Millwall and Brentford had lost points, and they had exited the FA Cup in early January at Charlton Athletic. This defeat, although narrow and disappointing, had led to a loss of form for the rest of January, but gradually the team rallied and recovered from the loss of Shackleton (there is a certain indication that one or two of the players were by no means as devastated as the fans at the loss of him), and the team began to tighten up.

Luton Town scored at St James' Park on 3 January. They would be the last team to do so until the vital game against Sheffield Wednesday in April. Away form improved. There was one defeat at distant Southampton in March, but generally visits to other grounds tended to end up as draws, and in 1948, with one point for a draw and only two points for a win, an away draw was looked upon as a good result. Draws at the war-devastated Coventry, at Nottingham, Barnsley and Cardiff were generally viewed as acceptable performances.

To a large extent, the person responsible for all this was Frank Brennan. Frank took few prisoners and was one of the traditional 'no road this way' centre-halves who also had the ability to inspire and bring out the best in his other defenders. Around him he had a solid pair of full-backs in Bobby Cowell and Benny Craig, two local boys from County Durham. They were largely unsung and unspectacular players, but totally reliable. At right-half there was Joe Harvey from Yorkshire. There was a cohesion in that side and a collective determination to do well.

Up front, young Milburn continued to impress with his goalscoring ability and there was also George Stobbart, by no means the silkiest of football players but certainly a hard worker and a man with the ability to pop up and score goals. He was also a good shoulder-charger of goalkeepers, and particularly in the last few weeks he had been scoring the vital goals. On the Wednesday evening before the Sheffield Wednesday game he had scored the crucial penalty which defeated Fulham.

The game against Sheffield Wednesday was all about a man called Frank Houghton, however. If Frank had been a dog, he certainly would not have been called 'Lucky'. His entry into first-class football was delayed by World War Two, when he served in the RAF, then his career at Newcastle was almost perpetually dogged by injuries and finally brought to a premature end when he picked up tuberculosis, which could, as late as the 1950s, kill. He survived but his career, at least at the top level, was over.

Houghton was no great football player, but he was hard working and he was a manager's dream in that he was versatile, being able to play happily in the forward line and the half-back line on either side of the field. He had joined Newcastle in January and had played a few games in the half-back line, but now he found himself on the right wing for this vital game.

It was the third-to-last game of the season. Newcastle still had an outside chance of catching Birmingham City to win the title, but second place was a more realistic option. They were two points ahead of third-place Sheffield Wednesday. With two points for a win, a victory for the Geordies would virtually guarantee promotion, although they still needed three points to be absolutely certain. The Wednesday were a team like Newcastle, with a glorious past but a slightly less satisfactory present. Like those of Newcastle, their fans expected them to be in the top flight, and they had some great players in Frank Froggatt and Eddie Quigley.

The game was a classic, with the fans left exhausted at the end. In the early stages it was Wednesday who had the better of the exchanges, twice almost scoring and denied only by clearances off the line by Benny Craig. Craig conceded a penalty, however, when he handled a third effort on the line and Doug Whitcomb converted. Newcastle came more into the game, though, and by half-time were on level terms thanks to a goal by George Stobbart.

The second half saw more of the same, with Joe Harvey heading Newcastle ahead and the Owls attacking vigorously for all of the second half. Newcastle, well organised by Frank Brennan, seemed to have weathered the storm until late in the game when right-winger Jackie Marriott drew the Yorkshiremen level. This plunged St James' Park into a temporary depression, because it meant that promotion was back in the melting pot and Newcastle would have to do well in their remaining fixtures away at Tottenham Hotspur and at home to Millwall.

This is when Frank Houghton came into his own. Three minutes were left and St James' Park became bedlam as he ran in from the wing to score what looked like the winner. The Wednesday defence had rather ignored Houghton, preferring to concentrate their attention on the far more dangerous (as they thought) Jackie Milburn and George Stobbart, but it was Houghton who scored the third goal, colliding badly with a defender and needing treatment from the trainer so that he could continue.

There was now a collective holding of breath from the Newcastle supporters. There were still a few minutes left, and everyone felt that it would be all hands to the pumps to defend against a now desperate Sheffield team. It did not turn out like that, though, because amazingly Houghton did the same again, both scoring a goal for his side and again injuring himself in the process. This time it was a post with which he collided and his injuries were far more serious, in the shape of a damaged leg and a broken arm. The hero of the hour subsequently spent his moment of glory in a hospital bed while all of Newcastle went crazy and celebrated in a way which recalled VE Day only three years before. Although promotion had not yet been secured, a 1–1 draw at Tottenham the following week would give them the extra point they needed. On that evening of 17 April 1948 everything looked bright.

Poor Frank Houghton did come back, but he took a long time to recover and played only a few games for the side after that. But this was his moment of glory!

18

Date: 28 April 1951

BLACKPOOL

Match: FA Cup Final **Venue: Wembley**

Score: 2–0 **Attendance: 100,000**

Newcastle United:	Blackpool:
Fairbrother	Farm
Cowell	Shimwell
Corbett	Garrett
Harvey	Johnston
Brennan	Hayward
Crowe	Kelly
Walker	Matthews
Taylor	Mudie
Milburn	Mortensen
Robledo	Slater
Mitchell	Perry

Referee: W. Ling

The 1951 FA Cup Final was meant to be Stanley Matthews's Final. Everyone loved Stan, the greatest right-winger of them all, renowned for his devastating play and his gentlemanly demeanour on the field. It was his wish to win an FA Cup-winner's medal before he retired (the FA Cup then being looked upon as the most prestigious trophy in the world), and this wish was shared by most people in the game. He had been around for a long time and he was now 36. He had already played in one Cup Final, ending up on the losing side in 1948 when Blackpool went down to Manchester United.

Tyneside shared in the general admiration and respect for Matthews, but clearly wished his Cup medal to be delayed. Newcastle themselves had had a good season. They were more then respectably placed in the League (they ended up fourth) and in Jackie Milburn they had someone special. Already called 'Wor Jackie', he was a local boy who had emerged from the pits at Ashington in the dark days of World War Two, and his goalscoring ability marked him out as a great player. He was an England internationalist as well, but like Matthews what he really craved was a Cup medal.

1951 was the start of the years of prosperity. The Labour government had been in office since the end of the war and had laid the foundations of the Welfare State. Yet Attlee's government was struggling – in recent weeks Ernest Bevin had died and Aneurin Bevan had resigned – and the whole country and indeed the world was becoming more and more concerned about the war which was going on in Korea and to which there did not seem to be any easy solution. In addition, although the

Milburn scores the second goal following Ernie Taylor's famous back-heel.

country was moving in the right direction in terms of social policy, it was clear that there was still a long way to go, not least on Tyneside where there were huge areas of sub-standard housing.

But unemployment had gone and wealth would not have been an obstacle to the Geordies migrating southwards en masse to see the Cup Final. The lack of tickets was a far more serious problem. Newcastle United and Blackpool were given 12,500 tickets each – a quarter of the capacity of Wembley. Considering that Newcastle's average home gate was 47,693 in those boom years of the early 1950s, the allocation was less than substantial. Season ticket-holders were given the opportunity first, then there was a huge drawing of lots from all the applicants. The local press reported a great many sad stories about men who had seen the Cup won in 1910, 1924 and 1932 but who had missed out this time. It was indeed a very lucky fan who would have a ticket, and a great deal of speculation took place about where the tickets, other than those given to Newcastle United or Blackpool, went.

A lot more than 12,500 supporters would head southwards on one of the many special trains which left Newcastle Central Station on the Friday night or even early on the Saturday morning. Some would be lucky enough to get tickets, albeit at a ruinous price from ticket touts (reports of 3 shilling tickets going for £5 were not unheard of), but there was little alternative in 1951 if one wanted to see the game. Television barely existed and most supporters would be listening to the game on the wireless.

There was a great deal of confidence in manager Stanley Seymour and his team. Seymour himself had a personal target in that he could become the first man ever to win the FA Cup both as a player and a manager. He was, in fact, in a strange position. He was actually a director, but had taken over as manager in the middle of the season when George Martin had left to go to Aston Villa. Tyneside was not short of those who claimed that Seymour's game plan all along had been to unsettle Martin, make him leave and get the job that he really coveted. He had won the Cup in 1924 as a player, and this was now as good an opportunity as he was likely to get to complete this unique double.

Even leaving Jackie Milburn aside, good players abounded in this team, and it was the unanimous opinion of all Tyneside (and a few respected pundits as well) that England had lost to Scotland a fortnight previously only because there were no Newcastle players in the team when several, Milburn in particular, might have been included. Blackpool, on the other hand, had had three men in that England team.

Milburn turns away after slipping the ball past Farm for Newcastle's first.

Newcastle's defence was sometimes accident-prone – they had on one occasion in the previous November conceded seven goals at Tottenham Hotspur – but generally was tight, particularly with the introduction of Bobby Corbett at left-back. Full-backs Cowell and Corbett were both local lads, and they were supplemented by the mighty Scotsman Frank Brennan at centre-half, a man for whom the phrase 'took no prisoners' is not quite sufficient to describe his determination. Known as the 'Rock of Tyneside', Frank's seven caps for Scotland might well have been many more.

In the forward line there was the fast and direct right-winger Tommy Walker, who often suffered in comparison with left-winger Bobby Mitchell, whose play was more flamboyant, and he was arguably one of the best players Newcastle have ever had. Mitchell was to earn a couple of caps for Scotland that summer and would surely have been an automatic choice for his country if his career had not coincided with that of Billy Liddell of Liverpool. The inside-forwards were the impish Ernie Taylor, whose greatest moments were yet to come in the resurrection of Manchester United after the Munich air disaster of 1958, and George Robledo, the man from Chile, whom South American politics had brought to England as a boy. He was a tremendous goalscorer and a foil for Milburn.

Milburn had scored in every round en route to Wembley, though not in every game as there had been a couple of goalless draws, notably a shocking performance in late February when Bristol Rovers had held the Magpies to a draw in front of more than 60,000 fans. They had been comfortably disposed of in the replay the following Wednesday. That had been the quarter-final, and in the semi Newcastle had been paired against the great Wolverhampton Wanderers team at Hillsborough. Only Bert Williams in the Wolves goal had denied Milburn in the first game, but the replay saw a 2–1 win for the Magpies with goals from Milburn and Mitchell.

The 1951 Cup Final is generally regarded as being one of the least interesting for a neutral. Blackpool's attempts to neutralise Milburn depended on an offside trap – something which leads to sterile football and which does not always work because it needs slick coordination and a good, eagle-eyed linesman. Newcastle's considerably more successful plan to stop Matthews was to employ a double left-back, in that left-half Charlie Crowe would drop back to help Bobby Corbett and prevent the ball reaching the dangerous veteran. Seymour reckoned that Newcastle could do that because Blackpool had lost Alan Brown to injury and were, therefore, a little short of firepower up front.

Half-time came with no score and many of the 100,000 were wondering why they had tried so hard to get tickets for this disappointing encounter. The radio commentator Raymond Glendinning was taxed to the utmost to describe what action there was and to encourage the nation to keep listening. Milburn had had the ball in the net in the first half, but the goal had been disallowed for handball – something that Milburn went to his grave denying, claiming that he had chested the ball down.

The game all hinged on the goal scored by Milburn in the early stages of the first half after Matthews had shown signs of getting moving for Blackpool. For once Matthews got the better of Corbett and crossed for the other Stan – Stan Mortensen – but George Robledo got there first and his long ball found Milburn just inside the Blackpool half and with the Blackpool defence caught unawares. There was a half-hearted appeal for offside, but Milburn turned on the speed, charged goalwards and, as Wembley took a collective intake of breath, drew goalkeeper George Farm and beat him to put the Geordies one up.

This goal released mayhem in the houses of Newcastle. Even those who did not have a wireless knew by the noise from their neighbours that something dramatic and exciting had happened. Five minutes after that the same man scored again. This was another great goal, made famous as much by little Ernie Taylor's back-heel as it was by Milburn's shot. Newcastle had the ball on the right just outside the penalty area, with Taylor in possession after a good run up the wing by Tommy Walker, but as defenders converged on him he realised that Milburn was standing behind him. He did not have time to turn, so he simply back-heeled the ball into Milburn's path and Milburn needed no second bidding to hammer home an unstoppable shot.

Blackpool now rallied, but it was all in vain as the Newcastle defence, with Brennan outstanding, gobbled up everything that came their way, and Matthews never got enough of the ball to make any kind of difference. The full-time whistle came with Newcastle well on top. Blackpool, disappointed and demoralised, nevertheless were chivalrous at the end, and even the hardest-hearted Geordie had to feel a sense of sorrow for Stanley Matthews, who still did not have an FA Cup-winner's medal. He would eventually win one in 1953 when he was 38.

Joe Harvey then collected the FA Cup for the fourth time in the history of Newcastle United. The trophy was presented by King George VI, that shy, stammering and nervous man, who nevertheless had played his part in guiding the country through its darkest days. He was now clearly ailing (this would be his last FA Cup Final for he died the following February) but he managed to stumble out a few words of congratulations to the proud Newcastle team.

Newsreel footage shows the Newcastle team returning home with the FA Cup in the luggage rack of the train before showing the trophy to the exultant fans. It was a tremendous triumph for the twin heroes, Seymour and Milburn. No one knew it, but there was a lot more of this to come.

19

Date: 3 May 1952

ARSENAL

Match: FA Cup Final **Venue: Wembley**

Score: 1–0 **Attendance: 100,000**

Newcastle United:	Arsenal:
Simpson	Swindin
Cowell	Barnes
McMichael	Smith
Harvey	Forbes
Brennan	Daniel
E. Robledo	Mercer
Walker	Cox
Foulkes	Logie
Milburn	Holton
G. Robledo	Lishman
Mitchell	Roper

Referee: A. Ellis

Season 1951–52 was spent with the backdrop of Newcastle's epic FA Cup win of the previous year. League form was good enough after a dodgy start, and the final position of eighth was what one would have expected and settled for, as a few new players came into the team. These included Ronnie Simpson in goal, Alf McMichael at left-back and Billy Foulkes at inside-right – an impressive trio and, as some supporters pointed out, a Scotsman, an Irishman and a Welshman. This was something that the Geordies had always taken pride in, namely that men from all over Great Britain were welcome on Tyneside.

There were two from even further afield than that. The Robledo brothers from Chile were further proof of the internationalisation of Newcastle United in an era long before the influx of foreign players. The Robledos had arrived in England as refugees from Chilean politics in 1932 following a revolution which was none too sympathetic to those who disagreed with it. George had been at Wembley the previous spring, and he had now been joined by his brother, Eduardo, commonly known as 'Ted', who had developed throughout the season as a proficient left-half.

The veterans of last year's triumph were still there – Joe Harvey, Frank Brennan, Bobby Mitchell and, above all else, Jackie Milburn, as prolific as ever and still as chivalrous, sporting and as much loved as he had always been. The 'Wor' in the 'Wor Jackie' tag did actually mean something. He came from Ashington, to the north of the town, and he was, in the eyes of the Geordie supporters, 'wor' or 'our' Jackie.

Prime Minister Winston Churchill shakes hands with Jackie Milburn.

Following the success in 1951 the team had said they would be back the following year. Of course, everyone says that but the results of Christmas 1951, including a 4–1 defeat of Sunderland at Roker on Christmas Day, followed by a 2–2 draw at St James' Park on Boxing Day, led to speculation that this Newcastle team might just have the ability to do that. There was such a buzz around the town at last year's success that everyone not only wanted, but even expected them to do it again.

History was not on Newcastle's side. Not since Blackburn Rovers in 1890 and 1891 had any team won the FA Cup two years in a row, and despite Manchester City, Preston North End and Charlton Athletic all having been there two years in a row since the start of the Wembley era in 1923, they had each only won on the second occasion, the first being a 'dress rehearsal' for the second time. No team had ever successfully defended the trophy at Wembley.

With 10 minutes to go on 12 January at St James' Park, it had looked as if Newcastle's dream had turned to a nightmare. A third-round exit looked probable as Aston Villa, a good side in 1952, were 2–1 up and looking likely to hang on. Milburn was having a dreadful day, marked and tackled (not always too gently) out of the game, but then with all the defensive attention switched to Milburn, Bobby Mitchell took over. He equalised to earn a replay, as everyone thought, but then scored again to save the Geordies the bother of a midweek trip to Birmingham. Then, with time up, Mitchell ran through an exhausted and defeated Villa defence to pass to George Robledo to emphasise the point.

There followed a trip in early February to White Hart Lane to play Tottenham Hotspur, then embroiled in a three-way struggle with Arsenal and Manchester United for the Championship. The pitch was a quagmire after a great deal of heavy rain in the capital, but once again it was Bobby Mitchell who starred, giving Alf Ramsey (the future manager of England) a tough time. The crowd was an astonishing 69,009, and it was estimated that at least 15,000 and possibly as many as 25,000 had travelled down from the North East to support the Geordies.

Action from the 1952 Cup Final as two Arsenal defenders converge on Bobby Mitchell.

Newcastle's travels would continue to Wales, where they beat Swansea in an unimpressive but competent 1–0 victory, and then to Portsmouth, where they had already lost earlier in the season in the League. It proved to be an astonishing occasion. The all-ticket 46,000 crowd contained about 12,000 Newcastle supporters who had travelled the length of England to follow their team, leaving the previous night from Newcastle station. They joined in the anthem of the friendly Portsmouth supporters, the words none too difficult to learn, going 'Play up, Pompey! Pompey, play up!', although the reciprocal *Blaydon Races* would present more of a problem to the men from the south.

Milburn, whose form had been suspect of late, scored a hat-trick that day. In spite of being injured twice he scored three magnificent goals, the third often described as the best he had ever scored and earning him all sorts of accolades from the press. Newcastle then avoided Arsenal and Chelsea in the semi-final draw and were paired with Second Division Blackburn Rovers, a team whose glory days had passed but who remained the only team still in existence to win the FA Cup two years in a row. A replay was needed at Elland Road, Leeds, after a goalless draw at Hillsborough, and 54,000 managed to attend on a Tuesday afternoon to see Newcastle edge back to Wembley after a 2–1 victory.

It all hinged on a penalty as time was running out. A Blackburn player handled the ball and a penalty-kick was awarded. Normally it would have been 'wor Jackie' who took the spot-kick, but he had injured his knee earlier in the game and was reluctant to do it. Eventually, as skipper, Joe Harvey shaped up to take it, on the grounds that he was captain and he had a sense of obligation. As no one else wanted it, Bobby Mitchell, arguably Newcastle's best player this day, offered his services. With the weight of history on his shoulders and looking even more pasty-faced than usual, Bobby took the kick and scored. Newcastle were back at Wembley.

The opponents in the Final were Arsenal – rich, affluent, establishment, London Arsenal, with their posh stadium and fans in high places. Until their wealth tempted Herbert Chapman from Huddersfield in the late 1920s, they had won nothing at all and were, in fact, something of a laughing stock in London circles for that reason. But Chapman's arrival changed all that, and they dominated English football in the 1930s with players like Alex James and Cliff Bastin. Since the war they had done well under Tom Whittaker and had won the League in 1948 and the Cup in 1950. But there were many Gunners fans with long memories and a sense of injustice about the 1932 Cup Final and the 'over the line' incident.

It was thus a classic North versus South confrontation and there was the usual scramble for tickets, with many disappointments. Newcastle CID had to investigate allegations of forgery and black marketing, with one of the players supposedly involved. The FA decided that there would be no live televising of the game, but this was hardly a huge blow because so few people had access to a television. For the ticketless it was the radio, then a wait until the film arrived at the local cinemas.

The squad went to their normal retreat at Brighton the week before the game. The team was chosen and it was as expected. The players were as trained and as committed to the occasion as one could have expected, and so to a large extent the emphasis was on relaxation, with golf, snooker and other things.

The formal side of the occasion saw a few changes. King George VI had died in February, and it had been hoped that the young, as yet uncrowned Queen Elizabeth might present the Cup and be introduced to the players, but in the event it was Winston Churchill, re-established as Prime Minister the previous autumn, who did the job. As they were introduced Churchill apparently said to Milburn, 'Are you going to grab the honours again this year?'

It was generally looked upon as a poor Cup Final as regards the standard of play, and it was marred from an Arsenal point of view by the severe injury in the first half to right-back Wally Barnes. He sustained ligament damage and this effectively ended his career. A few years later he became an excellent BBC commentator, but this injury in this Cup Final was a particular blow to the Gunners because they were relying on Wally to stop Bobby Mitchell. Left-winger Don Roper had to be drafted back to perform that task.

It had been Milburn who was the unwitting cause of Barnes's injury. It was as early as the 18th minute when Jackie tried to back-heel a ball and his foot caught Barnes on the knee. In 1952 substitutes were not allowed and this was a shame because Arsenal could do little other than defend and hope for a replay. In fact, they played very well and were probably the better team for long spells, but it was Newcastle who got the only goal of the game. A Bobby Mitchell cross found George Robledo who, after a curious movement, managed to head the ball wide of goalkeeper Swindin. It was so late that 10-man Arsenal had little chance to get back.

George Robledo scores the only goal of the game.

The victorious Newcastle team with Joe Harvey, hoisted on the shoulders of two of his teammates.

The return home.

A fine picture of the first team to win at Wembley in successive Cup Finals.

Even the hardest-hearted of Geordie fans would have to admit that all this was hard on the Gunners, whose 10 men had fought so gallantly to give themselves a chance to fight another day with 11 men. Barnes had tried to come back and had hobbled about on the left wing for a spell, but eventually he had to withdraw altogether.

Ronnie Simpson, Newcastle's goalkeeper, had a very quiet game, but what he had to do he did well. At the full-time whistle, he found it hard to believe that he was now the proud possessor of an FA Cup medal. His father, Jimmy Simpson, looked on approvingly from the stand, as Simpson Snr thought that the English Cup medal would look nice alongside the Scottish Cup medals that he himself had won for Rangers. No one realised that Ronnie Simpson's astonishing career was just beginning.

The triumphant team returned to Brighton after a banquet at London's Savoy and eventually got home to Newcastle on the Monday. The whole city seemed to have turned out to greet them as they arrived at Newcastle's beautiful old station with its classical façade. They then boarded an open-top bus for what would normally have been a very short trip to St James' Park. With detours and traffic jams it took them a very long time indeed.

Date: 13 May 1953

20
ABERDEEN

Match: Coronation Cup quarter-final **Venue: Ibrox Park**

Score: 4–0 **Attendance: 13,000**

Newcastle United:	Aberdeen:
Simpson	Martin
Cowell	Mitchell
Batty	Shaw
Harvey	Harris
Brennan	Young
Crowe	Allister
White	Boyd
Mulgrew	Hamilton
Milburn	Buckley
Hannah	Yorston
Mitchell	Hather

Referee: R.M. Griffiths, Wales

Coronations do not happen very often. There were only four in the 20th century: in 1902, 1911, 1937 and 1953. To celebrate the crowning of Queen Elizabeth, it was decided to have a football tournament involving the eight best teams in Britain. To ease pressure on the congestion in London, and also perhaps to keep the rebellious Scots on side, it was decided that all the games should be played in Glasgow at the very establishment-orientated Hampden Park and Ibrox Stadium (conspicuously not at Celtic Park, where the natives were rumoured to have sympathies for the Irish Republic rather than the crown).

It is hard to imagine what the Coronation meant in 1953 to the people of Great Britain. It was a very joyous occasion, much looked forward to and welcomed by a people who had had it rough for many years through wars and depressions, but had now turned the corner and were beginning to deal with the horrendous problems of poverty, bad housing and ill health. Mass unemployment had now gone and there was a remarkable social union in the country, symbolised in the arrival of a new, young and pretty Queen with two charming children.

Every effort was made by the government and the establishment to keep everyone sweet. Bars of chocolate (a treat in 1953; until recently chocolate had been rationed) and Coronation mugs were given to children, several days holiday were given to workers and the whole country was decorated with red, white and blue and signs saying 'God Save The Queen'. On the other hand, it was often felt that all this was merely hiding the still-prevalent slums and the recent horrors of what had happened in Korea.

Those who advocated an all-British football League were encouraged by the idea of an all-British Cup, and there were those who suggested that it should be an annual event. This was too early for any European dimension to the game as floodlights and air travel, the two necessary components for the European Cups, were not yet sufficiently developed, but a competition within Britain seemed no bad thing.

To say that the best eight teams in Britain were chosen is perhaps not quite true. On the basis of League form the four English teams should have been Arsenal, Preston North End, Wolverhampton Wanderers and West Bromwich Albion, and the Scottish ones should have been Rangers, Hibernian, East Fife and Hearts. This emphatically did not happen. For reasons of sheer greed, Tottenham Hotspur, Manchester United and Newcastle United, teams with high profiles and a large support, found themselves in, as did Aberdeen and Celtic. This was difficult to justify on footballing grounds, but it certainly made financial sense. In Newcastle's case they had had a dreadful season, having finished 16th in Division One and made an ignominious early departure from the FA Cup at the hands of Rotherham, but it was clearly hoped that because of the comparatively short distance to Glasgow fans would travel to support them. Sadly, very few Geordies availed themselves of the opportunity.

The draw was arranged so that every quarter-final game was Scotland versus England, and Newcastle found themselves up against their geographical equivalents. In the same way as Newcastle were the team of the north-east of England, Aberdeen represented the north-east of Scotland. It would be fair to say that the Dons had under-performed in Scotland since their inception in 1903, with only one Scottish Cup to their credit in 1947, but they had had bad luck this year after taking Rangers to a replay in the Scottish Cup Final. They were not a bad side under manager Davie Halliday and would be a strong test, it was felt, for the Geordies.

Connections between the two clubs were few and tenuous, but they did have in common the tremendously talented Tommy Pearson, who had played for Newcastle in the 1930s and had his career badly disrupted by the war before moving to Aberdeen in 1948. He had just recently retired, but had the odd distinction of having played for both Scotland and England. Admittedly, his England appearance was in emergency circumstances during the war, but it is unusual and remarkable nevertheless.

Aberdeen had other fine players too, notably the veteran inside-right George Hamilton, Paddy Buckley, an enterprising centre-forward and a very speedy left-winger in Jackie Hather. Their goalkeeper was Fred Martin, who would soon be capped for Scotland. Newcastle, on the other hand, although having disappointed this season, still had Jackie Milburn, now no longer an automatic England choice but still the idol of the Tyne. George Hannah had appeared this season and had a few good games, and there was an unfamiliar name in Tommy Mulgrew, whose appearance in Glasgow would give his family a chance to come from nearby Motherwell to watch him.

When Newcastle lined up against Aberdeen at Ibrox on the evening of Wednesday 13 May, Scotland were already two up on England, as it were. Celtic had delighted and amazed their fans by beating Arsenal, and Hibs, after a replay, had got the better of Tottenham Hotspur. The crowd at Ibrox was a paltry 10,000 (sometimes given as 13,000 and the *Glasgow Herald* goes as low as 5,000) and it had a strange atmosphere in the large bowl that was Ibrox, the attendance being less than a third of Rangers' average League attendance.

There were reasons for this, notably the counter-attraction of Rangers playing Manchester United at Hampden a couple of miles away. This game attracted 75,000 and clearly accounted for most of the missing thousands at Ibrox. The 10,000 thus consisted of a few Geordies, a few Aberdonians (Ibrox being a long way away from both cities), a few Celtic supporters who could not face watching Rangers and a few Glaswegians wishing to see the great Newcastle United, who had won the FA Cup twice in the last three years. Lovers of Queen's Park and Third Lanark would have an opportunity to see their old boys, Ronnie Simpson and Bobby Mitchell.

It is a shame that so few Geordie supporters were at Ibrox that Wednesday night, because they missed a tremendous display of Newcastle at their best, with Bobby Mitchell showing Glasgow what they had been missing and inviting yet more speculation about why he tended to be ignored by the Scotland selectors. From an early stage wing-halves Joe Harvey and Charlie Crowe took a grip on proceedings, spraying passes to the eager forwards and drawing gasps of admiration from the meagre crowd. Their performance was particularly praiseworthy given the unsatisfactory state of the pitch, which had been played on all season and was in urgent need of rest and attention.

For their part, Aberdeen, after a bright start in which they three times hit the woodwork, fell away badly in the face of a determined Newcastle onslaught. The first goal came in the 15th minute when, in the aftermath of an indirect free-kick (which the *Glasgow Herald* thought should have been a penalty), the ball came to Len White, who hammered home though a ruck of players' legs. Five minutes later Newcastle went two ahead when George Hannah lost his marker, Tony Harris, and fired in a great shot from 20 yards. It was 2–0 at half-time and the rout was completed when Alec Young, challenged by Milburn, conceded an own goal before Milburn himself picked up a White free-kick to score a trademark goal. Newcastle were now well on top and showing a great deal of composure and sheer class.

It was one of the rare occasions in 1953 when everyone played to their potential, and the delight of the small group of Newcastle supporters was plain for all to see. The Aberdeen fans had departed the scene to get an early train back home, and the game finished to the cheers of the Novocastrians, the polite claps of the neutrals and the lugubrious tones of the Ibrox announcer telling everyone in a melancholy voice that in the other quarter-final at Hampden, Rangers had gone down to Manchester United.

Newcastle returned to their hotel delighted and must have fancied themselves to win the tournament. Both League winners, Rangers and Arsenal, had bitten the dust. One of the other favourites, Manchester United, had to play Celtic, while Newcastle seemed to have a slightly easier run against Hibs, who were certainly a better side than Celtic but lacked their fanatical support. Celtic and Manchester United would play at Hampden, and Newcastle returned to Ibrox to take on Hibs.

It being a Saturday, more Newcastle supporters treated themselves to a day out in Glasgow. In addition, Edinburgh is a lot closer to Glasgow than Aberdeen is, so there was a respectable crowd of over 35,000 at the semi-final. Once again, however, it would appear that the tournament organisers did themselves less than justice by holding both semi-finals at the same time, as Celtic were taking on Manchester United at Hampden.

The game at Ibrox will not feature highly in any history of the Toon, and it was all the more disappointing after the fine performance on Wednesday night. The score was also 4–0, but this time it was the other way round, as Newcastle had no answer to Hibs' Famous Five forward line of Smith, Johnstone, Reilly, Turnbull and Ormond, and were ruthlessly hammered. Newcastle's own forward line were simply not able to get going and the wing-halves were totally outplayed by the devastating football of Hibs. Newcastle might have made the scoreline more respectable if Milburn had not missed a golden opportunity after some fine work from Mulgrew, and if Mitchell had not missed a penalty, but the truth was that Hibs were by far the better team.

In some ways it was typical of the Jekyll and Hyde performances that supporters had seen rather too much of that year, and plans that anyone had to return to Glasgow for the Final on Wednesday were immediately forgotten about as Newcastle limped off the field to the jeers of the Scottish supporters and the silent indifference of their own fans, at least those who had not yet left to rejoin their wives, who were buying Coronation souvenirs in the city centre.

Thus it came about that we had the bizarre sight of the Coronation Cup Final being watched, not by the establishment royalist supporters of Rangers and Arsenal, nor even by the craggy Geordies of Newcastle or the strident lovers of Manchester United, but by the two Scottish teams, whose supporters were unmistakably Irish in their sympathies. For the record, it was Celtic who won 2–0.

Date: 30 March 1955

21
YORK CITY

Match: FA Cup semi-final replay

Venue: Roker Park

Score: 2–0

Attendance: 59,239

Newcastle United:	York City:
Simpson	Forgan
Cowell	Phillips
Batty	Howe
Scoular	Brown
Stokoe	Stewart
Crowe	Spence
White	Hughes
Davies	Bottom
Keeble	Wilkinson
Milburn	Storey
Mitchell	Fenton

Referee: J. Kelly, Chorley

York is a beautiful and interesting city, with York Minster, the Railway Museum, the Jorvik Viking Centre and other areas of interest. The Romans were there first, calling it Eboracum, but others followed and the result is a fascinating place with good shops, fine architecture and what the locals call 'snickets' – lovely little alleyways that date back many centuries. But football was never been a major part of its culture in the way that the sport took over the more industrialised parts of the country like Manchester, Liverpool, Glasgow and indeed Newcastle.

Spring 1955 saw Britain in gradual and obvious economic and social improvement from the post-war days. The Welfare State continued its irreversible progress even under the Conservatives. Churchill was still Prime Minister, but now that he was over 80 it was becoming clear that he was struggling. Anthony Eden was waiting in the wings, but the stubborn old war leader showed little signs of wanting to depart. He would eventually do so in April, leaving Eden to begin his disastrous Premiership. It would be foreign affairs that would be Eden's downfall, but the more immediate problem was a rash of strikes of bus drivers, train drivers and – annoyingly for the football historian – newspapers.

1955 also made everyone sit up and take notice of York City. Under manager Jim McCormick they were in what was called Division Three North, which meant that they had to participate in the early rounds of the FA Cup before having a chance of meeting the big guns. They duly disposed of local rivals Scarborough and then Dorchester Town before pulling out a plum in the draw with a

Len White scores Newcastle's first goal in the replay at Roker Park.

trip to Blackpool – Stanley Matthews, Stanley Mortenson, Jackie Mudie and all. Blackpool had won the trophy 18 months previously in a famous Final against Bolton, but on this occasion York beat them 2–0.

This was impressive enough, but then they collected another scalp. The famous amateur team from the north, Bishop Auckland, were disposed of without a great deal of fuss, but then they drew Tottenham Hotspur to Bootham Crescent. Spurs were a great and wealthy side, with men like Danny Blanchflower and Alf Ramsey on board. In a few years time, in 1961, they would win the FA and League double for the first time for any club this century, and there would be those who claimed that they were the best team of all time. Not in 1955, however, as Spurs were beaten 3–1 with surprising ease on a hard but playable pitch, and Danny Blanchflower was wholesome in his praise.

Notts County were disposed of next, and this brought York up against Newcastle United in the semi-final at Hillsborough on 26 March 1955. As this was by some distance the most important game ever in York's sometimes rather sad history, and Hillsborough was not too far away, it would be safe to say that York was a fairly empty place that afternoon.

Newcastle had won the Cup in 1951 and 1952, but League form in 1954–55 had been mediocre and unpredictable. A 5–1 spanking of Arsenal in December indicated that the team might be turning the corner, but on New Year's Day they managed to go down 6–2 to Sheffield United. They had also managed to lose twice to Sunderland, something that hurt the Geordie faithful, and their progress in the FA Cup had been none too impressive, with prolonged, painful and rather lucky victories over Notts Forest and Huddersfield Town. The game against Huddersfield, in particular, had been tough, with Newcastle needing a late Len White goal to earn a replay and being heavily indebted to Ronnie Simpson (patronisingly referred to as 'the little Scot' in the club programme) for many saves.

But they did have Jackie Milburn and Bobby Mitchell, two of the best forwards in the British game, and on their day they would be hard to beat. They also had a Cup tradition, having won the trophy five times, and they had their massive and fanatical support, now in the mid-1950s sharing a little in the general affluence of the times and able to travel in ever-increasing numbers to away games. They were intrigued by the possibility of an all North East FA Cup Final, as Sunderland were in the other semi-final, playing against Manchester City.

It would be easy, when one looks at the Pathé News pictures of the first semi-final at Hillsborough, to put up a strong argument that the game should not have been played. The rain was incessant, the pitch was muddy in places and in some areas of the field it bordered on the unplayable. It was the conditions that played a part in the incident that has all of York convinced to this day that they were robbed.

The game was tied at 1–1 as it entered its final stages with two exhausted teams throwing everything at each other. A goal at either end would have been no surprise, but it would also have been a gross injustice for the team who lost it. During a scramble in the Newcastle goalmouth, the York player with the unfortunate name of Albert Bottom (he would play for Newcastle a few years later) headed for goal, and Ronnie Simpson dived and clawed the ball back from the line. York claimed it was over, but Simpson, an honest man (who would win a European Cup medal with Celtic 12 years later), insisted to his dying day that the ball was not entirely over the line. Bottom, years later, would admit that he did not think the ball crossed the line, but he was mystified by what happened next. Intriguingly, as controversy raged, the referee awarded a free-kick to Newcastle for reasons that the press were at a loss to explain. It couldn't have been for offside and must have been for a foul on a Newcastle defender – something that Bottom denied. For whatever reason, Newcastle were saved.

In the last minutes, even after that moment of drama, both teams might have scored, but it was to be a replay at Sunderland on the Wednesday. Relief was the order of the day for the Newcastle faithful, tinged with joy that rivals Sunderland had lost in the other semi. The choice of Roker Park for the replay might have caused a few palpitations for Newcastle, but then again anyone who analyses derby rivalry will realise that such things are only skin deep and that there was a huge advantage for Newcastle here in that most of their massive support lived within 20 miles of Roker Park. It was a home game in all but name.

For York the day was looked upon as a triumph as well, in spite of any pain that might have been experienced for the Bottom/Simpson incident. There was a certain amount of feeling that if it had been the other way round, and if it had been the First Division team on the attack, the goal would have been given. York had the consolation of being the first team from either of the two Third Divisions (North or South) to have forced a semi-final replay, and they still had the chance of appearing at Wembley, although wiser opinion and bookmakers tended to believe that Newcastle, for all their indifferent form, would not let them off the hook again.

Both teams made changes for the replay. Sid Storey returned from his back injury for York City and for Newcastle, while Tommy Casey returned to displace Charlie Crowe. The crowd was only a few hundred short of 60,000 and it included about 15,000 from York. One of the benefits of supporting York City is the railway connection and many took advantage of this, even though it was a Wednesday afternoon. Wembley was now beckoning.

The astonishing crowd says something about devotion to a team. It is unlikely that as many people as all that were on holiday or had Wednesday as their day off. It can, therefore, be assumed that many people were willing to put their jobs at risk, and that there would have been a fair number of uncomfortable interviews with employers and headmasters the following morning. What was remarked upon by the newspapers, though, was the number of Newcastle fans who were seen to be walking to the ground. It was a good day and the distance was not all that far!

The conditions were as good as the first game's were bad. It was a fine, dry spring afternoon, still with a hint of coolness in the air, but as good a day for playing football as one could have wished. Newcastle started playing towards the 'sea' end of the ground, and within a few minutes were ahead. It was right-winger Len White who scored, latching onto a cross from the right (where arguably he should have been if Newcastle had been strict in their field dispositions) and getting to the ball before the York defenders did. White had been with the club for two years and would become a long-serving Newcastle player with enduring popularity among the fans, many of whom felt that he would have graced an England cap.

If Wembley had been beckoning before, it was now positively opening its arms in invitation, but there was still a long way to go. York, with nothing to lose, tried hard but without often troubling Ronnie Simpson. They were hampered by a bad injury to centre-half Alan Stewart (ironically a Newcastle boy) after a bad clash of heads, but earned a great deal of praise in the following morning's newspapers for their pluck.

Newcastle remained the better team, however, and this was confirmed when they scored their second goal towards the end of the game. It was a strange, unsatisfactory, but nevertheless welcome goal. A long, floating ball from the left, where Bobby Mitchell had been his normal outstanding self, found Vic Keeble rushing in. The ball was just too high for his feet and too low for his head, so it was his chest that he used. The final whistle went soon afterwards and Newcastle were at Wembley for the third time in five years. It was a happy return to Newcastle that night.

In some ways, though, all the glory belonged to York. They had been a credit to the Third Division and might even have reached Wembley, particularly in the first game where they had many chances and the Arthur Bottom incident, in which every York supporter remains to this day convinced that the ball was over the line. Even those who were born many years later will argue that a goal should have been given.

Date: 7 May 1955

22

MANCHESTER CITY

Match: FA Cup Final   **Venue: Wembley**

Score: 3–1   **Attendance: 100,000**

Newcastle United:	Manchester City:
Simpson	Trautmann
Cowell	Meadows
Batty	Little
Scoular	Barnes
Stokoe	Ewing
Casey	Paul
White	Spurdle
Milburn	Hayes
Keeble	Revie
Hannah	Johnstone
Mitchell	Fagan

Referee: R.J. Leafe, Nottingham

There were exciting times on Tyneside in spring 1955. Newcastle United were on their way to Wembley for the third time in five years. They had won the trophy in 1951 and 1952, and now, after a prolonged and epic struggle to defeat Plymouth Argyle, Brentford, Notts Forest, Huddersfield Town and York City, the Toon were back at Wembley.

For the third time in the 1950s, the city's obsession with football and its team grew even deeper, with everyone talking about tickets (3s 6d for the cheapest ones), trains, TV coverage and everything to do with the game as if there were no other event worth talking about. Certainly there was nothing else in the city and the surrounding area. Other things, like the appointment of a new Prime Minister in Anthony Eden and his immediate calling of a General Election for 26 May 1955, passed almost without being noticed. The FA Cup was the thing that really mattered.

League form had been acceptable but not outstanding. The team had won 17 games and lost 16, with the normal tendency to do better at home than they did away. The average home attendance was 42,987, well above the national average for 1955. There had been a bad spell in the autumn when the team went a couple of months without a win, but they had then rallied to have a better winter and spring. Form at Easter had been splendid with three wins in four days against Everton, Sheffield Wednesday and Everton again, and this was on the back of their qualification for the FA Cup Final at the end of March.

Newcastle United in the mid-1950s.

The route to the FA Cup Final had been difficult, to put it mildly. The draw for the third round could have been kinder, in that it sent United to Devon to play Plymouth Argyle on the second Saturday of the New Year in the middle of an icy spell, and Newcastle were grateful to Vic Keeble, who gave them a narrow 1–0 victory. Amazingly, a large percentage of the 28,585 crowd was from Newcastle. Even in the 1950s, when the railway network was at its height and tolerably efficient, it would have been a very lucky supporter who would have reached home before midnight. Those brave enough to travel by road in the dreadful conditions and several years before the motorway system came into being would have had a nightmarish trip.

An undistinguished home victory against Brentford followed before the fifth round threw up a prolonged tussle with Nottingham Forest. Two draws led to a third game being played at St James' Park, Newcastle having won the toss for venue, and there was a moment of glory for Alan Monkhouse, who was given a game for the injured Vic Keeble and scored twice before an astonishing Wednesday afternoon crowd of 36,631. (38,573 had been at St James' Park on the Monday for the second game.) Huddersfield Town came next: a fairly lucky draw at Leeds Road after Huddersfield scored first, then were denied what looked like a penalty before Len White grabbed a late equaliser to take the game to St James' Park. A crowd of 52,449, just short of the number at the first game, saw Newcastle win 2–0 with goals from Vic Keeble and Bobby Mitchell in extra-time.

One would have thought that this was enough to be going on with, but even more excitement was to come in the semi-final. By the time that the sixth-round replay had been played, Newcastle knew that they had avoided Sunderland in the semi-final and that an all North East Cup Final was, therefore, a possibility. As it was, Sunderland travelled to Villa Park to take on Manchester City and Newcastle went to Hillsborough to play York City, the giant-killers of the Third Division North who had already disposed of Tottenham Hotspur and the winners of 1953, Blackpool. Newcastle needed a replay to triumph over them.

Sunderland had been beaten by Manchester City in the other semi-final, and thus the prospect of a derby Final had been avoided. Manchester City were probably still considered to be the more prestigious of the two Manchester sides in 1955, even although United had won the FA Cup in 1948 and had done better than City in the League this year, clearly developing a talented young side under Matt Busby. City's manager was called Leslie McDowall and he had a good side, relying on what was known as the 'Revie plan' with Don Revie, nominally the centre-forward but in fact playing behind the two inside men of Joe Hayes and Bobby Johnstone, then charging forward to devastating effect. It had been quite effective, and City had ended up seventh in the English League – a good performance in most seasons, but not in the season that Manchester United had finished fifth. Pressure was on City to deliver the goods.

There seemed to be problems with the management at Newcastle. The manager was Duggie Livingstone, a Scotsman from Dumbarton who had played for Celtic and Everton in the years immediately after World War One and had since done a great deal of coaching all over Europe. He was a great believer in continental training methods. In this he was a man ahead of his time, too far ahead for men like Jackie Milburn, who went on record as saying that Newcastle needed such methods 'like a man needs a hole in the head'. They included bizarre things like chalking Bobby Mitchell's boots to improve his passing.

It would be fair to say that Livingstone did not enjoy the total confidence of all the playing staff at Newcastle – George Hannah had asked for a transfer in February but had thought better of it – and increasingly the directors, particularly the very powerful Stanley Seymour, were beginning to wonder whether Livingstone was a good idea. But the Cup run and the general good form had solidified the team, the directors and the supporters were behind the manager, and an uneasy peace reigned. Livingstone deserves a great deal of credit for getting United to the Final.

In the run-up to the Final, a crisis arose. Jackie Milburn was suffering from a slight injury and also had a dose of laryngitis. This was enough, in Livingstone's eyes, to rule him out of the Final. It may be that Livingstone did not like Jackie (and perhaps the feeling was mutual) and perhaps a wiser

The iconic picture of Newcastle's early goal in the 1955 Cup Final.

manager would have waited until the very last minute before making a decision, but Livingstone, when the team were staying at the Royal Albert Hotel on the outskirts of London, presented the board of directors with a forward line which read: Davies, Hannah, White, Keeble and Mitchell.

Seymour was now in a quandary. Milburn seemed quite fit to him. The injury was slight, and while laryngitis would be a problem for an opera singer, it isn't really that serious for a footballer. In Seymour's opinion Milburn should play, but could he overrule his manager and provoke an almost certain resignation?

Seymour took the bold step, realising that Milburn was the man on whom everyone depended, but the story now became more complicated when Reg Davies, the Welsh inside-right, also caught laryngitis. In his case, however, he became quite ill and had to be isolated and removed from the squad. This was rotten luck for Davies, who would have been asked to play out of position in any case, but it meant that Len White had to play on the right wing after all instead of the centre. The burly Vic Keeble was put in the centre and Milburn was included at inside-left. Honour was, for the moment at least, satisfied as far as Livingstone was concerned, but it was the first step towards his departure.

How appropriate it was that a combination of White and Milburn scored the first goal. The jittery Manchester City defence conceded a corner on the right in the first minute and failed to mark Milburn adequately as the corner was taken by White. Jackie headed home off the newly painted

Queen Elizabeth II presents the FA Cup to Jimmy Scoular.

crossbar at the near side of the penalty box in what has become an iconic Milburn goal. Len White would admit later that the true target had been Vic Keeble rather than Jackie Milburn, but that mattered little. It was the earliest goal ever scored in an FA Cup Final, and the royal party had barely managed to settle down after meeting the players. Stan Seymour, sitting beside the Queen and Princess Margaret, wondered if they understood Geordie!

Often an early goal determines the course of the game and this one had its effect, but far more significant to Manchester City was the loss of Jimmy Meadows, their right-back, in the 20th minute through ligament damage. There were no substitutes allowed in 1955, and this meant that City had to play with 10 men for the rest of the game. Sympathy for Meadows was tempered, however, by the thought that it had been a somewhat crude lunge on Bobby Mitchell that had led to his injury.

City's purple patch came just before half-time when, after Ronnie Simpson had twice saved (once with his legs), a great diving header from Bobby Johnstone brought an equaliser and gave City hope for the second half, even with 10 men. It was a good goal as well, well worked and brilliantly finished off by a man who had been part of the Famous Five forward line of Hibs.

The second half saw the triumph of the Newcastle half-back line of Scoular, Stokoe and Casey as they simply took charge, with Jimmy Scoular in particular playing brilliantly and neutralising any Revie plan. The other Scotsman, Bobby Mitchell, was also superb and it was he who scored the second goal from an impossible angle at 60 minutes. A few minutes after that he shot again. The ball was parried by German goalkeeper Bert Trautmann, and George Hannah was on the spot to net the third goal.

Newcastle finished the game well on top, and Wembley was in a Geordie uproar as Jimmy Scoular lifted the FA Cup to bring it back to Tyneside for the third time in five years. The team returned to an exultant city on the Monday. The players were awarded a bonus of £25, not exactly a king's ransom, but still a considerable sum in 1955.

Jimmy Scoular shows the trophy to Newcastle's fans.

Date: 26 December 1955

23
SUNDERLAND

Match: League Division One   **Venue: Roker Park, Sunderland**

Score: 6–1   **Attendance: 55,723**

Sunderland:	Newcastle:
Fraser	Simpson
Hedley	Batty
McDonald	McMichael
Anderson	Scoular
Daniel	Paterson
Aitken	Casey
Shackleton	Milburn
Fleming	Davies
Purdon	Keeble
Chisholm	Curry
Elliott	Mitchell

Referee: A.W. Leuty, Leeds

Football fans would have certainly enjoyed their Christmases in the mid-1950s – five games were scheduled over the festive period in 1955, on Christmas Eve (a Saturday in 1955), Boxing Day, 27 December, New Year's Eve and 2 January. It was generally agreed that this was, by any standards, a heavy schedule, and a similarly hard programme would be arranged for Easter, but there seems to have been a distinct lack of moaning and complaining about how ill-treated professional football players were. It was accepted as part of the game.

What added spice to the programme was that a team would play one team on Boxing Day and then the same team with venues reversed the following day. In 1955 the North East was particularly enthralled by the idea that the games were Newcastle versus Sunderland. Letters to Father Christmas would often include requests for a derby double over the local rivals, and it would be a fair guess that the topic of conversation at the Christmas dinner table would centre on the football.

The relationship between Newcastle and Sunderland was complex. They were from separate cities, so the games were not derbies in the strictest sense that one would find in Manchester, Liverpool or Glasgow, but increasingly, as both cities expanded with the demand for houses, it was becoming more and more difficult to see daylight between the cities. Geordies and Mackems worked together, generally spoke the same dialect, shared the same outlook on life, and 'mixed marriages' without any Romeo and Juliet problems that one might have found in Glasgow, for example, were not uncommon.

Yet it is a mistake to romanticise the 1950s and say that in that era football was football, and violence and thuggery played no part. This is not quite true, although the 1950s probably saw a slight dip in the football violence that had been common in the 1920s and 1940s (the immediate aftermath of wars where young men learned all too readily how to be and remain violent) and which would resurface with all its ugliness in the 1970s.

Whether there was violence or not, there was certainly passion and desire for victory. One had to face workmates after the Christmas holiday and it would be nice to be in a position to talk about football rather than have to change the subject when it came up, or pretend not to be interested or not to be too upset about what had happened. It was what is now called 'bragging rights'.

One often feels, however, that the rivalry between the two great sides of the North East has not always worked to the advantage of either side in that it has often prevented them from seeing the broader picture. There is often the impression, for example, that the supporters are satisfied whenever their team finishes higher up in the League than the other or makes more progress in the FA Cup than the other, whereas the focus should surely be on being the best team in England, as Newcastle had been 50 years previously.

The Toon was still on a high after the Cup Final victory of 1955, the third in five years, and the FA Cup of 1956 was looked forward to with a great deal of relish. A trip to Sheffield Wednesday beckoned on 7 January. League form had been inconsistent. There had been injuries to key players like Crowe, Stokoe, White and Mitchell, and although home form had been tolerable, away form meant that Newcastle spent Christmas in mid-table mediocrity. Their supporters agreed that the FA Cup represented a better chance of success that the League did.

Cars were a new phenomenon. More and more people owned one and used them to go to football matches, so much so that it was very difficult to find a space to park one's Austin, Zodiac or Somerset. From an early hour that Boxing Day morning it was becoming obvious that the crowd was going to be a huge one, and as the players ran out it seemed that the black and white rattles, rosettes and scarves of Newcastle were at least as prevalent as the red and white ones of the Sunderland fans. As this was before the days of segregation, fans of both sides mingled with each other exchanging banter or at least maintaining a 'peaceful coexistence', to use the Cold War phraseology.

Under manager Bill Murray, who had been with the club since before World War Two (this was in the days when managers tended to last a little longer in their jobs than they do today), Sunderland were doing well. They would finish higher up in the League than Newcastle and had some fine players. There was Len Shackleton, a man whom the Geordie supporters would never forgive for his leaving of Newcastle and moving to Sunderland, but the real hero of the hour was Charlie Fleming, who had joined Sunderland a year earlier from East Fife, with whom he had won a couple of Scottish League Cup medals.

Charlie was called 'Legs' Fleming because of his speed, and his ability to shoot earned him the other nickname of 'Cannonball Charlie'. He was a great foil to Shackleton, who was now beginning to slow down, and it was a happy combination for the Wearsiders. A feature of Sunderland's play was their excellent wing-halves in Stan Anderson and George 'Dod' Aitken. Aitken, like Fleming, had joined the club from East Fife – it had been he who had recommended Fleming – and no one would have predicted that the ubiquitous Stan Anderson, a traditional 'take a grip of the game' wing-half, would one day join Newcastle.

Sunderland still felt that they were in with a chance of the League Championship and had shown welcome initiative in arranging fixtures against foreign opposition. They had travelled to Paris to play a game against Racing Club, and the great FC Dynamo Moscow had appeared at Roker Park in November to play a friendly. There was clear ambition in the air at Roker, more so than at St James' Park, where complacency at the recent FA Cup successes was more the order of the day.

It was in the tradition of holiday fixtures, and indeed local derby fixtures, for there to be freak results. There were reasons for this – probably not the widely held popular view that the losing side had enjoyed Christmas rather too much, but more because of the desire of players to raise their game or to respond to the large crowd. Not many supporters, however, would have predicted what was about to happen.

Roker Park lay on the 'Newcastle' side of Sunderland and was comparatively easy to access, but even so many Newcastle supporters were late and missed the first goal. In Newcastle's first attack, Sunderland conceded a foolish and unnecessary free-kick. Irish left-half Tommy Casey took it and found the head of Vic Keeble, who headed home with vigour. He was allowed what was virtually a free header, for several defenders had instinctively shadowed the dangerous Milburn, who was quite happy to play the role of a decoy.

It was the great Bobby Mitchell who created the next two goals, so that with less than 20 minutes on the clock, Newcastle were three goals up. Mitchell created the opening for Jackie Milburn to rifle home a low drive then, with the Sunderland defence still reeling, Mitchell again created the opening, this time for the little-known Bill Curry to tap in from very close range. This was only Curry's third game for the club this season, because his career was much disrupted by his National Service and injury.

Roker Park was rocked by all this, and Sunderland simply could not get any counter-attack going, such was the power of the Newcastle half-back line of Scoular, Paterson and Casey. Neither Shackleton nor Fleming received any service worth the name, and it was no surprise when Newcastle went even further ahead before half-time. This time it was a corner on the right taken by Milburn (more famed for being on the receiving end of corners) that found Vic Keeble, who once again rose high above the hapless Ray Daniel and headed home.

Neither set of supporters could quite fathom what had happened, as both teams trotted off at half-time with Newcastle winning 4–0. Sunderland's fans could not believe that their team would not make some sort of fight-back in the second half, and Newcastle's fans, for their part, feared that this success was transient and illusory and that their defence, which had been criticised in the first part of the season, would yet let them down.

Their fears appeared to be justified when Sunderland, coming out with their tails up and obviously having been on the wrong end of manager Murray's wrath, pulled one back through Fleming within five minutes of the restart. But it was the next goal that would be the one that mattered, and it was Milburn who scored when he picked up a delightful ball from the grossly undervalued Reg Davies and scored first time. Mitchell then got into the act once again, beating a couple of men and crossing for Curry to score his second and Newcastle's sixth.

Shortly after this, Mitchell, who had been the greatest architect of Sunderland's destruction, was injured and finished the game as a passenger. Had this not happened double figures might well have been achieved, because Newcastle were running through this panic-stricken defence at will. As it was, a halt was called at 6–1, and irreversible damage was done to Sunderland's League challenge the following day when the teams met again at St James' Park in front of a crowd in excess of 61,000. Newcastle won again, this time only 3–1 after Sunderland had scored first, but Newcastle finished the game as much on top as they had been the day before.

Newcastle fans enjoyed their biggest and most complete defeat of their local rivals. New Year was spent in an atmosphere of euphoria, with the FA Cup ties and the possibility of yet another trip to Wembley much looked forward to and relished. But it was Sunderland who were fated to kill this particular dream. The teams were drawn together in the quarter-final at St James' Park, and Sunderland quite simply played better that afternoon and won 2–0. It was as well that the triumphant Newcastle hordes on Boxing Day 1955, heading home in their triumphant cavalcade of cars with black and white scarves hanging out the windows, did not know what was coming to them.

24

Date: 28 January 1956

FULHAM

Match: FA Cup fourth round   **Venue: Craven Cottage, Fulham**

Score: 5–4   **Attendance: 39,200**

Fulham:	Newcastle United:
Black	Simpson
Wilson	Woollard
Lawler	McMichael
Smith	Stokoe
Brice	Patterson
Lowe	Casey
Hill	Milburn
Robson	Davies
Jezzard	Keeble
Haynes	Curry
Chamberlain	Mitchell

Referee: J. Mitchel

The winter of 1955–56 saw stirring times for Newcastle. Still living off the triumph of the previous May and installed as favourites for their fourth FA Cup in six years, United were very much in the spotlight, attracting headlines in the national press, being mentioned first on the sports programme on the radio and having everyone on the trains as they passed through Newcastle hoping to catch a glance of Jackie Milburn, a man talked about endlessly.

The early part of the season, in which the Magpies had hoped for their first League challenge since the days of Hughie Gallacher nearly 30 years ago, had seen a few injuries. Bobby Cowell, for example, the hard-working right-back, had not played all season and would have to give up, and injury was also troubling Jimmy Scoular and Len White. As a result, League form had been inconsistent but there had been some very good days as well. Christmas had been particularly merry on Tyneside that year; Christmas Eve had seen a 5–0 defeat of Preston North End, then on Boxing Day the team had travelled the short distance to Sunderland to win by the astonishing margin of 6–1. The following day, the venue was reversed but it was the same winners – Newcastle, by 3–1 this time – before a staggering crowd of 61,058.

These were the boom times for football. There was prosperity, full employment guaranteeing that there was lots of money for football matches, and also very few other outlets for amusement other than the cinema. Television was there, with a football programme hosted by Kenneth Wolstenholme called *Sports Special*, but it was not yet the dominant force of British cultural life that it would become in a few years time, although it was advancing rapidly. In football itself there were changes, with more and more clubs getting floodlights so that midweek matches could be played at night, and a new concept had arrived in the European Cup, which the Football Association seemed to disapprove of but was powerless to stop.

In Newcastle's case the FA Cup remained virtually the be-all and end-all. Newcastle had now won the trophy six times, a record shared with Aston Villa and Blackburn Rovers. It would be nice to win it again. Progress had been made in the defence of the previous year's FA Cup with a trip to Hillsborough in Sheffield to beat Sheffield Wednesday, and then the draw threw up another away trip, this time to Craven Cottage, Fulham. In his notes in the programme for a League match, Stan Seymour, by this time the general factotum of the club, cannot conceal his disappointment. He would have liked a home draw and unfortunately Craven Cottage was 'on the small side', but his real cause for concern, one assumes, was the talent at Fulham's disposal.

Fulham did indeed have some fine players, but there was another dynamic here as well. This was Duggie Livingstone. Livingstone had been the nominal manager when Newcastle won the FA Cup in the previous year. One says 'nominal', for Stan Seymour ran the show, particularly when Livingstone picked the team for the FA Cup Final, which, astonishingly, did not contain Jackie Milburn and, mercifully for all concerned, Seymour overruled him. In addition, he did not enjoy any popularity with the players for his new continental training methods, which did not sit very well with the tough, conservative men of the North East like Milburn and Keeble. He was described by one player as a 'nutcase', and it was no surprise when he was put in charge of the reserve team – a humiliating demotion. When Fulham made an enquiry about him, it was with general relief on all sides that he accepted. He relished this home draw with Newcastle as an ideal opportunity to pay off one or two old scores.

Perhaps to avoid any unpleasant scenes, the official news of Livingstone's departure was released only after the end of the game, but everyone knew that he had been with Fulham for some time. He had certainly not been seen at St James' Park since before Christmas. The Fulham that Livingstone took over was a fine one with some particularly good forwards. They were a good Second Division side, possibly under the shadow of the bigger London sides like Tottenham Hotspur, Arsenal and last season's champions, Chelsea, but they did not lack support. In particular there was the famous comedian of the time, Tommy Trinder, a great radio comic but a lot less impressive on television.

The forward line of Hill, Robson, Jezzard, Haynes and Chamberlain was a young one and as good as one could get in the Second Division. On paper at least, it looked superior to the Newcastle one, which was perpetually being juggled about because of injuries. Fulham's three inside men in particular were impressive. In the centre was a great goalscorer with the unlikely name of Bedford Jezzard, called 'Beddy' for short. He was a great player who could score with both feet and fed off the promptings of Johnny Haynes, still surely one of the greatest forwards there has ever been. Both Jezzard and Haynes had already played for England, and later that year, in April 1956, Haynes would become 'the man who hushed Hampden' when he scored the last-minute equaliser that denied Scotland a win. At inside-right was a man from Durham called Bobby Robson, about whom one felt that one would hear a great deal more in years to come.

Craven Cottage, that quaint ground on the banks of the Thames where there is indeed a cottage in the corner, was thronged that dreary wet January day. On a fine day in summer there was a touch of 'rus in urbe', or 'the countryside in the city' about this ground, with its proximity to the river and its abundance of trees, but this was a grim day in January with the rain not heavy but unrelenting. The pitch would be heavy and the conditions would be ideal for a great, traditional Cup tie with no holds barred: a game that was somehow typical of that era when perhaps Cup football was at its best.

Newcastle started off in breathtaking style and it all came from the Scottish wizard, Bobby Mitchell. The man who had joined them from Third Lanark in 1949 and played such a huge part in the FA Cup successes of previous years was at it again. Those who wondered at the folly of Scotland's selectors in not giving him a permanent berth at international level would repeatedly shake their heads as they saw 'Mitch' ripping defences to shreds as he set up chances for the other forwards, and so it was that day.

Vic Keeble shoulder-charges the goalkeeper. To modern eyes this looks like a foul.

By the half-hour mark Newcastle were 3–0 up and apparently coasting, with Mitchell virtually unstoppable. First he took a corner for Jackie Milburn to shoot home, then he passed a delightful through-ball for Bob Stokoe to score the second, and then he was involved in a glorious passing movement which ended with Tommy Casey, the grossly undervalued left-half from Northern Ireland, adding the third.

The game would have appeared to be over to the disappointed Fulham fans, who nevertheless appreciated the good play of the Magpies, but Fulham were not finished. Before half-time Tosh Chamberlain pulled one back. It did not seem much more than a consolation goal, but no one could possibly have predicted the excitement that was to come in the second half.

Fulham began the half surging forward. Huge gaps appeared in the Newcastle defence as their midfield and forward line fatally relaxed and became complacent. First Chamberlain scored halfway through the half and then, with Craven Cottage in an uproar, he scored again to make the score 3–3. The massive Geordie contingent in the crowd were stunned into silence.

Immediately after that Chamberlain scored again, but this time Newcastle were saved by a linesman's flag. The decision was marginal, to put it mildly, and the following day the Newcastle-based *Sunday Sun* admitted graciously that the goal should have stood. The goal seemed to have been given until the referee, Mr Mitchel, saw the linesman with his flag up. There was no reprieve, however, and a minute or two after that Fulham scored again, this time through winger Jimmy Hill. Newcastle were now behind and ran the risk of being known as the Cup-holders who could not hold on to a three-goal lead. Yet 15 minutes still remained, and there was always the chance that Fulham had shot their bolt.

Luckily, Newcastle still had Bobby Mitchell. He was responsible for Newcastle equalising, although the manner of the goal was controversial. Mitchell beat a few men on the left then crossed a hanging ball, which goalkeeper Ian Black went up for but was then bundled over the line by a shoulder-charge from Vic Keeble. This method of scoring a goal was legitimate and even common practice in 1956, but this particular goal did seem to be a rather nasty foul. The referee allowed the goal, which seemed to have given Newcastle a replay at St James' Park the following Wednesday.

But the game was not yet over. With only minutes remaining, Keeble scored once more, this time a far more aesthetically pleasing goal following a move involving Bobby Mitchell, yet again, for whom this must have been his best game in a black and white shirt. Even then the excitement was not finished, in spite of the energy-sapping conditions, and both teams had half-chances before the full-time whistle came to the exhausted players and spectators. It was one of the best games ever seen at Craven Cottage.

It is interesting to reflect on what happened to some of the participants: the linesman who disallowed the Fulham goal was Jack Taylor, who refereed the 1974 World Cup Final; Fulham's right winger was Jimmy Hill, the famous (perhaps notorious) BBC pundit of later decades; Bob Stokoe, Newcastle's right-half, managed Sunderland in their winning of the 1973 FA Cup Final; Ronnie Simpson became the goalkeeper who won the European Cup in 1967 with Celtic and thus was the first British goalkeeper to win a European Cup medal; and Fulham's inside-right, Bobby Robson, became a very familiar name on Tyneside in the early years of the 21st century.

25

BOLTON WANDERERS

Match: League Division Two **Venue: St James' Park**

Score: 2–0 **Attendance: 59,960**

Newcastle United:	Bolton Wanderers:
Marshall	Hopkinson
Craig	Hartle
Clark	Farrimond
Anderson	Rimmer
McGrath	Edwards
Iley	Hatton
Robson	Lee
Hilley	Hill
Cummings	Davies
Penman	Bromley
Knox	Taylor

Referee: G. McCabe, Sheffield

The early 1960s, the era of the Beatles, is not a time that Geordies look back upon with any great degree of pleasure. The balance of power, in football as in pop music, had shifted noticeably and definitely to the north-west of the country, with Liverpool in particular beginning to make an impact on things. Newcastle United, on the other hand, were now in the Second Division, much to the chagrin of the legions of supporters who now descended on towns like Swindon, Norwich and Rotherham in the way that they used to go to Old Trafford, Highbury and Goodison.

The fault lay back in the 1950s, when complacency reigned in the St James' Park boardroom as the directors seemed to be content to rest on their laurels of the great days of 1951, 1952 and 1955. Milburn and Mitchell grew old and moved on, and little was done to arrest the decline of a great club. FA Cup exits to teams like Scunthorpe, Millwall and Peterborough followed, and the stadium itself was not developed at a time when there was still money to do something about it. The club was slow to read the signs of the changing society and European football and to adapt to the television era, and the price was paid when St James' Park was conspicuously not chosen as a venue for the 1966 World Cup. Roker Park and Ayresome Park, the homes of Sunderland and Middlesbrough, were.

On the field of play itself, Newcastle's traditional inability to handle the transfer market became evident as all sorts of mediocre players arrived at exorbitant prices in attempts to fill the gaps left by the great men of the early 1950s. Some, like Ivor Allchurch, for example, were good enough but perhaps older than one would have liked, and the one quality player of the time, George Eastham, was so badly handled that by the time the whole 'Eastham Affair' was settled Newcastle were well and truly ensconced in the Second Division. Eastham, a brilliant forward, requested a transfer in 1959. Newcastle said no and used the retention clause to prevent him signing for anyone else. They then changed their mind and sold him to Arsenal in 1960, but Eastham subsequently took the club to court and won a great deal of money in damages. It did no one any good, not even Eastham himself, but had the affair been better handled on a personal level, Eastham might well have stayed. It did not need to escalate into the *cause célèbre* that it became. It was a classic case of a feudal board of directors unable to realise that the world had changed, and that Newcastle United were not coming to terms with it.

It had been a very sad day in 1961 when Newcastle were relegated, but it had been coming for a long time. Worse still were the futile attempts to rise again when the team looked for all the world to be a good, respectable Second Division team, but the huge Geordie crowd, and more importantly the massive latent support who now had the financial wherewithal to play golf or do other things on a Saturday afternoon, demanded more than that. There were still a considerable number of older supporters left who remembered the great days of before World War One, more could recall Hughie Gallacher in the 1920s and almost everyone could remember where they were when Wor Jackie scored his wonder goals against Blackpool in 1951 and against Manchester City in 1955.

There was no real excuse for this sorry state of affairs. It is true that other teams were now doing well, but Geordie fans, with their inclination to be curmudgeonly insular and even paranoid on occasion, found it difficult to accept that there are other teams better than they were – even when it was transparently true. There was the feeling that Newcastle should be doing better.

Slowly, in season 1964–65, there were signs that the wheels were turning. Joe Harvey had arrived as manager in 1962. It had taken him some time to get things going the way that he wanted them to (during which time Newcastle supporters, to their annoyance, had seen Sunderland promoted), but a strong run round about the turn of the year and another good spell in March and April had brought them to the very cusp of promotion. There had been early exits from both Cup competitions, but that was hardly unusual at Newcastle in those days, and many supporters thought in any case that promotion was the important thing. On 10 April, when England and Scotland were drawing 2–2 at Wembley (in previous and better times, Newcastle might have expected to supply a couple of players to each team for that fixture), a 1–0 win at home over Swindon meant that if Newcastle could beat Bolton Wanderers on Good Friday at St James' Park, promotion would be assured.

The goal had been scored by Dave Hilley, one of the successes of that era. He had joined the Toon from Third Lanark, as Ronnie Simpson and Bobby Mitchell had in days gone by, and had been a reliable goalscorer. There was also Bryan 'Pop' Robson who could take a goal, as could Willie Penman, and, on occasion, centre-half or centre-forward Bobby Cummings. Although none of these men could realistically be expected to be mentioned in the same breath as the heroes of old, they were causes for optimism in the support as they approached the Good Friday fixture.

Bolton Wanderers were also flying high in the Second Division. They were a team with an astonishing similarity to Newcastle United in that they had a glorious past, particularly in the FA Cup, which they had won four times – three times in the 1920s and again recently in 1958 – but had fallen on bad times since the Nat Lofthouse days of the 1950s. Like Newcastle, they felt that they belonged in the First Division.

The weather was fine this Good Friday, although, as often happens in April, there was a strong blustery wind, and the pitch, having been played on relentlessly since August, was bare in patches. The crowd was an astonishing 59,960, the numbers swelled by the fact that it was a holiday, and that did not include a few who managed to climb the wall at the Gallowgate end. For safety reasons the police allowed a few boys to sit on the running track round the field – a wise precaution, because there were places where the crowd was swaying dangerously. Bolton did not lack support either, and the stage was set for a classic encounter.

It never reached such dizzy heights, however, as the conditions were not favourable to good football and there was too much tension around. If anything, Bolton were the better team in the first half, with a young, fair-haired man called Francis Lee attracting attention with his fast running and deadly accurate crosses looking for the head of Welshman Wyn Davies, a huge giant of a man who had already won international recognition for Wales. But the Newcastle defence was on top form and the teams went in at half-time with Newcastle 1–0 up. This was because of a goal scored from a free-kick on the right in front of the main stand. Robson was fouled, took the free-kick himself and Willie Penman won one of his few moments of glory in an injury-dogged career when he got his head to the ball before anyone else did, leaping high to head downwards. This was hard luck on Bolton because they had threatened the Newcastle defence on more than one occasion, and although Wyn Davies was injured following a clash with McGrath, they still seemed capable of scoring. But the Newcastle full-backs, Craig and Clark, were up to the task.

In particular Gordon Marshall in goal was having a great game. He was one of the few men on either side who had already won something: a Scottish League medal with Hearts in 1960 and a couple of Scottish League Cup medals with the same team. He was a very reliable goalkeeper for a variety of teams between 1956 and 1975, and his son also played for a few Scottish clubs, notably Celtic, Kilmarnock and Motherwell.

It was felt by the BBC radio reporter in his half-time summary that Bolton deserved to be on level terms. A draw would have suited neither team particularly well, but as Newcastle were ahead of Bolton in the League it could be assumed that the points divide was progress towards promotion. A win would guarantee promotion (although not yet the Championship because Northampton Town were still very much in the equation) and 59,960 representatives of the Geordie nation demanded no less than that.

Gradually, with Newcastle now playing towards the Leazes End of the ground, wing-halves Stan Anderson (a man who had been a legend with Sunderland until his amazing transfer to Newcastle 18 months earlier) and Jim Iley (instantly recognisable because of his bald head) began to take a grip on proceedings, and Newcastle were awarded another and this time decisive goal. How appropriate it was that the hard-working Jim Iley should score the crucial goal. It was, in essence, a very simple one. The ball was bobbing about the penalty area and Bobby Cummings passed it onto Iley. Before the Bolton defence could close him down he shot and scored, leaving veteran Eddie Hopkinson with no chance in the Bolton goal.

Half an hour remained but Newcastle now closed things down at the halfway line, with Bolton now recognising that they were a beaten team. Full-time brought scenes of chaos, with police hard pressed to keep fans out of the dressing room area. The players appeared at the front of the stand, and in an era long before players did such things as a matter of course, Stan Anderson took his jersey off and threw it into the crowd. Other players did the same. It was a fine gesture and showed that players and fans were fighting the same battle – a battle that they had now won. Newcastle were back where they belonged.

There was little rest for the players, however. Promotion may have been won, but there was still the Championship to be annexed. The team had to fly (a rare method of transport in 1965) to London that night to play Crystal Palace on the Saturday, then back to Bolton on the Monday before finishing the season off when Manchester City arrived on the following Saturday. Three draws (in decidedly unimpressive performances, it would have to be said) were enough to ensure a limp towards the Championship. But anyone who was at St James' Park that fateful Good Friday will remember it. The Second Division and Newcastle United are phrases that sit ill with each other.

Date: 21 May 1969

26
RANGERS

Match: Inter-Cities Fairs Cup semi-final second leg   **Venue: St James' Park**

Score: 2–0   **Attendance: 59,303**

Newcastle United:	Rangers:
McFaul	Neef
Craig	Johansen
Clark	Mathieson
Gibb	Greig
Burton	McKinnon*
Moncur	Smith
Scott	Henderson
Robson	Penman
Davies	Stein
Arentoft	Johnston
Sinclair	Persson
	Provan*

* Denotes substitution

Referee: J. Gow, Swansea

It was slowly becoming fashionable for English teams to win European competitions. Since Tottenham Hotspur had shown the way in 1963, Manchester United, West Ham United and Leeds United had all been successful, and the belief was beginning to grow on Tyneside that Newcastle might just win this year's Inter-Cities Fairs Cup.

No one could claim that the 1969 season was a vintage one for the Toon. The team had finished ninth in the League, which was respectable but no more than that, but there had been early and predictable exits from the two English domestic trophies. Yet there were some good players around – not least Wyn Davies, sometimes called 'Wyn the Leap' for his prodigious ability to jump. His yield of 11 League goals was none too impressive, but there was always the feeling that with Wyn around, something might happen. Supporters took a current pop song called *The Mighty Quinn* and changed it to

'Come on without. Come on within,
You'll not see nothing like the mighty Wyn.'

More goals were likely to be forthcoming from Bryan 'Pop' Robson, and there could be little doubt that Pop and Wyn worked well as a pair, looking particularly good in Newcastle's previous home games in the Fairs Cup, when one or other of them had scored in each game as Feyenoord, Sporting Lisbon, Real Zaragoza and Vitoria Setubal were put to the sword.

Newcastle should never have been in the competition, but they qualified on the 'one city, one club' rule, and they had surprised themselves by reaching the semi-final. Their opponents were near at hand – Glasgow Rangers, a tie that at first glance seemed to be a good one in that it provided no insuperable travel problems and was by European standards virtually a derby. It also gave Newcastle's sizeable Scottish support a chance to watch them in an away fixture.

By any objective standard it could not be said that Rangers were a bad team, but they came from the unnatural football city of Glasgow. Big city rivalries are common throughout the world and provide healthy competition, but throw in a few extra ingredients like religion and dreadful living conditions, and one has a recipe for a poisonous cocktail. Rangers and their fans came to the two games against Newcastle carrying a great deal of baggage. Uncomfortably aware that Celtic had won the European Cup two years previously, and even more unhappy at having seen Celtic win a Scottish treble this year, lifting the Scottish Cup in an emphatic 4–0 beating of Rangers, the Ibrox players were determined and their fans were bitter. Winning a European trophy would not in itself lift the Celtic monkey off their shoulders, but it would at least give them something to hurl back at the Celtic fans.

Both the Scottish and the English seasons had finished by the time that the semi-finals were to be played. The first game at Ibrox on 14 May attracted 75,000. It had ended in a goalless draw, but how different things might have been had Willie McFaul not saved a penalty from Andy Penman in the first half. Rangers were the better team at Ibrox – it was one of their better performances of the season – and really should have scored on several occasions, but McFaul was brilliant in goal and the Newcastle defence had John McNamee at his best. McNamee had played for Celtic and Hibs, and didn't the Rangers crowd remind him of that!

McNamee was injured for the return game at St James' Park on 21 May, and it was the red-haired Olly Burton who lined up alongside Bobby Moncur in the centre of the Newcastle defence for a game which would be remembered for all the wrong reasons. Since early in the morning, the Scots had seemed to take over Newcastle. Some were pleasant and cheery, others were less so, with an occasional edge to the banter in the city centre as each set of supporters reminded the other about how poor they had been at gathering trophies in recent years or what a drunken disaster had hit Sunderland when Jim Baxter had arrived from Rangers. England had beaten Scotland at Wembley 10 days previously and this was mentioned, as well as some wholesome praise for what Celtic had achieved. Sometimes a less than totally pleasant remark was made about the Pope, and as the consumption of alcohol continued the atmosphere began to become a lot less enjoyable. A few Newcastle fans suddenly appeared to become Roman Catholics and even planned to join the IRA.

The all-ticket crowd of 59,303 was augmented by 100 or so brave Rangers fans who had managed to scale the walls, and the atmosphere, electric at the start, became even more charged as the game was played at a terrific pace, with tackles going in thick and fast. Newcastle were playing towards the Gallowgate End. Both sides had men who would not be bullied, and there was now in this game the added ingredient of desperation, in that this game represented the last chance that either team would have of winning an honour. No quarter was sought or given, nor was any protection or respect afforded to men like Newcastle's Jim Scott, whose brother, Alec, had played so well for Rangers at the start of the decade. It was a wonder that referee John Gow had not invited a few of the participants to depart the scene in favour of an early bath as the first half headed towards its end.

Four minutes remained of the first half when there was what papers euphemistically called a 'clash' between Rangers centre-half Ron McKinnon and Wyn Davies. There was 'a flurry of fists and boots', with players on both sides running yards, not to separate the two of them but, shamefully, to

Jim Scott scores Newcastle's first goal against Rangers.

participate in the action. This was bad enough, but then some supporters from the Rangers end decided to join in. Play had to be suspended while police restored order, and it was possibly just as well for the offending players that everyone had a chance to calm down. This did at least ensure that both teams finished the half with 11 men, when a case might well have been made out for a couple on either side getting the long walk for this incident.

Half-time settled things down and Newcastle now began to play a little football and to take control of the situation. Moncur was immense in midfield as he blotted out the menace of the Rangers attackers, and slowly Newcastle's two Scottish wingers, Jim Scott and Jackie Sinclair, began to create problems for the Rangers defence. In the 52nd minute, Newcastle went ahead. Tommy Gibb, playing the game of his life at right-half, found Jim Scott. Scott made a little space for himself then angled a shot into the Rangers net past Gerry Neef. It was a classic goal, but unfortunately it triggered another invasion of the pitch, this time a 'friendly' one of Newcastle supporters. Friendly it might have been, but it was enough for play to be suspended yet again and referee Mr Gow made it quite plain that he was considering abandoning the match if the pitch were not cleared. In the circumstances of Newcastle being 1–0 up, this was the last thing that anyone on Tyneside would have wished, and once this thought permeated the thick Geordie skulls of those still on the pitch, the game proceeded.

By now Newcastle, clearly the calmer of the two sides and having heeded the wise advice of Joe Harvey to 'cool it', were very much in the ascendancy. Rangers did fight back, but the hysterical Scottish pressure that might have cracked a defence at Falkirk or Raith Rovers was unable to break through Moncur and Burton, especially as the Newcastle full-backs, David Craig and Frank Clark, had now mastered the potentially dangerous wingers of Willie Henderson and Orjan Persson.

Newcastle went further ahead with 15 minutes to go. It was, in essence, a very simple 'route one' goal. Burton cleared from defence, and either by luck or by design the ball found the head of Wyn Davies, who jumped over everyone to nod the ball on to Jackie Sinclair to fire Newcastle two ahead. Newcastle supporters now realised that they were on course for the Final, but it was all too much for the men from Glasgow, who invaded the field in their hundreds with bottles and other instruments flying through the air, a particularly dangerous one being a bottle opener that was sharp and difficult to spot.

Some of the Rangers players pleaded with their own supporters that they weren't doing the cause any good at all, but it was in vain, and when it became obvious that this was a major break in an attempt to stop the game, referee Mr Gow, with the safety of the players his paramount consideration, took them off the field. The concern of the crowd was now whether the game would be awarded to Newcastle or not, because it did not seem likely that the crowd could be cleared from the field.

Heroically, the police cleared the pitch with the help of Alsatian dogs with whom one would not have argued, and, to the delight of the Geordie crowd, the game restarted in front of massed ranks of cheering exultant Newcastle supporters and a half-empty end of Rangers supporters kept in place by police and dogs. Most, however, had gone home.

The game finished after an anodyne last 15 minutes or so. Rangers had given up and Newcastle were quite content to pass the ball around and await the whistle that would tell them that they were in the Final. Full-time came, the players shook hands, and shamefaced Rangers directors had to talk abjectly and contritely to their Newcastle counterparts.

The Toon was not sorry to see the last bus and train depart northwards that night. Oddly enough, there was not a great deal of damage done to shops and houses in the Gallowgate area, but it was nevertheless a salutary reminder of what football hooliganism can do. Much ink was spilt about this game in the press and politicians all mucked in to enjoy themselves, but for Newcastle fans the affair very soon took second place. What was more important was the fact that Newcastle United were in the Final of a European trophy.

Date: 29 May 1969

27

UJPEST DOZSA

Match: Inter-Cities Fairs Cup Final, first leg   Venue: St James' Park

Score: 3–0   Attendance: 59,234

Newcastle United:	Ujpest Dozsa:
McFaul	Szentmihalyi
Craig	Kaposzta
Clark	Solymosi
Gibb	Bankuti
Burton	Nosko
Moncur	Dunai
Scott	Fazekas
Robson	Gorocs
Davies	Bene
Arentoft	Dunai
Sinclair*	Zambo
Foggon*	

Referee: J. Hannet, Belgium

An audience of 59,234 saw a marvellous game of football at St James' Park on the very late date of 29 May 1969 (a Thursday, to avoid a clash with the European Cup Final the night before) as Newcastle met the Hungarian side Ujpest Dozsa in the first leg of the Inter-Cities Fairs Cup Final. This trophy is now better known as the Europa League and has undergone a few changes since 1969. It was then, as now, a prodigious tournament with a great deal of money involved and was much pursued by those teams who had not made it into the European Cup or the other great tournament of the day, the European Cup-Winners' Cup.

Since the defeat of Rangers in the semi-final, excitement had been high on Tyneside. Truth to tell, there had been little else to excite anyone for the past 14 years since the FA Cup had been won. The team had been in the Second Division and had returned to the First in 1965, but success in the Second Division, however much celebrated, was a hollow triumph for a club whose supporters expected so much. Since their return there had not been much to boast about on the domestic scene. The club had seen predictable, weak exits from the FA Cup and mediocrity in the League. The previous season they had finished up 10th (good enough to qualify them for the Inter-Cities Fairs Cup), this season it was ninth, and that was some sort of success, one would imagine, but the adulation given to the players by a support that had been so starved of success was hardly justified by events.

It was in some ways a typical Newcastle team with its sprinkling of Scotsmen and, to a lesser extent, Irishmen; lots of grimly determined defenders who would take no prisoners, and a personality goalscorer. Tyneside has always needed a personality goalscorer like Hughie Gallacher and Jackie Milburn. In this case, they had Wyn Davies, an introverted Welshman whose goalscoring potential always seemed to outstrip his actual yield, but who filled the role of goalscoring hero so craved and demanded by the fans.

European football was comparatively new on Tyneside, but the experience had been a pleasant one so far, with some fans even able to travel abroad to follow the team. Some 2,000 apparently had plans to go to Hungary to see the second leg. In the 14 years that had passed since Newcastle's last honour, life both in football and on Tyneside generally had changed immeasurably. Prosperity had been slow to reach Newcastle, but now it was clear that things were booming. Almost everyone owned a television, working-class boys and girls went to university and the Beatles were in full swing, as were people protesting against the Vietnam War and the selling of arms to South Africa. The traditional Geordie lifestyle of working down a mine and going home to a miners' village like Ashington or Boldon, where everyone lived in carbon-copy houses, had not gone completely but was now blended with other modes of living.

The ground was virtually unrecognisable from what it is today. There was the old stand, which would survive for another 20 years but was already in 1969 the deserving butt of the jokes of opposition supporters, looking as it did like a coal shed. The terracing was uncovered, apart from a leaky shelter at the Leazes End of the ground, which was a great deal smaller than it is now. It was a wonder that the ground could hold a crowd of 60,000. The Hungarian players, used to far smaller crowds behind the Iron Curtain and with very few supporters with them in Newcastle that night, were visibly overwhelmed by the presence of a huge fanatical crowd in close proximity.

It was a curious experience to be at a Cup Final at one's own ground and knowing that, however well the team did, the Cup would not be presented that night because this was only a first leg, the second leg being due a fortnight later in Hungary. Hungary still was a name to be dreaded in English

Action from the Final. Observe the crowds on the roof.

Jim Scott scores the third goal for Newcastle.

hearts – it was not so long ago (around the time that Newcastle were doing so well in the FA Cup in the early 1950s) that their national team had beaten England with high scores both home and abroad, and the name Ferenc Puskas was still bandied about with respect and admiration. Hungary had reached the Final of the 1954 World Cup, but their aborted revolution and its brutal suppression by the Soviet Union in 1956 had changed everything for the worse. Ujpest Dozsa, however, had defeated Leeds United in the quarter-finals, a highly popular result in Tyneside and the rest of England because no one liked Leeds! But then Don Revie's side had gone on to win the English League that season and, therefore, Ujpest Dozsa would be difficult opposition.

It was a dull night on Tyneside as Newcastle started playing towards the Leazes End. It being close to midsummer, trees outside the ground were in full bloom, but this did not prevent the occasional brave young man who did not have a ticket from climbing up and enjoying a vantage point. From an early stage it became apparent that the Hungarians would settle for a draw in Newcastle and hope to win at home. There was nothing unusual or unexpected about this – it was normal practice in European games at this time – but it did tend to make for a rather one-sided game, in appearance at least, and led many people to wonder what all the fuss was about concerning Europe when the games could be so dull.

Newcastle, with Tommy Gibb on top form and Bobby Moncur charging forward, pounded the goal in the first half, but goalkeeper Szentimihalyi was on top form, earning the prerogative of good goalkeeping – luck. On the few occasions that he was beaten, another of his defenders would appear to help out, and Newcastle's shooting was occasionally wayward. Half-time came with the score still at 0–0, but with everyone under the impression that the real action was still to come.

The hour mark had been passed when Newcastle at last scored. It came from the unlikely source of Moncur, who scored his first goal of the season when Wyn Davies shot from a distance after picking up a pass from Gibb. The ball hit a defender but came to Moncur, lurking just inside the penalty area, and he had no hesitation in putting the Geordies one up. This proved the old adage that when you are up against determined European defences, it is the unusual that often does the trick – a good defence has learned how to deal with your best attackers, but is not so good at dealing with your defenders.

The Geordie crowd was now wild with excitement, but after everything had settled down opinion was split in the stand and the terracings as to whether Newcastle should sit back and hold on to what they had, or whether they should attack all the more. Manager Joe Harvey was in no doubt and was seen in the dugout waving his men forward. One goal might not be enough behind the Iron Curtain. Another, at least, would be required.

The desired goal was forthcoming, and this time it was Preben Arentoft who played a vital part. Preben had yet to convince his doubters at the Gallowgate – he had only played 12 games for the club – but he certainly went a long way towards it on this night. He was an old-fashioned inside-forward who acted as fetch-and-carry man to the centre-forward. He was a Dane who had joined the Danish invasion of Scotland in the mid-1960s, joining teams like Morton and Dundee United. Preben had joined Morton in September 1965 and had impressed there in a team who tended to yo-yo between the Scottish First and Scottish Second Division. When Newcastle showed an interest in February 1969 he jumped at the opportunity, even though at £18,000 he was hardly in the superstar category. Injuries had given him his chance in April and he had seized it.

This time Arentoft, who had the unlikely nickname of 'Benny', read the situation perfectly. Ten minutes had passed since the first goal. With the Gallowgate crowd yelling for more, Benny saw Moncur, exulting in his first goal and itching for a second, come charging through the centre of the field. Arentoft moved slightly to one side, picked up a pass from Moncur, returned it immediately in as neat a one-two as one is ever likely to see, and Moncur crashed home his and Newcastle's second.

If St James' Park had been noisy after the first goal it was now absolute bedlam, and Ujpest Dozsa visibly wilted. The rest of the game was a remarkable account of missed chances, heroic defending and, once again, brilliant goalkeeping from Szentimihalyi. Just as it was beginning to look as if the Magpies would have to be happy with a 2–0 lead to take to Hungary, Newcastle, well into the last 10 minutes, added a third.

Once again Arentoft was involved, but this time he fed Jim Scott for the third goal. Jim played in the outside-right position and was a man who had played well for the Geordies since he joined them from Hibs. He suffered in comparison with his brother, Alec, who played for Rangers, Everton and Scotland on the right-wing, but Jim was no bad player. This was one of the easiest goals in his career, a tap-in from fairly short range, but it sent the whole of Newcastle into overdrive.

Newcastle might even have added another, so much were they on top over this demoralised team, but 3–0 it remained. Newcastle were cheered to the echo as they left the field by a crowd who clearly thought that the job had been done, but the sobering thought remained that the second leg was still to come in a fortnight's time in Hungary. One of the Scottish players recalled the example of Celtic, who had defeated MTK of Hungary in 1964 by 3–0 at Parkhead, but had then gone to Hungary, where there were problems with the crowd and in particular the referee, and had lost 4–0. This must not be allowed to happen to the Toon.

Newcastle was a happy city that night, but a collective intake of breath would be needed for the agonising second leg on 11 June.

Date: 11 June 1969

28

UJPEST DOZSA

Match: Inter-Cities Fairs Cup Final, second leg   **Venue: Budapest**

Score: 3–2   **Attendance: 34,000**

Ujpest Dozsa:	Newcastle United:
Szentmihalyi	McFaul
Kaposzta	Craig
Solymosi	Clark
Bankuti	Gibb
Nosko	Burton
Dunai	Moncur
Fazekas	Scott*
Gorocs	Robson
Bene	Davies
Dunai	Arentoft
Zambo	Sinclair
	Foggon*

Referee: J. Heymann, Switzerland

The 'Iron Curtain' was a phrase that terrified and awed Western society in the late 1960s. It had been a phrase first coined by Sir Winston Churchill in 1946 to describe the barrier from 'Stettin in the Baltic to Trieste in the Adriatic' that had descended on Europe and behind which lived the brooding, despotic and prickly tyranny called the Soviet Union (loosely described as Russia sometimes) and its allies, some willing, others a lot less so.

Hungary, where Newcastle United would be travelling to play Ujpest Dozsa in the Inter-Cities Fairs Cup Final, was behind the Iron Curtain. It would be Newcastle's first trip to the Eastern bloc in the campaign (they had previously travelled to Holland, the Iberian peninsula and a short trip up the road to Scotland) and their first visit on serious business to the area controlled by the vicious jackboot of the Soviets.

If anyone had the slightest doubt about the grim sincerity of the Soviet Union to defend its own interests, one had merely to consider the events of the previous August when Czechoslovakia, which had shown signs of being interested in democracy, had been invaded by the Soviets in an event which shocked the world.

Hungary itself had, 13 years previously, been a victim of savage repression when they had rebelled against the Soviets and had been brutally stamped upon. This had happened in early

November 1956, when the world's attention had been focused upon Great Britain's mad attempt to invade Egypt in what became known as the 'Suez Affair'. For a football fan, the Hungarian crushing had been all the more poignant because Hungary had impressed the world so much with their fine football team, and although Ferenc Puskas escaped to play for Real Madrid (there had been stories that he had been shot) others were less lucky.

Newcastle were wise enough to know what to expect in Hungary. Joe Harvey was no fool. The trick was to expect the worst in terms of spartan hotels, poor food and gamesmanship, brutal tactics and unhelpful refereeing, and then one would not be too disappointed. At times the three-goal cushion gained at St James' Park did not really look to be enough, and the press did not help by repeatedly quoting all the examples of teams who had built up a good lead at home only to have it cancelled out in the totally different circumstances of the second leg. There was, however, the happier and more recent precedent of the previous year when Leeds United had beaten Ferencvaros 1–0 at home then held out for a goalless draw in Hungary.

It was odd that the Final of this tournament was played on a home and away basis. It would continue like this for almost another 30 years, the arrangement surviving the change of name of the trophy to the UEFA Cup, but no one in 1969 seemed to want to challenge the idea, certainly not the 2,000 brave and rich Newcastle supporters who travelled out to the two beautiful cities, one called Buda and the other Pest, which had now joined together. The rest of the Geordies would face the agony of listening to the game on the radio.

The ground was on the small side and had a capacity of 37,000. Neither side had changed personnel, although Newcastle had reverted to a slightly more defensive formation, and the attitude of the Ujpest team was entirely different. They had left the field at St James' Park 13 days ago looking like whipped jackals, and their officials had graciously and charmingly said that the second leg would be a formality to their Newcastle counterparts. Joe Harvey knew that this was rubbish and told his players to expect an onslaught in the first half.

The football played by the Magyars in the opening stages that balmy night was breathtaking, with even the English press overwhelmed by the magnificence of the passing, the strength of the running, the ball-control skills and the ability of 11 men (some of whom had been totally anonymous in Newcastle) to play together as a team. The crowd roared their approval – being Hungarian, they knew what good football was when they saw it – and frankly Newcastle were given the run around, with even experienced men like Burton and Moncur throwing out the distress signals and fouling far too often and goalkeeper Willie McFaul, who might have been sitting in the stand in the first leg for all the work he had to do, compelled to pull off some fine saves.

The half-hour mark had been reached and Newcastle were beginning to congratulate themselves on having weathered the initial storm when Ferenc Bene scored from a more or less impossible angle, proving yet again that you have to expect the unexpected in European football. Newcastle now bit their lip and braced themselves for their duty, watching the huge clock go round and willing the referee to blow his whistle and offer them the haven of half-time. He had already looked at one of his linesmen when Janos Gorocs broke through, evading several men and, with everyone expecting a pass to Bene or Dunai, ran through to score himself. This was more or less half-time, but there was still time for the key moment of the tie. This was when Dunai shot and McFaul saved. Had that one gone in before half-time the aggregate score would have been 3–3, and it would have been difficult for Newcastle to come back. As it was, Newcastle were still marginally ahead, although it would have been difficult for even the most ardent of Geordie supporters to be sanguine about the second half.

It was at this point that Joe Harvey showed himself to be the master psychologist. He had never been a great tactician, but his love for the club ran deep. Intensely worried about what was happening in this game, he decided to put on a brave face. He had already shown the players before the start of the game the champagne that was waiting for the celebrations, and he kept it there. Some of the players, particularly the defenders for their ignominious failure to stop that second goal, may have expected a rough shouting at of the Yorkshire kind from the rugged Joe, who normally had little sympathy for poseurs and shirkers.

Instead, Joe was charming and reassuring, telling them to remember that they were not really 2–0 down. In fact, they were 3–2 up. The Hungarians had played well, but would never be able to keep this up in the intense heat that slowed down the pace of both sides. The opposition had already shot their bolt and Willie McFaul's great save on the half-time whistle would have discouraged them. All that Newcastle really had to do was score a goal and the Hungarians would collapse, as would their crowd, who were with them as long as they were playing fast, attacking, entertaining football, but who would lapse into silence when things turned against them. Newcastle should go all out for a goal and then they could start on the champagne, said Joe. His calm was all an act, but never has any actor on stage done a better or a more convincing job.

Newcastle went out to renew the contest and within a minute had regained the initiative. Incredibly, it was Moncur, the unlikely goalscoring hero of St James' Park, who did the trick. A corner had been forced on the left, the goalkeeper punched out Jackie Sinclair's kick back to the same person, who sent the ball over for Bobby Moncur to fire home a left-foot drive into the back of the net. The crowd were stunned into silence apart from the cheers of the tiny travelling support, who could now see that deliverance was at hand.

Soon afterwards, the tie was effectively over when Preben Arentoft volleyed home a second, the point being acknowledged by the sporting Hungarian crowd, who allowed themselves a generous round of applause for the Newcastle side. Any hope that the Hungarians might have had was finally extinguished when substitute Alan Foggon, on for Jim Scott, beat a couple of men to score a great individual goal off the bar to release chaos among the Newcastle support and the back-room staff.

Harvey was delighted and gave interviews to the press about how exciting a game it had been. It was a tremendous triumph for him on his 51st birthday. He had taken his beloved Newcastle to triumph in their first-ever season in Europe, when absolutely no one would have tipped them at the beginning (they had been lucky to even qualify, and it was only the 'one club per city rule' which gave them precedence over teams from London and Liverpool, for example) and he had moulded together a team that lacked any really brilliant or charismatic players. However, by the same token, there had been no one in the side (as there would very sadly be in later decades) who had talent but lacked any discipline or ability to work with others. In that respect there had been a certain similarity between the team that Harvey managed and the teams in which he played in the early 1950s.

The team then partied, and when they did fly back to Newcastle a huge crowd, an open-topped bus and a triumphant return to St James' Park awaited them. Reports are given of about 500,000 people thronging the streets of Newcastle on that occasion. This seems to be a gross exaggeration – or at least it would seem to be so to someone who has never experienced the atmosphere in this crazy city when football is involved. Supporters travelled from as far as Manchester, Birmingham and Edinburgh, with even a few from Sunderland and Middlesbrough, to see the combination of Newcastle and silverware.

The future must have looked good in those bright days of June 1969. One hopes that those who were there enjoyed themselves because it remains, more than 40 years later, the last time that Newcastle United lifted a major trophy. Is there a sadder story than that in the whole of football?

Date: 30 September 1970

29

INTER MILAN

Match: Inter-Cities Fairs Cup first round, second leg   **Venue: St James' Park**

Score: 2–0   **Attendance: 56,495**

Newcastle United:	Inter Milan:
McFaul	Vieri
Craig	Righetti
Clark	Facchetti
Gibb	Bellugi
Burton	Giubertoni
Moncur	Cella
Robson	Jair
Dyson	Fabbian
Davies	Boninsegna
Arentoft	Archilli*
Young	Corso
	Bordon*

Referee: J. Minnoy, Belgium

Even as early as 1970, Inter Milan inspired some mystique. They had won the European Cup twice, in 1964 and 1965, and although they had lost in the Final of 1967 to the magnificent Celtic team of Jock Stein, they and their legendary boss Helenio Herrera were much feared and respected. Thus, when they were drawn against Newcastle in the Fairs Cup, everyone on Tyneside expected a great game. Unfortunately, although it was a fine triumph for Newcastle, the game is remembered for reasons that reflect little credit on a team that were now losing out to their city rivals, AC Milan, and that would take some time to recover.

If the Edwardian era, the late 1920s and the early 1950s are the golden ages of Newcastle United, then the early 1970s could well be looked upon as a silver age. They had won the Fairs Cup in 1969, an honour much prized and valued by everyone, and their performances at home were respectable, although they repeatedly broke the hearts of their fans by consistent fecklessness in the FA Cup.

Manager Joe Harvey had been in charge since 1962 and he retained the respect and support of the players and fans, even though there was the normal moaning when things did not go as well as they would have liked. There were some fine players – 'Pop' Robson, Bobby Moncur, Preben 'Benny' Arentoft and the mighty Wyn Davies, whose aerial power was a sight to behold on occasion. There was, however, a lack of superstars. Not a single man had played in England's 1970 World Cup side, and sadly for them, Wales, Northern Ireland and Scotland had not qualified. This was in total contrast to the star-studded Inter Milan. They contained men like Boninsegna, Facchetti and Mazzola who had played successfully in the Mexico World Cup for Italy, losing only in the Final to the mighty Brazil team.

The first game at the San Siro stadium, played in front of a very poor crowd of 14,460, had been a very low-key affair, and this suited Newcastle, because the mighty ground was a lot less intimidating when it was half empty. Wyn Davies had scored with a brave effort in the first half, diving through a forest of legs and boots to head home, and Newcastle were slowly killing the game by sensible defending, neutralising all the star players, until defender Cella tried a shot from the edge of the penalty area. It was not all that well hit but it deceived goalkeeper McFaul and was good enough to earn Inter a draw. Nevertheless, although disappointed at losing the late goal, Newcastle had every reason to feel proud of themselves. A draw was definitely a good result to achieve in Italy.

By the time that Inter appeared at Newcastle, United's domestic form had caused concern. They had played 10 games and had won four, lost three and drawn three, and the goalless draw against

Even the Newcastle police have to help the referee sort out Inter Milan.

Coventry City at home the Saturday immediately before the Inter Milan game had been singularly unimpressive. They had also lived up to their pedigree in the League Cup with an ignominious 2–1 defeat at an incredulous Bristol Rovers. All would be forgiven, however, if they could only collect the scalp of Inter Milan.

The game was all-ticket and a virtual sell-out. The ground was still almost all-standing, apart from the Main Stand, and this led to a tremendously noisy atmosphere with flags, scarves and even a few fireworks in the crowd. The crowd had assembled early, and the Italians were visibly perplexed and disturbed by the sheer atmosphere and theatre of it all. They had seldom heard of Newcastle before and clearly did not realise that this was a football-mad place. Even those who had recently played in the World Cup Final were bewildered and disorientated – something that was plain in their body language and facial expressions as they walked out.

The Italian method of playing this game would be to hold Newcastle by stringing men along the edge of their penalty area, frustrating them, making them play men out of position, perhaps bringing forward a few defenders, then hitting them on the break, silencing the crowd and then holding out. It was the classic way of frustrating spirited British teams, and various names like 'catenaccio' (the door chain) were given to it.

Manager Joe Harvey had watched the way Brazil had got the better of Italy in Mexico. Newcastle lacked the sort of players that Brazil had, but Harvey phoned his old friend, Jock Stein of Celtic, who had famously beaten Inter in the European Cup three years previously. Stein's advice to Harvey was to be patient, to play his own game, to use his talented ball players and only to go hell for leather in the last quarter of an hour.

Controlled and competent defending was only one part of the Italian game. There was also another, less welcome, side to the game. This was the dirty face of Italian football – the spitting, the sly kicking and punching when no one was looking, the murderous challenges made by men who knew exactly how to hurt, and the looks of feigned innocence afterwards. Sadly St James' Park was to see a fair amount of that.

Black and white television (the game was relayed live to Italy, but live football was a rarity in Great Britain in 1970) meant that one of the two teams had to change. Newcastle amazed their fans by coming out in all red, while Inter played in their normal blue and black vertical stripes. The game started peacefully enough, in spite of the rabid, pumped-up atmosphere, and there was little indication of the mayhem that was to come.

It became clear that both sides looked upon Wyn Davies as a key man for his aerial power. Newcastle tried to get high balls into him, and Facchetti, the big Italian centre-half, was equally determined to stop him. It was this obsession that was to be his undoing. Just on the half-hour mark, Newcastle, while attacking the Gallowgate End, forced a corner for 'Pop' Robson to take. While Davies acted as the decoy he was naturally followed by Facchetti, and the other Italian defenders took a man each. This left centre-half Bobby Moncur unchallenged, something he had made a habit of in Europe, as he ran in to meet the ball cleanly and to head Newcastle into a 1–0 lead.

With the ground still in a ferment, the game exploded a minute later. It was all about the issue of shoulder-charging the goalkeeper. In the same way as British teams complained about Italians spitting and feigning injury, the Italian teams had often complained about shoulder-charging the goalkeeper. This was an accepted and traditional part of the British game, still technically legal, but frowned upon after a few well-publicised incidents, notably in the FA Cup Final of 1958. Over the years, Newcastle had excelled at this, with Bob Appleyard of long ago a great exponent, and, to a lesser extent, Vic Keeble and Jackie Milburn of more recent years. It was now, however, thankfully perhaps, dying out.

Goalkeeper Lido Vieri, still smarting from the loss of the goal for which he was at least partly to blame, had picked up a harmless ball as Wyn Davies ran in on him. Davies, still on a high after the goal and unable to resist a little gamesmanship, feinted to shoulder-charge Vieri but did not actually do it. Vieri failed to see the funny side of it all and pushed Davies in the chest with his elbow. The incident was still not all that serious, but when the referee, Mr Joseph Minnoy, a little man with a moustache, who looked not entirely unlike his famous Belgian compatriot Hercule Poirot, intervened, goalkeeper Vieri suddenly, and to the amazement of all concerned, punched him on the chin and knocked him out.

The next few moments were chaotic, with the referee lying semi-conscious and stunned, the two linesmen on the park trying to control the players, who were pushing each other around in what is now called 'handbags', and eventually the local policemen intervening. The game teetered on the verge of being abandoned, but referee Minnoy recovered after attention from the Newcastle trainer to a cheer from the Newcastle crowd, and the first thing he did was to order Vieri off. More tantrums followed, but this time there was a clear indication that the game would be abandoned if he would not go, and off he went to the cacophony of boos from the Newcastle crowd as Anglo-Italian relationships on the Tyne hit an all-time low.

It would be nice to say that the game calmed down after that, but sadly it didn't, with several Italians seeming to wish to join their goalkeeper in his early bath. Facchetti in particular (some Newcastle players called him 'hatchetti') had several goes at Davies and other players in episodes that would have seen red cards today. The phrase 'kick off the park', much used in speech among football fans to exaggerate a few fouls, was totally applicable in its literal sense that night.

Newcastle were told by Harvey at half-time that they were a goal up, a man up and that Inter had a non-specialist goalkeeper. All they had to do was play the game, do nothing stupid, not retaliate, and all would be well. This was, indeed, what happened, and it was Davies who scored the second and decisive goal. It occurred in the 70th minute. He headed the ball against the bar, and when it came back out to him he headed it again, this time past the despairing arms of the deputy goalkeeper.

Davies then ignored a few more kicks and punches, and finished the game laughing at those who had tried to maim him. It was a sweet triumph for the Geordies and they were deservedly lauded all over Europe for their honourable part in what was a dreadful occasion for the game of football. One of Newcastle's directors, with an admirable knowledge of the Apostles' Creed, talked about 'the quick and the dead', because if you weren't quick that night, you would have been dead.

Newcastle had defeated Inter Milan to advance into the next round. Sadly, they would not last much longer in the competition that year, but they could look back with pride on that night as the time when football beat thuggery.

30
BURNLEY

Match: FA Cup semi-final   **Venue: Hillsborough, Sheffield**

Score: 2–0   **Attendance: 55,000**

Newcastle United:	Burnley:
McFaul	Stevenson
Craig	Noble
Clark	Newton
McDermott	Dobson
Howard	Waldron
Moncur	Thomson
Cassidy	Nulty
Smith	Casper
Macdonald	Fletcher
Tudor	Collins
Hibbitt*	James
Kennedy*	

Referee: G. Hill, Leicester

There were stirring times for the Magpies in 1974. There was nothing to write home about in the League form, which was mediocre at best and dire at worst, but two things excited Tyneside in spring 1974 and they were both intimately connected. One was the Cup run – the team had now reached the semi-final for the first time since they last won the Cup in 1955 – and the other was that charismatic character called Malcolm Macdonald, or 'Supermac'. He was not the first nor the last on Tyneside to be cursed with the name 'messiah'. Was he to be the man who would bring back the glory days and the FA Cup? 1955 and Jackie Milburn were fast becoming a distant memory.

The FA Cup had seen some dismal exits in the past 19 years to teams like Scunthorpe, Carlisle United and, perhaps worst of all, Hereford United on that terrible day of little more than two years before. Yet everyone was aware of the great days of 1951, 1952 and 1955. Every fan of a certain age would claim with varying degrees of veracity to have been there at all three of these Wembley occasions, and there were still a few around who could recall 1932, 1924 and even 1910.

The 1960s, in some ways, had seemed to pass Newcastle by. There had been a sojourn in the Second Division from 1961 to 1965, and the team and the city had seemed to go into a collective sulk as a result. St James' Park was pointedly not used as a venue for the 1966 World Cup, while Roker Park and Ayresome Park were – something that seemed to indicate to the outside world that

Newcastle was now a backwater of English football – and although the team had come back to the First Division, there had been no sustained success in the top flight. More poignantly for the faithful, attempts on the FA Cup had been decidedly puny, and relentlessly so. True, there had been the European success of 1969 and a reasonable run the next year, but little else as teams like Leeds United and Liverpool had risen to take the place that the Geordies all felt that they should be. The FA Cup of 1974 might change all that.

Other world events were dramatic in themselves, but they nevertheless took second place in the Geordie focus. A month earlier the Conservative government of Ted Heath had fallen and had been replaced by a Labour one of Harold Wilson, albeit with no clear majority. Across the Atlantic Ocean the net was tightening on President Richard Nixon for his part in the Watergate affair; further south on that same continent England were embroiled in a Test series against the West Indies, and on the very day of the semi-final they were starting the fifth Test match, one down in the series. In addition, there was rampant and seemingly uncontrollable inflation, with the pessimists and the depressives, especially the ones who wrote in the Sunday newspapers, comparing things to Germany in 1923, asking alarmist questions like 'Is Britain governable?'

Football itself had problems in the 1970s. Attendances were falling, hooliganism was rising and stadia were outdated, decrepit and (as later events would prove) downright dangerous. The game had suffered from England's inability to qualify for the World Cup in West Germany, and it often seemed that skill had gone out of the game, as the long-haired, facially hirsute and highly-paid exponents, looking anything other than professional football players, tried vainly to match the standards of a previous generation.

It was almost as if Newcastle United deliberately went out of their way to tease and torment their fans in the early two rounds of the FA Cup in early 1974. Hendon came to Newcastle on the first Saturday of the year and earned a draw before 33,840 incredulous fans. Few problems were encountered in the replay (played at Vicarage Road, Watford, with a midday kick-off because of power restrictions due to the miners' work to rule, which also caused a three-day week in many industries and eventually brought down the Conservative government), but then Scunthorpe revived horror memories of 1958 by scoring first, holding on to their lead until half-time before Terry McDermott saved the blushes. Then, in the fifth round for a change, the team put on a

Malcolm Macdonald scores for Newcastle.

sterling Geordie performance at West Bromwich Albion, when Tudor, Macdonald and Barrowclough produced the goods to delight the vast travelling support in the 42,699 crowd.

There were many people who believed that Newcastle United should not have been in the semi-final and that they should have been expelled from the tournament following the untoward events of 9 March at St James' Park, the quarter-final of the FA Cup against Nottingham Forest. Forest were 2–1 up at half-time, then early in the second half they were awarded a penalty kick when David Craig brought down Duncan McKenzie. It was a marginal decision, it would have to be said, and Paddy Howard disagreed vehemently, pushing the referee in the chest and getting sent off for his pains. Forest then scored the penalty and Newcastle were 3–1 down with half an hour to go and a man short.

It looked like curtains for yet another FA Cup dream, and some members of the crowd invaded the park. This was the mid-1970s, the age of the hooligan, when sober newspapers like the *Sunday Times* and *The Observer* every Sunday told us about the 'breakdown of society' and 'the lack of social control', and men like Tommy Docherty, then manager of Manchester United, called for capital punishment to solve the problem. Many secretly agreed with Docherty, but what happened here was that a group of misguided, long-haired and none too intelligent young men, joined by a few other simpletons who wanted a bit of fun on a rather depressing day, tried to get the game stopped.

There was probably no real evil intent, but the referee, Mr Kew, had to take the players off for nine minutes. The ground was soon cleared of Tyneside's invaders and the game restarted, but not before some of the crowd, believing that the game had been abandoned, or simply despairing of their team or even fearing for their safety, had gone home. They missed something, for 10-man Newcastle now excelled themselves and won 4–3, seemingly putting themselves into the semi-final with a penalty from McDermott and two excellent counters from Tudor and Moncur.

The matter did not end there, however. Forest claimed, not without cause, that the pitch invasion caused the game to change character and that their players were unreasonably intimidated by the hostile crowd. The FA considered and might well have awarded the tie to Nottingham Forest, but they instead ordered a replay at neutral Goodison Park. That replay was a sterile 0–0 draw, and yet another game had to be held at Goodison, which Newcastle edged with a Macdonald goal. By this time they knew that the opponents in the semi-final would be Burnley, the other semi being contested by Leicester City and Liverpool.

It would be fair to say that after all this (and the club, to its credit, was suitably embarrassed and disowned the morons), quite a lot of uncommitted people would have been happy to see Burnley beat Newcastle in the semi-final. Burnley, managed by Jimmy Adamson, a Geordie through and through, were having a good season. They had not yet met Newcastle in the League, but they were comfortably placed in seventh spot and were probably more consistent and reliable than Newcastle. They were favourites, but only marginally, because the Geordies still had the much-vaunted 'Supermac', who was now an established internationalist for England.

The 55,000 crowd might have found it hard to get a drink before the game, because many publicans in Sheffield had decided that the danger of trouble outweighed any financial profit and closed for the day. The abstemious crowd, however, saw a great game of football with two absolutely super goals which sent the Geordie crowd home in a rare state of euphoria.

Both teams came out to the music of a pipe band – something that might have brought a tear of nostalgia to the eye of Newcastle's Scotsmen Bobby Moncur and Jimmy Smith. Burnley were by far the better team in the first half, playing good passing football, and it was a wonder that they were not ahead by half-time as Newcastle's midfield struggled to get any sort of control of the game. Jimmy Smith looked particularly out of sorts. Burnley had been distinctly unlucky when Nulty hit the bar, but McFaul was having a good game in Newcastle's goal, and it was just as well.

Joe Harvey's team talk at half-time must have worked wonders. Now attacking the Leppings Lane end of the ground, Newcastle gradually gained some sort of control over the midfield, and slowly managed to get Supermac involved in the action. Twenty minutes had elapsed when Macdonald picked up a long ball from Howard and charged towards the goal, showing all his power to run all the way, even with Waldron fouling him repeatedly, and he shot at goal. It was saved at the first attempt by goalkeeper Stevenson, but he netted the rebound.

That was good, but his and Newcastle's second was even better. Macdonald once again supplied the brilliant finish, but this time it was a well-developed goal with a contribution from Moncur, Tudor and Hibbitt before Supermac finished things off. By this time the second half was well advanced, and Burnley really did not have time to come back and equalise the two goals. In any case, the defence was outstanding, Moncur in particular and goalkeeper McFaul radiating confidence. The final whistle came with the Toon well on top, and the Geordie fans in great voice, relishing the thought of their first visit to Wembley since 1955 or, in the case of the majority of the young fans, their first visit ever.

The trains northwards were happy places that night, and the local press rightly praised the performances of the team and Macdonald in particular. Everyone knew, however, that the great test was yet to come. Leicester City and Liverpool had drawn the other semi-final. Both of these teams had recently earned draws at St James' Park, but neither of them looked totally unbeatable. Either would be a severe test of Newcastle United at Wembley.

31

Date: 4 May 1974

LIVERPOOL

Match: FA Cup Final	**Venue: Wembley**
Score: 0–3	**Attendance: 100,000**

Newcastle United:	Liverpool:
McFaul	Clemence
Clark	Smith
Kennedy	Lindsay
McDermott	Thomson
Howard	Cormack
Moncur	Hughes
Smith*	Keegan
Cassidy	Hall
Macdonald	Heighway
Tudor	Toshack
Hibbitt	Callaghan
Gibb*	

Referee: G. Kew, Amersham

The sleeping giant had arisen. Newcastle United were back in the Final of the competition that had meant so much to them in the past – the FA Cup. Absolutely everyone on Tyneside talked about the forthcoming game – in the Toon itself, obviously, but places like South Shields, Cleadon, Ponteland, Jarrow and Boldon also seemed to be bothered about little else. Everyone was painfully aware that it had now been a long 19 years since the Cup had last been at St James' Park, and everyone was even more painfully aware that Sunderland, managed by one of Newcastle's heroes of 1955, Bob Stokoe, had won it last year. Surely this had to be Newcastle's year – if only to quieten the gloating Mackems.

The Toon had, of course, changed a great deal since 1955, but the centre of Newcastle still bore a remarkable resemblance to 20 years before, particularly the railway station, with its classical façade, pillars and other tokens of Victorian empire building. It seemed to have been built for no other purpose than to allow black and white bedecked Geordies to go to London to watch Cup Finals and for triumphant teams to return, then pile into open-topped buses and circulate the town centre, with all its grimy, sooty buildings, to show off the magnificent piece of silverware to the huge crowd that always loved them.

Newcastle had the undivided love of their city. Since the amalgamation in the 1890s, there had only been the one team that any young Novocastrian would support. Unlike most 'Uniteds', like

The team, in the horrendous fashions of the 1970s, walk over the Wembley turf.

those of West Ham, Manchester and Dundee, there was something appropriate about the word because it had been a genuine amalgamation in the first place and also because the city was definitely joined in its love for its team. Those who professed to know little about football or to be uninterested in the sport all knew who Supermac was, and all knew who Milburn and Gallacher had been. They would all be in front of a television on 4 May 1974, joining in the constant refrain of

'Supermac, Superstar,
How many goals have you scored so far?'

In the run up to the Cup Final, Newcastle United actually won some silverware. This was the Texaco Cup, played for by teams in Scotland and England who had not made it to Europe. It became the Anglo-Scottish Cup for a few years then disappeared into its deserved obscurity. Nevertheless, it was something tangible, and Newcastle, having disposed of Morton, Birmingham City and Dundee United in late 1973, tackled Burnley in the Final at St James' Park on 24 April, some 10 days before the 'real' Cup Final. A total of 34,540 went along and saw Newcastle lift the trophy, with goals from Moncur and Macdonald.

This was good, but ultimately didn't matter. What really did matter was the FA Cup Final. The allocation of tickets provoked its usual cries of unfairness and favouritism, added to in this particular year by a complaint of inefficiency in the distributions. Some people did not know as late as the Friday whether or not they had been allocated a ticket. One lost count of the number of letters that one read in newspapers, or statements in pubs and on street corners to the effect that 'I've been going to St James' Park for years, and after this I am not going back.' It was all talk, of course – Geordies do not give up on their team as easily as that.

The team were staying at the Selsdon Park Hotel in Surrey. This was decidedly swish and had been the venue for the Conservative Party in the late 1960s when they had their 'think tank' meetings to unseat the Labour government. Manager Joe Harvey, with a nostalgic hankering after the old days, had wanted to go to Brighton, where the great teams of the 1950s had gone before big Wembley

Action as John Tudor challenges the Liverpool goalkeeper.

occasions, but he was persuaded otherwise, on the grounds that Brighton was just too far away from London and Wembley, and that times had moved on.

Joe Harvey was a traditional Geordie – not by birth as he was a Yorkshireman from the Doncaster area – but now definitely a Geordie by inclination, temperament and commitment. A chain smoker and a man invariably described in newspapers with words like 'rugged', 'crusty' and, in particular, 'craggy', he possessed a keen football brain and was generally loved by the fans in spite of the many disappointments they

Bobby Moncur watches Willie McFaul clutch the ball in a Liverpool attack.

had had since he took over in June 1962. He had taken them out of the Second Division and led them to success in Europe, but could he now lead them to what would be the peak of his career, the FA Cup?

Objective analysis would point to Liverpool as the more likely winners. They had ended up second in the League to Leeds United, were notoriously consistent and determined, and they had some fine players like Kevin Keegan, Emlyn Hughes and John Toshack. They also had as manager the charismatic Bill Shankly, a Scotsman with a permanent chip on his shoulder but who could nevertheless inspire players, and they now had a long pedigree of success. They had only won the FA Cup once though, in 1965, and this tournament meant a great deal to them and to their supporters as well.

Liverpool were the favourites and the *Sunday Times* of 28 April, the week before the Final, stated that it expected *You'll Never Walk Alone* to drown out *The Blaydon Races* at Wembley the following Saturday. The *Daily Mirror* said that while Newcastle were basing their optimism on intangible things like 'tradition' and 'luck', Liverpool had a more realistic base in 'their football'. Shankly kept feeding the press comments about how good Liverpool were, but the feeling persisted on Tyneside that there was a bit of romance in the air, and with Supermac on board Newcastle could silence the Liverpool crowd.

A key man, the Magpies felt, would be Jimmy Smith. On his day 'Jinky', the nickname that he shared with Celtic's Jimmy Johnstone, could be the best player on earth with his trickery, passing ability and old-fashioned dribbling, and if he and Supermac were on song together nothing on earth could stop them, certainly not Emlyn Hughes. Since his arrival from Aberdeen in 1969 Smith had entertained and infuriated the supporters in equal measure. His attitude, one felt, was sometimes not all that it could be, and earlier in the season he had bizarrely got himself sent off in a game against Birmingham City within the first minute with a shockingly ill-timed tackle. Yet he was such a great player. Could he turn it on?

Half-time saw the teams level at 0–0. Liverpool were the better team according to the TV pundits, but that counted for nothing. A goal could change that, and even if the technically more proficient team were controlling the game, as long as Newcastle could hold them until late in the

The expressions on the faces of the Newcastle defenders tell the whole story.

game then a goal by Supermac could then win the game. This was what the Geordies said, at Wembley and in their thousands back home in front of the TV.

Sadly, it was not to be. David Coleman, the BBC commentator, talked about Newcastle being 'stripped naked' by Liverpool. Quite a few people found this offensive, but it would have to be said that Newcastle were overrun in that second half. Seldom in the Liverpool half of the field, it was desperate defending all the time, with two goals from Kevin Keegan and one from Steve Heighway (and another disallowed) killing off Newcastle with the 3–0 scoreline one of the biggest in Wembley history, and, in truth, it should have been a lot more.

Although the fans at the game bravely tried to raise their team with *The Blaydon Races*, everyone knew that it was a lost cause. Back home the game finished with everyone staring morosely at the TV screens, seeing in dumb admiration just how good Liverpool were, as the TV pundits, some of them showing their true colours, fawned all over them. The Toon was a sad place that night. How we hated that Kevin Keegan!

Three Newcastle careers never recovered from that. Jimmy Smith, humiliatingly taken off by Joe Harvey, had now shown that talent in itself was not enough. Character was also required. Never popular with his teammates, he was publicly described as 'finished' by at least one of them. And Malcolm Macdonald, whose moment it was supposed to be, had failed to deliver when he had to. He had two chances in the game, both coming when Liverpool were already 2–0 up. He mis-kicked one and blazed the other one over the bar. He had not made life any easier for himself by allowing himself to be quoted in various newspapers about what he was going to do to Liverpool. (Shankly cut out what he said and pinned the cuttings on the Liverpool dressing-room wall to inspire his players.) His glorious goals against Burnley in the semi-final had been in vain It might have been better if the team had departed anonymously in the third round, as they normally did.

And finally, there was Joe Harvey himself, haunted by this result until the day of his death in 1989. He would be sacked a year later as manager but still remained very much a Newcastle man. That night at his hotel he received a phone call from his old friend Jock Stein, the manager of Celtic, whose team had won the Scottish Cup that day, funnily enough also 3–0, against Dundee United. Jock tried to tell Harvey that life was like that, and that was football, but Joe never really recovered his *joie de vivre*. He had let his fans down.

Jackie Milburn, the hero of long ago, pulled no punches. 'I was so embarrassed I tried to hide. It's not often I've been ashamed of the Magpies, but I was saddened and shocked by the performance. Only the goalkeeper and the full-backs played. The rest were rubbish!' Jackie was clearly upset. Like all the supporters, he had felt that this was the day that would herald the return of the glory days.

Incredibly the fans turned out to welcome the team back. Not only was there a parade through the city centre, but the ground itself was opened to allow fans in to greet their fallen heroes. It was moments like that which showed that Newcastle were a very special club, and those who were not of the Geordie inclination were amazed that a defeated team could be fêted like this. But that is because the Newcastle fans are very special.

32

TOTTENHAM HOTSPUR

Match: League Cup semi-final   **Venue: St James' Park**

Score: 3–1   **Attendance: 49,902**

Newcastle United:	Tottenham Hotspur:
Mahoney	Jennings
Nattrass*	Naylor
Kennedy	McAllister
Nulty	Pratt
Keeley	Young
Howard	Osgood
Burns	Coates
Cassidy	Perryman
Macdonald	Chivers
Gowling	Duncan
Craig	Neighbour
Barrowclough*	

Referee: R. Tinkler, Boston

This was unprecedented territory for the Magpies. Since the inception of the League Cup, Newcastle's record had been rudimentary and fitful, to be as kind as possible. In fact, it had been dreadful. The competition itself was only now, some 15 years after its creation, beginning to be considered important. It had not helped itself with the emphasis on home and away two-legged ties, something which slowed the competition down. However, for almost a decade now, the Final had been staged at Wembley – something which gave the competition a great deal of prestige and kudos, but the semi-finals were still (and remain to this day) two-legged affairs.

This had not been a problem for Newcastle in the past because their record had been lamentable since 1961, with teams like Colchester, Lincoln, Bristol Rovers and Chester all managing to lower the Magpie colours. Such had been the low profile of this tournament, though, that no one seemed to care very much. Yet for supporters, a defeat in any tournament is hard to take, even in a half-hearted midweek event that traditionally recorded gates of well below the average for the season.

This year, however, things had been a little different. Manager Gordon Lee was not everyone's cup of tea and Malcolm Macdonald would make no effort to hide his feelings on this issue, but the pair of them had produced a good Cup run in this tournament. Christmas was reached with

Newcastle still in business. Truth to tell, performances had been patchy, with the best one a win at Loftus Road against Queen's Park Rangers when Newcastle overcame their traditional London phobia to win 3–1 with goals from Macdonald, Burns and Nulty. Against that, the next round in early December had seen the Magpies distinctly lucky to edge past Notts County at home thanks to an own goal. This goal was one of the most remarkable ever scored and was barely legal. A long throw-in seemed to be heading nowhere in particular other than the arms of Notts County goalkeeper Eric McManus. Under no particular pressure, McManus went for it but allowed the ball to squirm out of his hands and to enter the net via the woodwork. It was only because McManus had touched it that the goal was legal, and it remains one of the few goals ever scored in the history of football direct from a throw-in – or almost direct.

There was also, this midwinter, a certain amount of local interest in that Middlesbrough had also reached the semi-finals. Boro, managed by Jack Charlton, had some fine players in Graeme Souness, Stuart Boam, Terry Cooper and, in particular, ex-Lisbon Lion Bobby Murdoch. It would have been good for the area if both the north-east teams had been drawn together in the semi-finals, but they were kept apart, with the Boro entertaining Manchester City, and Newcastle away to Tottenham Hotspur. There was thus the possibility of an all north-east League Cup Final, and so, although motivation had possibly been lacking in the past for this competition, this was no longer true on this occasion.

The first legs were played at Ayresome Park and White Hart Lane on 14 January, and after these games an all-North-East Final was still a possibility because the home sides won 1–0 in both ties. At Middlesbrough, John Hickton had scored the only goal of the game for Boro, and at Tottenham, Newcastle had reason to believe they were unlucky to go down to a goal from David Pratt and were not without confidence for the return leg the following week.

This was a Tottenham Hotspur side at the beginning of what would be a very sharp decline, leading to relegation at the end of the following season, but their recent history had been very good. There are still those who claim that the Spurs team that won the League and Cup double in 1961 was the best that British football has ever produced, and their team of the late 1960s containing the two Gs – namely Greaves and Gilzean – was a fine outfit as well. As recently as 1972 they had won the UEFA Cup and were the beaten finalists in 1974, and they had won the League Cup in 1971 and 1973. Their credentials were impressive, although this season, with one or two of their players having moved on, they were, like Newcastle, in mid-table. Newcastle had earned a draw when they met them in the League in October.

The Magpies were a goal down in this two-legged affair as 49,902 made their way to St James' Park on a fine January night. The weather was cold but clear, with a hint that there might yet be a touch of frost, and this attendance at St James' Park was, by some distance, a ground record for the League Cup, as the Geordies clearly fancied their chances of beating the mighty Spurs. Both teams were unchanged from the first leg, and on the Saturday in between both teams had drawn 1–1, against Aston Villa in Newcastle's case and Manchester United in the case of Spurs.

Newcastle started playing towards the Leazes End, with thousands still outside the ground. The latecomers therefore missed the first goal and the game's controversial moment, which had the Londoners in the crowd claiming that the referee and linesman had been influenced and intimidated by the massive Newcastle crowd. This was nonsense, but it would have to be admitted that the decision was marginal.

The goal came from the Macdonald/Gowling combination that had caused so much harm to opposition defences that season. Macdonald, from his own half, released Gowling with a fine through ball. Gowling read him perfectly and stayed onside until the ball was played, as television footage (such as it was) tended to indicate. Gowling then found himself in acres of space as the Tottenham defence all claimed offside, forgetting the golden rule that you must always play to the whistle. A less confident man than Gowling might well have made a hash of this opportunity, but he calmly rounded Irish international goalkeeper Pat Jennings and scored to put Newcastle one up on the night and to cancel any advantage that the first leg might have given Tottenham.

Newcastle's best player that night was undeniably Tommy Craig. The red-headed Scotsman, ludicrously under-capped by his country, had arrived at St James' Park a year previously. His career at Sheffield Wednesday had seemed to be heading inexorably for the scrapheap, much to the mystification of the Aberdeen supporters, who had admired and loved him so much at Pittodrie before he went south. At Sheffield Wednesday he had found the burden of being the only quality player in a poor team too much to bear and he had been glad to move on to Newcastle. He had taken a while to settle but now, under Gordon Lee, he was flourishing.

Playing on the left side of midfield, he was a constant source of passes to the forwards. He was a hard worker, a sturdy tackler and ball winner, but it was his passing ability that marked him out. His red hair seemed to reflect the lights that night, giving him some kind of aura, which dazzled and demoralised the Tottenham players, now visibly buckling under the constant noise from the Geordie faithful, who sensed the imminence of a trip to Wembley.

After a first half of fairly constant Geordie pressure with no tangible result, Newcastle went ahead on aggregate. In addition to Tommy Craig's other attributes he was a great taker of set pieces, and when Newcastle won a corner on the left at the Gallowgate End of the ground with virtually their first attack of the half, Craig took it. With some clever decoy work by Macdonald and Gowling, who took defenders with them out of the danger area, the ball came to the head of centre-half Glen Keeley. Keeley was virtually unmarked and had enough time to decide to head the ball downwards past the mighty Pat Jennings and to score his first goal of the season. Keeley, struggling to find a place and not, apparently, well beloved by manager Gordon Lee, was only in the team because of an injury to David Craig, but he was never more popular in the Toon than he was that night with that magnificent goal.

Newcastle's joy was tempered by the thought that there would be a Tottenham fightback, and they did have Martin Chivers, an England striker, in their line-up. But any threat from Chivers failed to materialise with Newcastle's well-drilled defence on top of their job, and in any case, about halfway through the second half, the Toon went further ahead. This was a fine goal made by the hard-working Irish midfielder Tommy Cassidy, who made space and sent a hard drive across in the direction of Gowling. While the crowd held their breath, Gowling unselfishly dummied the ball and it went to Geoff Nulty, who hammered home to a tremendous roar of acclaim from the black and white hordes all around the ground.

Newcastle now seemed to be coasting as they passed the ball comfortably around the park to each other to loud shouts of 'Olé', as they remained in control with minutes ticking away. News was coming through on the ubiquitous crackling transistor radios that the opponents in the Final were unlikely to be Boro, who were undergoing a spectacular collapse at Maine Road, Manchester – a result that was greeted with almost as much joy as Newcastle's own result – but then, just to prove that Newcastle are capable of putting their supporters through the horrors of hell, they conceded a goal to make the aggregate 3–2.

It was a header scored by full-back Don McAllister, as Newcastle paid the price for switching off and losing concentration. Ten minutes remained and it was a long 10 minutes for the Newcastle supporters as anxiety now began to replace confidence, with Wembley so tantalisingly close, yet just out of reach. But the players remained calm, knocked the ball about to each other and remained composed as the supporters counted down the minutes. After an unconscionable amount of overtime Mr Tinkler eventually pointed to the dressing rooms, and Newcastle were in their first-ever League Cup Final. Seldom had so many Newcastle supporters left the ground to get their trains, buses and cars in such a good mood. Manchester City would be difficult opponents, but if Newcastle could beat Tottenham Hotspur there was every chance that they could do the same to City. The fans' only concern was how they were going to get tickets for the Final.

33

MANCHESTER CITY

Match: League Cup Final   **Venue: Wembley**

Score: 1–2   **Attendance: 100,000**

Newcastle United:	Manchester City:
Mahoney	Corrigan
Nattrass	Keegan
Kennedy	Donachie
Barrowclough	Doyle
Keeley	Robson
Howard	Oates
Burns	Barnes
Cassidy	Booth
Macdonald	Royle
Gowling	Hartford
Craig	Tueart

Referee: J. Taylor, Wolverhampton

It would be fair to say that United's record in the Football League Cup was and continues to be disappointing. Words like 'dire' and 'woeful' have been used to describe their performances with only the run in 1976 earning any sort of praise. In 1976, they at least made it to Wembley.

Wembley represented something very special in the eyes and minds of most Geordies because it recalled the glorious days of 20-odd years before, but it also brought back the painful memories of the 1974 FA Cup Final, that infamous day 22 months previously when Newcastle had travelled to Wembley only to freeze on the day. For one player in particular, there was a point to prove.

This was 'Supermac' Malcolm Macdonald, who had talked himself into national ridicule by telling everyone how well he was to perform against Liverpool in that Cup Final and then failing to produce the goods. It was a chastening, humbling experience for Macdonald, and for all of Tyneside, and there were those who felt that it might have been better if Macdonald had departed in the wake of that particular day, because although he was still scoring the goals and enjoying some of his popularity, there was no doubt that his charisma had taken a severe beating.

Yet Supermac had proven that he could do it at Wembley. Ten months previously he had bagged five for England against admittedly weak opposition in Cyprus, thus equalling the record, and allowing Newcastle to boast that they had provided record breakers for both England and Scotland. Hughie Gallacher held the Scottish record, having scored five against Northern Ireland in 1929.

Manager Gordon Lee (third from right) takes his men for a walk on the Wembley pitch.

Now Macdonald had another chance. This time he was commendably quieter about what he was about to do, but the hopes grew in the hearts of the Geordies that at long last another triumph might be gained and that the ghosts of past horrors might be buried. Opinion remained divided about Macdonald. Some still called him Supermac, while other, possibly older, supporters would justifiably point out that he was no Jackie Milburn – 'You want ta hae seen Jackie Milburn, if you think that he's ony guid' cried one elderly female supporter when the adulation started, and others would shake their head and say to Macdonald's admirers 'You never saw Jackie Milburn!'

There were rumours – more than rumours, as little concerning football can ever be hushed up in the football-mad city of Newcastle – that Macdonald did not like manager Gordon Lee. Lee tended to play a team game with loads of method football at the expense perhaps of individual flair and talent. Macdonald felt threatened by this, particularly as there now seemed to be a rival for his position as the goalscoring king. This came from Alan Gowling, a talented, tall, loose-limbed striker who had arrived from Huddersfield Town at the beginning of the season. Even though the two of them seemed to team up well on the field and goals came from the partnership, rumours of disharmony, including one or two stories of fisticuffs, did not go away.

Lee, Macdonald and Gowling all shared one goal of wanting to earn a medal at Wembley. The fans were similarly keen on treating themselves once again to the now rare and elusive sight of black and white colours on silverware. Following a successful, even a triumphant, campaign against Southport, Bristol Rovers, Queen's Park Rangers, Notts County and Tottenham Hotspur, only Manchester City stood in their way. League form had been far from convincing, but there had also been progress in the FA Cup, albeit with some replays. Queen's Park Rangers and Coventry City had needed two games, and on the Monday before the Wembley Final Newcastle, on neutral ground at Elland Road, Leeds, had at long last disposed of Bolton Wanderers at the third attempt.

Manchester City were, not for the first or last time in their history, trying to assert themselves as the number-one team in the city. They had achieved that aim when United had been relegated in 1974 (City themselves had delivered the fatal blow), but both Manchester teams had been under the shadow of Liverpool for many years. Manager Tony Book had assembled a good team with fine players, like the rhyming pair of Mike Doyle and Joe Royle, a tenacious full-back in Willie Donachie and the occasionally controversial character Asa Hartford, who enjoyed a certain amount of popularity in Manchester but never quite managed to convince those in Scotland who watched the international team that he was able to step up a gear.

Newcastle's moment of triumph. Alan Gowling has just scored.

Like Newcastle, City were one of those teams whose supporters expected more. Although their record in the 30 years since World War Two had been acceptable, and markedly better than that of Newcastle, they had never really reached the dizzy heights of their pre-war sides. They had had a golden spell in the late 1960s when they had won the English League then the FA Cup in successive years, before having a glory season in 1970 when they won the English League Cup and the European Cup-Winners' Cup. In 1976 they were already out of the FA Cup, having flopped to Stoke City in the fourth round, and were, like Newcastle, in mid-table mediocrity in the League, so this Final represented their only realistic chance of winning anything for the first time since 1970.

Newcastle had had a heavy schedule and in particular a prolonged Cup run in both tournaments, and there were those among the support who suspected that a draw in the first game of an FA Cup tie was no bad thing for the finances of the club, with gates in the replays of 37,225 versus QPR, 43,445 versus Coventry City and 50,381 and then 42,280 versus Bolton Wanderers doing the club no harm at all in a year when everyone was prosperous enough, but when all financial institutions were threatened by the curse of inflation, which was showing every sign of getting totally out of hand.

This, however, had had its effect on players, and a particularly feeble performance had been witnessed at Anfield against Liverpool the week before the League Cup Final as the team clearly had their eyes on other things. The days between the win over Bolton on Monday 23 February and the League Cup Final were spent in the city in a mood of euphoria and optimism but tempered by the news that the local newspapers were putting about of injuries and outbreaks of flu among the exhausted players. Such stories must be taken with a very large pinch of salt, and with the possible exception of Mike Nulty, out with a broken jaw, the Magpies were at full strength for the League Cup Final.

It was Manchester City who scored first through young Peter Barnes. There was a touch of historical irony about this one because Peter was the son of Ken Barnes, who had played for City against Newcastle United in the 1955 FA Cup Final. The goal came in the 11th minute and followed a free-kick taken by Asa Hartford. Hartford floated the ball in over the Newcastle goal and it was headed back by Doyle. It was not adequately dealt with by the Newcastle defence and the ball came out to Barnes, who forced the ball home through a posse of Newcastle defenders before they could converge on him.

This was tough on Newcastle, who had started brightly, but they did not allow this early reverse to unsettle them too much. Both teams were playing attractive football, employing wingers, with Macdonald on the right causing a fair amount of havoc, and it was from Macdonald that the equaliser came. He was released by a fine ball from Irish international Tommy Cassidy, made ground and crossed for Alan Gowling to nudge the ball home at the near post before a defender could get there. It was a fine goal, and whatever the rumours may have been about Macdonald and Gowling not getting on behind the scenes, they certainly teamed up well for that goal, as indeed they had done many times that season.

Half-time was thus spent with the Geordie supporters in a state of excitement and optimism for the second half. The game had been good, and Newcastle had given as good as they had got. In fact, it was the opinion of the radio commentators and the summarisers giving their half-time reports (live television coverage was not allowed in 1976 lest it have a deleterious effect on other gates) that Newcastle had edged it.

It was early in the second half that Newcastle met their nemesis, and it came in the shape of Dennis Tueart, one of the long and lamentable list of Geordies who had grown up supporting Newcastle United but had been allowed to slip through the net and then returned to punish the Toon for their improvidence, causing all sorts of moral dilemmas to his friends, family and possibly himself. Dennis had been doing this for some time – he had played for Sunderland between 1968 and 1974 and had won the FA Cup with them in 1973.

On this occasion he scored a truly wonderful goal. In Manchester City's first attack, Willie Donachie crossed from the left and the ball was headed on by Tommy Booth, apparently out of reach of Tueart, but he launched himself at it and scored with a superb overhead scissors kick. Such brilliance wins Cup medals, and from then on Newcastle's chances began to evaporate.

Dennis Tueart's brilliant overhead scissor-kick.

Defeated but unbowed, Newcastle greet their disappointed fans.

There was the whole second half to be played, yet, for one reason or other, Newcastle now dropped out of the game. Magpie apologists will talk of heavy schedules, flu and injuries, but the reality was that Manchester City simply played better. They now had the confidence, they were faster to the ball and they passed it around a lot better. Newcastle tried, but in truth they were the second-best team on the day. The black and white clan watched the time ticking away and prayed and implored heaven for Supermac to produce a piece of brilliance to match the Tueart goal, but it was now becoming clear that Macdonald's moment was passing – indeed, it had long passed – and that the two great centre-forwards of the past, Hughie Gallacher and Jackie Milburn, were not to be joined by a third in the Newcastle pantheon. A few half-chances came Newcastle's way, one in particular from Micky Burns that might have gone in on another day, but the City defence was never breached.

Full-time came, and the broken-hearted Geordies clapped their team. It had, at least, been a good day out at Wembley. They had outshouted their Manchester City counterparts and impressed the media with their enthusiasm, and the following year's *Rothman's Football Yearbook* singles them out for praise. The tragedy would be that it would be some considerable time before they would have another visit to Wembley, and grim days now beckoned once again for Newcastle United.

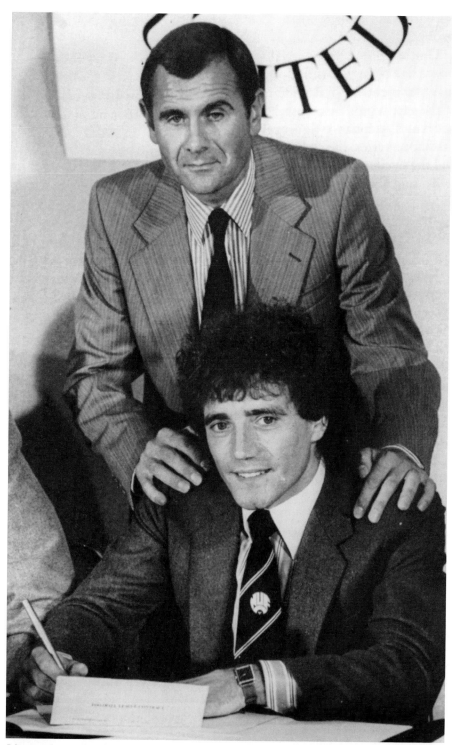

A long and convoluted relationship begins as Kevin Keegan signs with Arthur Cox looking on.

Date: 5 May 1984

DERBY COUNTY

Match: League Division Two   **Venue: St James' Park**

Score: 4–0   **Attendance: 35,866**

Newcastle United:	Derby County:
Carr	Cherry
Anderson	Burns
Wharton	Buckley
McCreery	Gemmill
Carney	Watson
Roeder	Powell
Keegan	Devine
Beardsley	Davison
Waddle	Garner*
McDermott	Harbey
Trewick	Robertson
	Wilson*

Referee: D. Richardson, Lancashire

1984 was meant to be, according to George Orwell and other prophets of doom, the year of the dictator and 'Big Brother', which was not the somewhat infantile television show that later bore that name but a vicious dictatorship in which everyone was spied upon. Fortunately, such predictions never came true, but 1984 was still an extremely difficult year for many people in Great Britain with the miners' strike, which hit the North East particularly hard.

There was one redeeming feature of 1984 for Geordie fans and that was the return of their beloved team to the First Division after a dreary exile in the Second Division. This period in the wilderness had lasted six rather painful years, with the team so out of touch and seemingly going nowhere that the danger was that English football would soon come to regard the Second Division as being Newcastle United's natural home. This, of course, will never be accepted by the fans, but the truth was that the early 1980s gave little cause for any kind of cheer on Tyneside as gloom descended on the whole Toon.

In 1982 the club at last showed some initiative by signing Kevin Keegan, one of the big names in world soccer, who had possibly reached his peak by this time but had been a superstar in his day with Liverpool and Hamburg in particular. While Tyneside seized on his arrival as some sort of beginning of a new millennium or a golden age (the word 'messiah' was sadly and inappropriately heard), and

Kevin went out of his way to impress everyone with his Geordie credentials – which were, in truth, somewhat tenuous because he came from Doncaster, although his father was from Hutton-le-Hole – the area did get some kind of a boost, but sadly, after a bright opening, promotion was not achieved in season 1982–83 with Kevin, fairly obviously, far from impressed by some of his teammates and the general set-up at St James' Park.

Manager Arthur Cox had been more successful in season 1983–84 in that two other great forwards, both still young and inexperienced, had emerged to supplement Keegan. An advantage was that both were local boys, Chris Waddle having come straight from local minor football league and Peter Beardsley having arrived via the scenic route of Canada. Waddle was the more exciting of the two with his gangling, ungainly run and his sheer unpredictability, whereas Beardsley was far more incisive in every respect.

There was also Keegan's old friend and associate from his Liverpool days, Terry McDermott. It was often felt that Terry's best days were behind him, and he did suffer from some terracing unpopularity at the start of the season, but significantly, when the team picked up, McDermott was on song and his contribution should not be underestimated. There was also David McCreery from Belfast, who won 67 caps for Northern Ireland. He was a tough midfielder who managed to combine tenacious tackling with good ball skills and distribution.

Sometimes the defence caused heartaches. The twin centre-half combination of Glenn Roeder, the classy Londoner, and local boy Steve Carney was generally more than adequate, but full-backs tended to be a problem for the Magpies, with a disturbing number of goals being conceded from the wings. The general problem, however, was one of inconsistency.

A disappointment had been the transfer of Imre Varadi to Sheffield Wednesday. A goalscorer and a personality player, his departure would have caused a great deal more angst if the team had not been doing better. As it was he did very well for the Owls, scoring twice against Newcastle in November, and Wednesday finished second in the League, some eight points ahead of Newcastle. The history of Newcastle is littered with irrational transfers which bewildered supporters. This was one of them.

It would be a mistake to think that 1983–84 was a triumphant charge to the top. The truth is that they were more than a little fortunate. They made a stuttering start, had a brighter autumn and then the odd shocking result and performance – Grimsby Town at St James' Park in February was a particular blow – but in general there were more good results than bad ones in a season when the Second Division race was very interesting indeed as teams like Chelsea, Manchester City and Sheffield Wednesday (all three of whom would have felt entitled to call themselves First Division teams) battled it out with United for the three promotion spots.

One could never expect a devastating performance on any one given week, but, like the famed little girl with the curl on her forehead, when Newcastle were good, they were very, very good. One such occasion came on 29 October 1983, when Manchester City were put to the sword in a 5–0 thrashing which left 33,588 patrons at St James' Park breathless and rendered City's manager Billy McNeill (no stranger to wonderful attacking football from his days with Celtic) almost speechless at how good Newcastle were. Beardsley scored a hat-trick, and one goal in particular will stay long in the memory. This was the fourth of the game, when Peter picked up a ball from Chris Waddle and sliced through the Manchester City defence to score brilliantly. An old timer in the main stand watched this, paused, and then gave Peter the greatest compliment of them all when he said, quite simply, 'Jackie Milburn'.

The performances in the Cup competitions had been disappointing, to say the least. The League Cup games against Oxford had been feeble, and any feelings that the Toon might have entertained that they were on the cusp of greatness were dispelled when Newcastle were drawn to play Liverpool at Anfield in the third round of the FA Cup. This was a high-profile, televised game on the first Friday night of the year, but Newcastle collapsed and went down 0–4 before a Liverpool team who may have expected a more robust challenge. In circumstances that reminded the broken-hearted Geordies of the FA Cup Final between the same two sides a decade earlier, the forwards failed to trouble the scorers and the buses home that night were quietly despondent.

It was thus clear at a very early stage in 1984 that it was promotion or nothing. Commendably, the team buckled to their task. Results were not always good, but it was clear that in Kevin Keegan, the Toon had the man who would take them into the First Division. His lay-offs, his chesting down of the ball and, above all else, his goals marked him out as a very special player – but then again we all knew that. The trouble was that he was 33 on Valentine's Day 1984, and it was no real surprise that he announced his retirement at the end of the season. He had clearly realised the truth of the old adage that a player should retire when people were still asking 'why' and before they began to say 'why not'. The supporters were unhappy about this, but he had made up his mind and he had clearly earned enough from the game to keep him in luxury all his life.

A disappointing defeat at the hands of Cambridge the previous week set up this game against Derby County as the game that might gain promotion for the Geordies. Derby County had an agenda of their own in that they were struggling to avoid relegation. They were a team with fine players. They had, for example, Archie Gemmill, scorer some six years before of Scotland's famous goal against Holland – the only bright spot of Scotland's otherwise disastrous Argentina campaign. Kenny Burns was another veteran of Argentina, and at centre-half there was Dave Watson, who had won 65 caps for England. They would be difficult to beat.

To be absolutely mathematically sure of promotion, Newcastle needed to beat Derby County and hope that Grimsby lost to Blackburn Rovers. However, the three points would possibly be enough, barring some mathematical improbability. The Derby County game would be significant. Certainly 35,866 Geordies thought so.

A stranger arriving by train at Newcastle Central Station will immediately know if there is a game on that day. The town will be animated, excited, and there will be lots of black and white scarves around, even on a day in early May when scarves are not necessarily required to keep out the cold. A feature of this day was the vast amount of what Homer's *Iliad* would call the 'far summoned allies', as trains from London and Scotland disgorged passengers talking in accents that were markedly other than the normal one from the North East.

The Gallowgate End was particularly full that day as the chant of 'Going Up! Going Up!' was heard ad infinitum. It would have been a tremendous disappointment if the team had under-performed on the day, but they chose to put on one of their better performances as poor Derby were put to the sword and beaten with four great goals.

Unusual behaviour from professional football players.

More scenes of celebration.

The first came in the 17th minute with Keegan scoring from a Waddle cross from the left. Five minutes later a slick one-two with Keegan saw Beardsley score with a low shot. Then a few minutes after the interval a delightful diagonal through ball after good play from Keegan and Beardsley found Waddle in the clear, and the rout was completed 12 minutes from time when Beardsley's low diving header after a McDermott miskick put the Geordie crowd into overdrive. In truth, there could have been a lot more goals, so dominant were Newcastle.

There could be little doubt as to who was the man of the moment. It was Kevin Keegan, whose distribution and general control of the game were indeed sights to behold. How appropriate it was that he led the celebrations at the end as *The Blaydon Races* was heard for the first time in triumph for many years at St James' Park, even though technically and mathematically promotion was not quite assured as the crackling transistors told us that Grimsby Town had also won that day. Nevertheless, the moment was only delayed.

Unfortunately the triumph would not last, for Geordie self-destruction would take over in a big way. Keegan fulfilled his promise to depart (which he did, theatrically, in a helicopter the following week) and then Arthur Cox, in some ways the hero of the hour, departed in circumstances which have never yet been completely explained. He went to manage – of all teams – Derby County, now in the Third Division, the side that had been so comprehensively defeated by Newcastle on that day, which promised so much future prosperity for the long-suffering Geordies. The truth was to be so tragically and devastatingly different.

Date: 25 April 1992

35

PORTSMOUTH

Match: League Division Two　　　　**Venue: St James' Park**

Score: 1–0　　　　**Attendance: 25,989**

Newcastle United:	Portsmouth:
Wright	Knight
Ranson	Awford
Neilson	Daniel
O'Brien	McLoughlin
Kilcline	Symons
Scott	Burns
Carr	Neill
Peacock	Doling
Kelly	Powell
Sheedy	Aspinall**
Brock*	Anderton*
Clark*	Wigley*
	McFarlane**

Referee: S. Bell, Huddersfield

1992 saw dire days for many people, not least those living in Newcastle. A few weeks before this game the General Election had returned the Conservatives to power for the fourth successive time, something which indicated perhaps that some people at least were happy with the status quo. Very few of them lived in Newcastle, however, where signs of decay and stagnation were all too obvious to the casual visitor and observer. Even from the train, the line to and from Sunderland past Felling, Pelaw and Boldon was a particularly depressing experience.

The club had made, and was still making, brave efforts to improve the stadium in spite of the obvious economic problems of the area, but the problem lay in the team. The nightmare phrase 'Division Three' haunted the city because Newcastle were already in Division Two and struggling. Life among clubs like Shrewsbury, Chester and Exeter (all respectable and decent clubs, but not in the category of Newcastle United) beckoned in the third tier.

There had been in the city an almost resigned acceptance that Newcastle had now 'had it'. They were now paying the bitter price for the short-sighted and money-grabbing selling of star players like Waddle, Beardsley and Gascoigne. There were even those who said that this was a good thing, as the area was far too obsessed with an activity that they were not good at, and that it was perhaps

145

better to move away from football and concentrate on other things. There was a good tradition of middle-distance running, the rugby team was not bad, and Durham County Cricket Club were now arriving on the scene, but Newcastle United, the team of Peter McWilliam, Colin Veitch, Hughie Gallacher, Jackie Milburn and Bobby Mitchell, was now dead. Milburn had died in 1988. His funeral had been impressive, but there was the sense that those who lined the streets were there not merely to honour this man, great though he was. There was also a certain amount of mourning for the death of a great club.

Yet was it all as bad as that? The manager for most of the 1991–92 season had been the charming Argentinian, Ossie Ardiles. He had, in his day, been one of the best players around, playing for Spurs after being a member of the 1978 Argentina team that won the World Cup, but as a manager of a declining giant like Newcastle United he had not had a clue. He was not the only guilty man, of course. The directors had been as feckless and as inefficient with him as they had been for the past 20 years and more, and there had been times when the players seemed to lack any drive, direction or even ambition and energy. Crowds had dipped to alarming levels – 13,077 to see Cambridge United in November and 14,740 to see Southend United, and the away support was shrinking to virtual invisibility.

There were clear signs that the Geordies had had enough. Even the strip they wore invited ridicule. It was black and white certainly, but the stripes were of unequal width and there was a big blue star. This pathetic attempt to appease a sponsor was an insult to all those who had worn the shirt in the past and, more importantly, was an insult to all those who had supported the club, as were the plethora of away strips of different hues and arrangements.

This was nothing like Newcastle United. It was naked Thatcherism and an attempt to join the revolution of the 'yuppies'. (Young, upwardly-mobile professional people). The trouble was that Newcastle were not moving upwards. They were, in fact, going downwards at an alarming rate, and even their enemies in Sunderland, Middlesbrough and London were not without their sympathies at the apparently terminal decline of a great club.

The revolution that took place in February 1992 was not as dramatic as, for example, the one that saved Celtic in 1994, but it was a total one as Sir John Hall took charge and unceremoniously sacked the lovely little Argentinian with the perpetually bemused look on his face. As frequently happens, he had been told 36 hours previously that his job was safe! Hall then brought Kevin Keegan in as manager. Tyneside rejoiced, the word 'messiah' was used, not for the first nor last time, and a glimmer of hope appeared – but Newcastle still had to be saved.

Keegan fairly soon went into the transfer market and came back with Brian Kilcline, a ferocious looking defender from Oldham Athletic who sported a ponytail and a moustache. He looked anything but a skilful football player, but his defensive skills came to be much appreciated by the Geordie faithful. There was also Kevin Sheedy, a player whose best days were behind him but who had been very much associated with the success of Everton in the mid 1980s, when they had won temporary bragging rights over Liverpool. Sheedy had been an extremely influential midfielder but was now struggling to hold on to a first-team place at Goodison.

For a while things went well. Good wins against Port Vale, Cambridge United, Swindon Town and (crucially for morale) Sunderland seemed to have solved the problem, but then the gremlins struck again. In the absence of Kilcline, the team conceded six goals to Wolverhampton Wanderers, and the horrors continued through the month of April with three narrow and unlucky defeats to Tranmere Rovers, Ipswich and Millwall.

But it was the Monday before Portsmouth arrived that saw real trouble. Newcastle went down 4–1 to Derby County at the Baseball Ground. That was bad enough, but three red cards were also distributed by an over-zealous referee to an over-committed Newcastle side. It never rains but it pours, and by some sort of vindictive decree by a malevolent deity Plymouth Argyle beat Oxford United 3–1. Thus, Newcastle found themselves in 22nd spot and in the relegation zone.

It was clear then that a victory against Portsmouth was an absolute necessity. Anything less would probably spell the unthinkable, and they were concerned that they might not be able to hold on to

Kevin Keegan in those circumstances. As the trains arrived that morning there was the same sort of feeling that the defenders of the Alamo would have had, namely that it was now or never. Even the sales assistants in shops and waitresses in restaurants would look upon a black and white scarfed customer with a mixture of admiration and pity and express their best wishes.

But cometh the hour, cometh the man, and this time it was David Kelly who turned up trumps. Kelly had joined the club in December 1991 after a career with several clubs where he had not set the heather on fire, although he had played a few good games for Ireland under Jack Charlton. He had scored for Newcastle in a few games, notably against Sunderland in the 1–0 victory in the local derby, but he had been off form recently. Today, however, would be the day that would earn him some sort of Tyneside immortality.

Portsmouth were a good team, now managed by ex-Geordie boss Jim Smith, who was given a good reception by the crowd. Like Newcastle, they had seen better days, but this year they would be destined to finish just short of the Play-off spots. They would not be easy to beat. A crowd of 25,989 were there to see if the Geordies could do just that.

The game was far too tense to be a good one, but by half-time Newcastle felt that they had more or less held their own. A draw would at least keep the issue open for the final-day game away to Leicester City, but half-time scores indicated that other games were going Newcastle's way and a win would more or less solve the problem. The public address system also informed the club of how Durham were doing. It was the first day of Durham in the County Championship. They were playing Leicestershire at Durham University, but even with Ian Botham and Dean Jones on board they were dismissed for 164.

But even the many cricket fans at St James' Park became more and more absorbed in the ongoing Newcastle battle against relegation. Time passed but no goal came. Kevin Sheedy looked good, and so did Lee Clark when he came on, but, now attacking the Gallowgate End, they still could not break the Portsmouth defence. Dissatisfaction and boos began to be heard, with Peacock being singled out for barracking. Then at last, with time running out, it came. It was a simple enough goal – a surge forward from Ray Ranson on the right was followed by a high ball, which Kelly missed but which went to Mick Quinn, who knocked it on to the advancing Kelly. Kelly struck it well with his right foot, obeying the golden rule of kicking the ball once, and only once, in the penalty area. It was his first for six games, but seldom has a goal been greeted with such glee and enthusiasm.

The final whistle came a few minutes later, and Newcastle had saved themselves. The scenes all the way from the ground to the railway station were more akin to a support whose team had just won the European Cup rather than having saved themselves from the third tier of English football. Strangers hugged each other, danced and sang *The Blaydon Races* and that most repetitive of chants 'New-cast-le, New-cast-le, New-cast-le'. It was a very sweet moment.

The scenes at Central Station were bizarre as the black and white hordes gathered. They were predominantly young men, singing raucously and loudly (with the odd obscenity about Sunderland), but there were one or two older men as well, middle-aged ones who used to listen to the results on BBC *Sports Report* to hear how Milburn had done that day, and there was at least one who looked as if he might have seen Hughie Gallacher. One or two middle-class, middle-aged women who looked as if they might sing in the choir at the chapel the next day and then be in front of their classes in school on the Monday were there, and they too had their black and white scarves round their necks. Everyone had that drained but happy look about them because the team that they loved was saved.

There was one nagging thought as the fans awaited the arrival of the trains to take them north, south and west – all that had really happened was that Newcastle had confirmed their place in the Second Division. There was the fear that this could still be considered their natural position. They need not have worried, though, for Newcastle now looked upwards. It all began with David Kelly.

Date: 4 May 1993

36
GRIMSBY TOWN

Match: League Division One   **Venue: Blundell Park, Grimsby**

Score: 2–0   **Attendance: 14,402**

Grimsby Town:	Newcastle United:
Wilmott	Srnicek
McDermott	Venison
Croft	Beresford
Futcher*	Bracewell
Rodger	Scott
Dobbin	Howey
Ford	Lee
Gilbert**	Cole
Groves	Kelly
Mendonca	Clark
Woods	Sellars
Smith*	
Childs**	

Referee: T. Lunt, Lancashire

Events in Cleethorpes on the evening of Tuesday 4 May 1993 confirmed that Newcastle were champions of the First Division for the first time since the days of Hughie Gallacher in 1927. It was the stuff that dreams were made of.

There was one important qualification, however, in that Division One sadly no longer contained the best teams. They had been creamed off to the Premier Division (England rather disappointingly and slavishly following Scotland's lead in its nomenclature and similarly fooling nobody) or 'the Premiership' as it was sometimes ridiculously called by those who should have known better. What all this meant was that when Newcastle won Division One in 1993, everyone knew that it meant Division Two. The real Division One was won by Manchester United, who were the champions of England for the first time in 26 years – amazing in the light of their subsequent history, but true.

All this was of little or no concern to the Newcastle fans who enjoyed their night out at Blundell Park, bringing a certain amount of congestion and therefore danger to the area, and alarming the authorities, who were all too aware of what had happened at Hillsborough four years previously. On two occasions after Newcastle scored the crowd had encroached and the game had

had to be delayed until such time as they could be cleared, and there had been one or two other minor incidents when youngsters had been compelled by the pressure of the crowd to move on to the field. There was no ill will or malice in all this, though, because Newcastle fans were happy.

Chants about Kevin Keegan resounded round the ground and a few attempts were made to sing *The Blaydon Races*, even though there was a major handicap in many supporters not knowing the words. In particular the road that they were travelling along seemed to present a few difficulties. Was it Scotswood, Scotshill, Scotston or even Scotland? What no one could doubt, however, was the sincerity and joy of the youngsters at the thought that their beloved side was back in the top tier of English football for the first time since the disastrous relegation of 1989.

In some ways it was merely the restoration of the position of 1984, except that Kevin Keegan was now the manager rather than a player and that this time he was here to stay. He was also working for a forward-looking chairman called Sir John Hall, who was not without his enemies both within football and within business, but he had put his money where his mouth was and had saved the sinking ship. At least as importantly, he had done something to rescue the fans from the depths of misery to which they had sunk when the club was in the hands, not for the first or last time, of those who did not understand what Newcastle United meant to so many people.

The years from 1984 to 1993 were years of under-investment, craven management and the weak selling of crack players who were replaced by men of inferior value. The years had seemed to present such a great opportunity, but the possibilities had been wasted. Jack Charlton had laudably stuck his neck out against the less well-educated of the support who booed black players of opposition teams, but he had then taken umbrage when the same idiots chanted 'Sack Jack' at a pre-season friendly and he handed in his resignation. Willie McFaul had been mediocre at best, the 'Bald Eagle' Jim Smith had landed to a great fanfare of trumpets but had been similarly ineffective, the charming Argentinian Ossie Ardiles simply did not seem to understand Newcastle United. But now we had Kevin Keegan. He had saved Newcastle from the third tier in 1992 and in one complete season had won Division One, and clearly he had not stopped yet. The future looked dazzlingly bright to those wearing black and white that Tuesday evening on 4 May; the football had been consistently good and forceful. Not without cause were the team described as 'the entertainers'.

Newcastle were aware that it had been Grimsby in October at St James' Park who had put an end to the incredible beginning of their League campaign, which had seen 11 straight wins. The football had been quite outstanding at times with a 5–0 defeat of Bristol City and a very welcome, if slightly tighter, win at Roker Park the week before. But Grimsby had thwarted Newcastle for a considerable part of the game before Jim Dobbin, a man whom Celtic foolishly let go, scored a wonder goal at the Leazes End for Grimsby. Would Grimsby frustrate Newcastle once more?

Defeats had been rare for Newcastle that year. Only eight defeats had been sustained and six of them had been by the odd goal. Closest challengers West Ham United had been well dealt with at home and drawn with at Upton Park, and any team who had beaten Newcastle in one game had been defeated in the return game, with the exception of Swindon Town, who had held the Magpies to a draw at St James' Park and then beaten them at the County Ground in Wiltshire. All this consistent form meant that a win at Grimsby would both secure automatic promotion to the Premier League and win the League Championship as well.

There were other encouraging things that season. In contrast to both campaigns in the past, both Cup competitions had seen respectable runs, ended by odd goal defeats by Premier League teams in Chelsea and Blackburn Rovers, and the club had not been afraid to spend money on players as well as on the ongoing ground development. Paul Bracewell, Barry Venison, Rob Lee and Andy Cole had all arrived either before the start of the season or in the middle of it, with the purchase of Cole from Bristol City for £1,750,000 in March looking like a particularly shrewd investment, but no more so than Rob Lee from Charlton Athletic for less than half that amount in the autumn.

The game kicked off a little late to allow the 14,402 fans to gain admission to a ground where normal attendance was a great deal less than half that. Newcastle's attendances had dwarfed those of anyone else that season, something that indicated that the Geordie support was on the march, and that it was high time that they were playing somewhere other than the second tier of English football.

The first half was all action but goalless with Grimsby, whose chances of making the play-offs had all but gone, nevertheless enjoying the frenetic atmosphere and contributing as much as Newcastle. Both sides had chances, and although the occasion made both sides a little nervous it had no noticeable effect on the standard of the play. It was early in the second half when Newcastle went ahead.

The goal came from the combined efforts of two of Keegan's signings. A through ball from the tall, dark and elegant Rob Lee found Andy Cole, who avoided any challenge and lashed the ball past goalkeeper Rhys Wilmott, who had defied Newcastle so bravely in the first half. This event caused major crushing behind the goal and saw several fans injured in the surge of the crowd. Some came onto the field to avoid the crush, others rushed on to celebrate and enjoy the sheer *joie de vivre* of a goal and the chance to run on a football field. They had to be pushed back gently but firmly by the local police, who handled the situation with admirable restraint and good humour when a heavy hand might have led to less pleasant consequences. It was also seen, however, that some fans were led away by the local ambulance men who attended to their injuries.

The second half was a long, nervous time for the Toon Army. A goal by Grimsby would delay, although in all truth would probably not prevent, the celebrations, but Newcastle retained control of the game. One or two chances to go further ahead were spurned, and at the other end Pavel Srnicek, Newcastle's Czech goalkeeper, who had had an outstanding season, was called upon to make a few saves.

With time running out and the supporters counting down to the full-time whistle, Newcastle finally settled the game and the Championship with a fine strike from David Kelly, the man who had scored the famous goal that had kept the Magpies in the second tier a year ago, now scoring the goal that took them out of it. Kelly and other players were engulfed by celebrating Geordies because, no sooner had the pitch been cleared and the game restarted, the referee pointed to the pavilion and blew for full-time.

A lap of honour followed as Keegan and his assistant Terry McDermott were fêted and adored by their grateful public. Keegan would be quoted as saying, 'I promised them (the Newcastle supporters) a team to be proud of and I think it is safe to say that we have provided it.' Indeed they had, although the picture that appeared in the *Daily Mirror* of Keegan wearing a crown and being called 'King Kev' struck fans as a little over the top, however much it mirrored their mood. The *Daily Telegraph*, admiring Newcastle's fans, wondered what they would be like if they ever did win anything of more prestige than the First Division.

The buses and cars more or less flew rather than drove back home north to Newcastle that night, carrying joyful supporters who were already saying that they were looking forward to the start of the new season. They still had a couple of games to play this season, both at home and both won comfortably, with the 7–1 defeat of Leicester City on the last Sunday looking like sheer bullying and punishment of Leicester for beating them earlier in the season at Filbert Street.

The summer was spent gloriously with the days being counted off until the start of the new campaign. Football, which had never been totally forgotten on Tyneside even in the bad days, now became the number-one topic of conversation once again, as anyone who went to a Durham county cricket match that summer would readily attest to. They never stopped talking about Andy Cole and Kevin Keegan. The future looked bright, and it seemed that a new force was about to enter the top ranks of English football.

37

LIVERPOOL

Match: Premier League

Score: 3–4

Venue: Anfield, Liverpool

Attendance: 40,702

Liverpool:	Newcastle United:
James	Srnicek
McAteer	Watson
Jones**	Beresford
Scales	Batty
Wright*	Albert
Ruddock	Howey*
McManaman	Lee
Redknapp	Beardsley
Collymore	Ferdinand
Barnes	Ginola
Fowler	Asprilla
Harkness*	Peacock*
Rush**	

Referee: M. Reed, Birmingham

It is dangerous, ultimately self-defeating and also incredibly painful to play the game of 'what if'. Most rational people will agree that if something has happened, one accepts it and makes the best of it. Nevertheless, it is difficult for Geordie supporters in all their many sleepless nights since this horrible evening to wonder what might have happened if things had been different.

The match has been described as the greatest Premier League game ever and even by a few hysterical people as the greatest game in any competition of all time, but Geordie fans are less magnanimous. It highlighted the age-old question of whether a team should entertain or whether it should win. It is fine, of course, if you can do both, but in the real world there are times when you have to make the choice. Kevin Keegan chose to keep trying to entertain and was quite unrepentant about it afterwards. Many pundits and neutrals gave him a great deal of credit for that. Newcastle supporters, even those who traditionally want to see flowing attacking football, wish that he had chosen to bore the pants off the nation in the final part of the game.

On this pivotal Wednesday night Newcastle had travelled to Liverpool for a rearranged game. They had led the League table for most of the season but had lost to Manchester United at home in early March and to Arsenal at Highbury at the end of that month. After this game at Anfield they would also lose to Blackburn Rovers and draw a couple of games at the end of the season. It is, therefore, unfair to blame the loss of the Premier League entirely on this game against Liverpool, a team who for the last few seasons were all too aware that they were losing out to their Lancashire rivals, Manchester United.

Manchester United were now turning on the heat in a big way. Since their defeat at Tottenham Hotspur on New Year's Day they had won every League game apart from two draws, and words like 'relentless' and 'juggernaut' were being used. Alex Ferguson was not slow to win every psychological battle, clearly needling Keegan on several occasions. A major (though unspoken) niggle between the two was Andy Cole, the man whom Keegan had inexplicably allowed to go to Manchester United in January 1995 and who was now teaming up with Eric Cantona to score the goals for the Red Devils.

The success of Manchester United did not need to have had any great effect on Newcastle, but football being the game that it is, it was played as much in the minds of players and managers as it is on the field of play, Newcastle began to show signs of cracking under the pressure, with the perception beginning to grow that they could not cope with playing the big teams. There was also the phenomenon that a team unused to success finds it difficult, at the death, to believe in themselves and feels that there is some unwritten law somewhere that one must, sooner or later, fall by the wayside.

This dynamic, so prevalent in Scotland, where a team challenges the Old Firm for about three-quarters of the season and then 'blows up', had been broken spectacularly in England during the previous year by Blackburn Rovers (although, goodness knows, they very nearly didn't do it) and it was hoped that this would be the start of a trend. It was really up to Newcastle to carry it on, and the game at Anfield, as we have shown, was possibly more important for the effect that it would have on the rest of the season. It would not, in itself, win or lose the League.

Newcastle were now three points behind Manchester United but had two games in hand, the game at Anfield being one of them. They had actually done well against Liverpool this season, having beaten them at St James' Park in the League and having also beaten them at Anfield in the League Cup in one of their rare successes in that tournament. On form and given that they had done well against them this year, one would have expected Newcastle to win.

Two men on the Newcastle team bus that night were returning to the scene of their former glories. One was Kevin Keegan, who had starred for Liverpool in the 1970s, and the other was Peter Beardsley, who had begun his career with Newcastle, had gone to Liverpool to the distress of his admirers, but now, after a spell with Everton, was back with his first love and playing as well as at any time in his career. He would have loved to win something for Newcastle to add to what he had done for Liverpool.

Newcastle started off playing towards the Kop End of the ground and by half-time had had the pleasurable experience of silencing the opposition twice. But it was Liverpool who had scored first with a fine goal, with Fowler heading downwards a cross from the left from Collymore and beating **Srnicek** by the bounce of the ball as much as anything else. However, Les Ferdinand, after some nice interchanging movement involving himself and Asprilla on the right and a neat turn, levelled the score. That was good, but the goal scored by David Ginola was a lot better as he picked up a good pass from Ferdinand halfway inside the Liverpool half, ran in with a tremendous amount of pace and composure, and scored.

That, incredibly, all happened inside the first quarter of an hour. One might be tempted to think that the game settled down after that, but that was emphatically not the case as play swung to and fro, keeping the 40,702 on tenterhooks and demanding the attention of everyone watching the game on TV in pubs up and down the country, even those who were not really football fans and were 'only there for the beer'. There are times when football simply takes over.

Chances were made at both ends but the teams, playing at full pace, were unable to add any more goals in the first half. The Sky commentators, normally seldom short of words, said things like 'Wow'.

Liverpool came back into the game with an exceptionally well-taken goal. Ten minutes of the second half had elapsed when the ever-dangerous McManaman found himself with the ball on the right and saw Fowler charging in. He crossed, the ball was not cut out and Fowler hammered home from the edge of the penalty box to level the score, then dived into the net to delight his fans in the Kop.

Within minutes, however, Newcastle were back in front and this one owed a great deal to the sheer brain power of Tino Asprilla. A fine pass from Rob Lee found the Colombian halfway inside the Liverpool half, and while most players might have run on and blasted the ball straight at the goalkeeper or over the bar, Asprilla had the brain to place the ball cunningly past David James and to send the Toon Army into overdrive with his trademark celebration.

It was at this point that Newcastle might well have decided to shut up shop. Certainly Liverpool themselves, one feels in such circumstances, would have done just that. They would have brought men back, passed the ball round to each other, slowed the game down, frustrated the opposition and generally killed the game. Such play does win European Cups, but Newcastle, perhaps because they did not have the players for this sort of game, or perhaps because they were simply enjoying the attacking game and felt they could score even more, singularly failed to do so. Neutrals applauded their determination to continue entertaining; Newcastle supporters, in retrospect and with the considerable advantage of hindsight, condemned the team for their naïvety.

Certainly the word 'naïve' would have to be used about the defending of the equalising goal. McAteer's ball into the penalty box did not in itself look all that dangerous because there were Newcastle defenders around. A more determined and confident effort from Srnicek would have grabbed the ball, or someone could have shouted 'mine', got to the ball and booted it clear. As it was, Collymore was allowed to steer the ball home from close range.

If that was bad, there was worse to come at the very death. A draw would have lost ground but would have left Newcastle still with a psychological advantage, having earned a point at the home of one of their most dangerous rivals. Even now, a concentration on defence might have paid dividends. As it was, fans now had a collectors' item in the long and lamentable catalogue of Geordie horror stories.

The ball was bobbing about the edge of the penalty area with McManaman and Fowler involved. Five Newcastle defenders converged on them, but the ball was slipped to Collymore, now unmarked and charging in on the ball, which he hammered home from a tight angle. No wonder that the Toon Army at the far end were stunned into silence and that Kevin Keegan, in what was an almost iconic moment of frustrated despair, sank in chagrin over the advertising hoarding, looking as if he had indulged in too much of the beverage that the hoarding advertised. Perhaps he wished he had, but no amount of anaesthetic would ever take away the pain of that night.

The supporters' buses going home that night knew that the game was up. The major credibility barrier had not been breached. The idea that Newcastle were not meant to win football trophies had taken an even firmer root. Kevin Keegan would have loved to have been the man who would kill that nonsense. Unfortunately it was not to be. And yes, the Geordies would have loved to have seen their team putting up the shutters, boring everyone, keeping it tight at the back and copying the Liverpool teams of old.

38

Date: 20 October 1996

MANCHESTER UNITED

Match: Premiership

Venue: St James' Park

Score: 5–0

Attendance: 36,579

Newcastle United:	Manchester United:
Srnicek	Schmeichel
Watson**	Neville
Beresford	Irwin
Peacock	May
Albert	Pallister
Batty	Beckham
Lee*	Butt
Beardsley	Cantona
Ginola	Poborsky***
Ferdinand	Johnsen*
Shearer	Solskjaer**
Clark*	Cruyff*
Barton**	McClair***
	Scholes**

Referee: S. Dunn, Bristol

The year 1996 brings back painful memories to Geordie fans, but it had its good moments too. There was no finer game than this one, played in front of Sky TV cameras and showing the world, including Newcastle fans in many nations, just how good they could be under the managership of Kevin Keegan.

The Premiership had been lost in bitter circumstances in the previous spring. Historians will point to the high-scoring game at Liverpool as the point at which the League was lost. This is true only up to a point, because that game could well have gone the other way. A more likely game to beat oneself up about was the game at Highbury some 10 days previously, when the traditional Geordie self-destruct button was pressed. It could be called a lack of self-belief, a feeling, based on decades of heartbreak, that the team are not allowed to beat the likes of Arsenal, especially in London. It was Keegan's task to rid the club and its supporters of this inferiority complex.

In autumn 1996 Keegan seemed to be doing just that. There had been a stutter or two at the start of the campaign, but the 2–1 win over Sunderland at Roker Park in early September had been the first of six wins in a row before this game, and the team were going well in Europe and even in the bogey tournament, the League Cup. This was beginning to look to the Magpies as if it were the start of something big and that the trophy famine was about to end.

There was much to be happy about, notably in the form of home-grown boys Peter Beardsley and Alan Shearer. Beardsley was in his second incarnation with the club, and how everyone regretted that he had been allowed to go in the first place. Alan Shearer, after winning the Premier League Championship with Blackburn Rovers in 1995, had now, in the immediate aftermath of England's exit from the Euro '96 competition, come back to play for the club that he always loved. With Les Ferdinand and David Ginola also on song, and with a steady reliable defence for the first time for a while, it seemed that few teams could live with Newcastle, and how agreeable it was to hear when one switched on a radio or TV sports programme that Newcastle were being talked about first. They were a breath of fresh air in the English scene. No longer were Newcastle the poor team with the big support. They were back and they meant business.

Today, however, they were up against Manchester United. If Newcastle were the team that didn't know how to win silverware, Manchester were the side that hardly knew how to lose. They had won three of the last four Premiership titles. They had that almost uncanny ability to be there at the end and to slip in when the opportunity presented itself. That had been exactly what happened in the year before when Newcastle blew up, and Manchester United had celebrated by winning the FA Cup as well.

They had not always been so successful, however. Before Alex Ferguson came in 1986 they had tended to be a very poor second to Liverpool (and often not even second), and even after his arrival things took a long time to come together with Ferguson, allegedly, being fairly close to the exit door on more than one occasion. But gradually things came together for the Red Devils, and by the mid-1990s they were the dominant team in England, although not yet in Europe. They radiated power and wealth and expected to win football games. They were an example that Newcastle would have done well to copy.

It would be fair to say that controversy and Eric Cantona were never very far away. He had just returned from a lengthy suspension from the game following an incident at Crystal Palace in which he kicked a fan – kung fu style – after he had been sent off, and on this particular day at St James' Park it was the opinion of several commentators and journalists that he might well have had a red card on one or two occasions. There was also a rather undignified squabble (a 'cat fight' someone unkindly named it) between David Batty and Nicky Butt, but fortunately these unsavoury incidents were forgotten in the tidal wave of praise and glory that came Newcastle's way.

The first goal came within the first quarter of an hour. It was a scrappy, dubious sort of goal following a David Ginola corner. Shearer won the header and knocked the ball on to Darren Peacock, who slightly mis-headed the ball over the line from close range before Denis Irwin hooked clear. It was the linesman who gave the goal and the referee took his word for it, although Manchester United and Irwin in particular threw prolonged tantrums about it. TV evidence proved conclusively that the ball was well over the line, but Manchester United's sense of being ill done by was emphatic.

This first goal may have unsettled them for the rest of the game. On the half-hour mark Newcastle went further ahead, and this time there was no possible doubt about it. It came from David Ginola, a man who had taken time to be accepted and loved by the Geordie faithful. A notorious diver inside the penalty box (and some of his efforts were far from convincing) and a man who often gave the impression of lacking a little of the heart that men like Shearer and Ferdinand certainly possessed, he comprehensively silenced his doubters that day. He picked up a good pass from the hard-working John Beresford on the left, cut inside to beat Gary Neville and hammered home with his right and weaker foot. All this was done so quickly that there was a delayed reaction before St James' Park exploded into noise and applause for such a brilliant piece of work.

The first half finished with Newcastle well on top and the game just beginning to simmer under the surface. It had been a tough, full-blooded encounter with one or two players on either side skating on thin ice as far as referee Steve Dunn was concerned. Newcastle fans were happy but there was an anxiety about them too. It would not be the first time that Manchester United had mounted a late comeback, and it certainly would not be the first time that Newcastle United had thrown away a winning position.

Keegan's half-time talk was simple — keep doing what you are doing. He knew that he had the players to win the game. The only problem would be in the mind. The team had to convince themselves that there was no divine law that said Manchester United had to win. Alex Ferguson, on the other hand, would have had one of his 'hairdryer' half-time talks, with everyone being shouted at and told to buck up their ideas, and try a little harder, although the language might have been more graphic than that!

In the second half Newcastle continued to dominate, with the midfield of Albert and Beardsley causing all sorts of problems, particularly Beardsley with his ability to run on and off the ball. The ball was knocked about with bewildering speed and accuracy in a way that had not been seen at St James' Park for many a long day. The third goal came on the hour mark, not long after Jordi Cruyff, son of the legendary Johan, had been brought on for Manchester United. It was a stunning goal, the sort that this generation of Newcastle supporters had become tired of hearing about in that it could have been a Jackie Milburn goal.

It was Shearer who made the goal. He beat Denis Irwin on the right and centred a high ball, which Les Ferdinand rose high to head home. It was perfect simplicity and St James' Park rightly erupted at such brilliance. It was hard now to see Manchester United coming back. They too, like the spectators and the TV viewers, were stunned at such a goal. And how nice it was to see a goal coming from Les Ferdinand. It had only been a decade previously that Newcastle fans had been taken to task by their then-manager, Jack Charlton, for hurling racist abuse. Now Les was one of the many black men proud to be a member of the Geordie team and equally proudly accepted by the fans.

The rout continued. The fourth goal, scored in the 74th minute of the game, was what might be called a 'ping-ball' or a 'rat-a-tat' goal, as first Beardsley drove for the net and was blocked by the hard-working Schmeichel. Then Ferdinand had a go and Schmeichel parried again before Alan Shearer eventually did the needful and scored.

Ferguson's squad were now beaten and they knew it. Men like Beckham, Scholes and Cantona were running about like headless chickens and were roundly abused and jeered at by the Geordie crowd, who have always hated poseurs, while their own travelling fans lapsed into brooding introverted silence. A fifth goal came near the end with a delightful chip from the Belgian wizard, Phillipe Albert. Not even fellow Belgian Hercule Poirot could have imagined what he was going to do as he seemed to be lining himself up for a blockbuster drive against Schmeichel. Instead, he lobbed it gently over his head and into the net.

Alex Ferguson was probably glad to hear the final whistle to save his demoralised side from further agony. For the Geordies it was an unbelievably good day and one that they would remember for a very long time. Nine days later they would be in similar ecstasy after they dumped Ferencvaros out of Europe with a similarly exhilarating display, and little seemed wrong with the world.

But this was Newcastle. Before they met Ferencvaros they appalled their travelling support by going down to Leicester City, and the rot soon set in. There would be one or two other great performances that season, but it would be the runners'-up spot yet again. And the champions? Manchester United.

39

BARCELONA

Match: European Champions League **Venue: St James' Park**

Score: 3–2 **Attendance: 35,274**

Newcastle United:	Barcelona:
Given	Hesp
Watson	Reiziger
Beresford	Celades
Batty	Nadal
Albert	Sergi
Barton	De La Pena
Lee	Figo
Gillespie	Luis Enrique
Asprilla	Rivaldo
Barnes**	Amunike*
Tomasson*	Anderson**
Peacock*	Ciric*
Ketsbaia**	Dugarry**

Referee: P. Collina, Italy

Season 1992–93 is a famous one in the history of Newcastle United. It was the year that the team returned to the top tier of English football. No less significant, however, was that it was the year that Channel Four, showing imagination and enterprise rare among the rather stodgy and predictable broadcasters of the time, decided on Sunday afternoons to show Italian football from Serie A.

This could not be anything other than a boon to the game, for fine players were on view every Sunday, with one of the better one being a young Colombian who played for Parma called Faustino Asprilla. He was a marvellous passer of the ball and goal scorer with a trademark backflip after he scored. It became so famous that it might have earned a place in the *Don't Try This At Home* TV show. Some did, but few were athletic enough to succeed.

Newcastle had paid a colossal £6.7 million pounds for 'Tino' in July 1995, and the years between 1995 and 1997 had been good ones for both Newcastle and Asprilla. This statement needs to be qualified, though, as Newcastle still had not won a trophy and Asprilla's form had been inconsistent, sometimes electrifying the Newcastle crowd but at other times looking anonymous and uninterested. It would be a fair statement to say that many supporters did not feel that they had as yet had their money's worth.

Newcastle's first crack at the group section of the Champions League was to be 17 September 1997. They had seen off Croatia's Dinamo Zagreb in thrilling style in a qualifying round in August and were now in a group that contained Dynamo Kiev, PSV Eindhoven and the mighty Barcelona. It would be Barcelona who would kick off the group at St James' Park.

Barcelona needed no introduction to anyone. Everyone was so familiar with them and their ground, the Camp Nou, and how they were the representatives of the province in the north-east of Spain called Catalonia. There were similarities between Barcelona and Newcastle in that both teams represented a large area and were a social institution rather than just a football club. There was a great deal more than that to Barcelona, though, whose rivalry with Real Madrid was legendary and involved issues like the Civil War of 1936–39, the alleged love of the late dictator Francisco Franco (a genuine football fan) for the other team, and the ability to speak in the Catalan language within the Camp Nou ground without fear of persecution by the odious Guardia Civil. These issues all belonged to a bygone age but they would not go away, in the same way as there are still absurd elements of religion and politics on view at Celtic versus Rangers games in Scotland.

In playing terms over the years, Barcelona had done surprisingly badly in the European Cup. Incredibly, they had twice gone out of Europe, in 1966 and 1987, to Dundee United, a club whose turnover was minute compared to the Spanish giants. They had won the European Cup only once, at Wembley in 1992, and even then needed extra-time to beat the luckless Sampdoria. Two years later they had been in the 1994 Final but had collapsed badly to an AC Milan team that had won 4–0 in one of the more one-sided European Cup Finals. They also trailed Real Madrid in the number of La Liga victories, but they always had a strong side and they would win La Liga this year. There was an aura about them, and very few Geordies would have expected their side to beat them.

In the Newcastle camp the big talking point was the injury picked up by Alan Shearer in a pre-season friendly at Everton from which he showed few signs of recovery, but at the start of manager Kenny Dalglish's first full season in charge things looked promising. As it happened the first three games had been home ones, and Sheffield Wednesday and Aston Villa had been well disposed of, but the previous Saturday's game against Wimbledon had been a disappointing 3–1 defeat. It was early days in the League so far, but it would be a real boost if they could get the better of the mighty Barca side.

There could be little doubt that Tyneside was now a different world from a few years ago. One recalled, for example, a game against Portsmouth close to the end of the season in 1992 when a late David Kelly goal had been necessary to take the team away from the fear of relegation to the third tier, and when teams like Grimsby and Port Vale were regular visitors. Now, at last, the club seemed to be going somewhere under the leadership of Sir John Hall. He would very soon take a step back from his high-profile role, but his contribution had been immense. Opinions varied about Sir John. Some thought of him as a chancer or a maverick, others were more positive. What could not be doubted was that he had given a moribund club a shot in the arm to such an extent that they were now playing in the European Cup against Barcelona. That would have been unthinkable 10 years earlier.

As much of an attraction as anything else that autumn night was the referee, the famous Italian Pierluigi Collina, generally reckoned to be one of the best around. A man who ate, drank and slept football, trained hard and whose preparations for any game included reading about the teams, their background, their players and other things, he was an imposing figure on the field. He was a huge man with a bald head, bulging eyes and protruding veins when he became angry. He stood no nonsense. He clearly enjoyed his job, refereeing the game with joy in his step, and although he was not always right, very few people disputed his decisions.

Newcastle started off playing towards the Gallowgate End of the ground, and it was a bright start with the Catalans perhaps a little intimidated by the closeness of the crowd and the fervent atmosphere. A few hefty challenges went in from both sides in the first few minutes, but it was obvious that referee Collina was going to have none of it. He was the man in charge.

It was Collina who made the decision to award a penalty in the 20th minute of the game following a collision between Asprilla and goalkeeper Hesp. This was after some fine football from the Newcastle forwards, with John Barnes and Jon Dahl Tomasson being particularly prominent. It was Tomasson who sent Asprilla away with the ball. Hesp came out to dive at his feet and sent Asprilla tumbling. The Catalans thought that this was a dive (and on looking at the video of the game, it would appear that they had a point), but the important person, Signor Collina, was otherwise minded and a penalty was given. Asprilla took the kick himself and scored, although Hesp did well to get a hand to it.

The second goal, on the half-hour mark, was made by Northern Ireland right-winger Keith Gillespie. Gillespie's career had stalled at Manchester United after a bright start and since moving to Newcastle he had yet to win over all his doubters, but tonight he was on song as he raced past his marker on the Milburn Stand side of the field and delivered a perfect cross for the spring-heeled Asprilla to jump high and head home. It was a glorious goal, reminiscent almost of a bygone age when wingers like Bobby Mitchell crossed for centre-forwards like Jackie Milburn to score. Little wonder that the ground was still in a turmoil of noise and appreciation as the teams went off for half-time, with Newcastle amazing all Europe by leading the great Barcelona 2–0.

Incredibly, the same thing happened again at the start of the second half. Barcelona had started the brighter side and had brought out a good save from Given, but with Newcastle now playing towards the Leazes End Gillespie picked up a ball from Robert Lee from well within his own half, made space on the right and crossed for Asprilla to score another. He seemed to be in mid-air, awaiting the cross. It was a brilliant piece of timing and execution. Asprilla, now clearly the darling of the crowd and revelling in the occasion, might even have scored again if he had had better luck with yet another header from a Gillespie feed, which Hesp saved well.

But then complacency, the age-old enemy of Newcastle and most football clubs, set in. When 3–0 up against most teams, one can afford to relax and take the foot off the pedal. But this was Barcelona. Players like Rivaldo, Luis Enrique and Figo can often appear to be out of the game but then suddenly, being the world-class players that they are, they can come back and in an instant change the picture.

At 74 minutes, Figo took advantage of some tired Newcastle defending and crossed for Luis Enrique to bundle the ball in. That gave the visiting supporters something to cheer about and, more importantly, gave their team some momentum as anxiety began to creep into the songs of triumph which had been reverberating around the stadium from the Geordie support. Newcastle were now very much on the back foot as the hitherto unemployed Shay Given had to pull off a fine save, and a free-kick conceded by a panicky Newcastle defence hit the bar.

Newcastle seemed to have weathered the storm, however, until, only a couple of minutes from time, Given didn't quite gather a cross properly. The ball was inadequately cleared and Figo fired home from the edge of the box. The last few minutes of the game were tense, but Newcastle were able to deploy their players to hold on to the ball and run the clock down before Signor Collina released a collective sigh of relief all around the ground and the city by blowing for full-time.

Newcastle, sadly, would not qualify from their group, collapsing miserably to PSV Eindhoven both home and away, and Barcelona did indeed get their revenge at the Camp Nou. But this game must remain one of the best games of Newcastle's recent past, and it did allow Geordies to walk tall for at least some limited time – their team had beaten the mighty Barcelona. An amusing postscript was added when it was revealed that hat-trick hero, the charismatic Tino Asprilla, almost missed the game because he was late back from international duty with Colombia. Manager Kenny Dalglish changed his mind after deciding to drop him – just as well!

40

ARSENAL

Match: FA Cup Final   **Venue: Wembley**

Score: 0–2   **Attendance: 79,183**

Newcastle United:	Arsenal:
Given	Seaman
Pistone	Dixon
Pearce*	Winterburn
Batty	Vieira
Dabizas	Keown
Howey	Adams
Lee	Parlour
Barton**	Anelka
Shearer	Petit
Ketsbaia***	Wreh*
Speed	Overmars
Andersson*	Platt*
Watson**	
Barnes***	

Referee: P. Durkin, Portland

The Geordies who cheerfully embarked on their trains, planes and coaches to take them to Wembley on Saturday 16 May 1998 were confident. This could be the end of the trophy famine, a state of affairs which had now lasted more than a lifetime for a great deal of them, maybe even more than half of the travelling Toon Army. 1955 had been the last FA Cup win and 1969 the last lifting of anything that could be described as first rate. The previous two years had seen the Magpies coming as close as they were ever likely to in the League Championship – lost in distressing, heart-rending circumstances – but this was now the FA Cup.

All that stood in their way now was Arsenal, already winners of the Premier League and a really great team under new manager Arsene Wenger with a great deal of emphasis on playing good football with, in particular, loads of pace. Rational analysis of the two teams would really have to favour Arsenal, who had Tony Adams, Patrick Vieira, Marc Overmars, Emmanuel Petit and many others in their side. Newcastle, on the other hand, did not lack good players and they had Alan Shearer, a home-town boy who had now returned from his travels with Blackburn Rovers.

He had been an outstanding success and had won the Premier League with Blackburn in 1995. Shearer would do anything to replicate his success with his beloved Newcastle United.

The bookies quite clearly favoured Arsenal, but neutral support would side with Newcastle. True, the Toon Army did not always do the side any favours with their inane chants about other players and their sad ability to turn on their own players when things were not going well, but general opinion in England was that the Geordies had now suffered long enough and that it was time to win something. Perhaps it was a day for long-suffering fans to be relieved of their pain. Across the border that day, in an almost exactly parallel situation, Hearts, whose tale of woe had gone back almost as far as that of Newcastle, were in the Scottish Cup Final against Rangers. Their fans too had suffered terribly. It would be nice if they could both do it.

Newcastle had not had a particularly impressive season. The Champions League had been a failure after a bright start. In the League Cup, they had, unusually, reached the New Year still involved and indeed in early January in the quarter-final had held Liverpool to a goalless draw for 90 minutes before collapsing woefully in extra-time. League form under Kenny Dalglish was dreadful after a bright start and the odd good performance, and they had ended up a piteous 13th, with the midwinter time being particularly bad. The sudden and unexpected loss of Faustino Asprilla in January back to Parma for £7 million was by no means the first or the last of the bizarre transfers in and out of St James' Park, but it was a blow which hit the fans hard.

The FA Cup campaign had given the fans quite a few heartaches as well. It had started with a good and competent victory over Everton at Goodison Park, but then they encountered difficulty at Stevenage Borough of the Vauxhall Conference and needed a replay at St James' Park to win through. Even then there was a tight finish. Newcastle were 2–0 up, then lost a goal and had to defend desperately while their fans suffered the horrors of hell. Next, Tranmere put up a great fight to lose 1–0, but Newcastle then got the better of Barnsley (a Premiership side in 1997–98 who had beaten Manchester United in the previous round) 3–1 to put them in the semi-final to play Sheffield United at Old Trafford.

Old Trafford housed a crowd of 53,452 and provided an image that will stay in the memory a long time. It was not in truth a great game – semi-finals seldom are, because there is too much at stake – but Alan Shearer scored for Newcastle on the hour mark. That did not seem enough to ensure a Wembley trip as the Blades piled on the pressure in the second half and threw everything at Shay Given's goal in the last few minutes. Sheffield United were also a team with a proud FA Cup history, but they had been breaking the hearts of their supporters for even longer. They had last won the Cup in 1925 and had not seen Wembley since 1936.

Television picked up a few spectators of both sides tearing their hair out and urging on their team and then they honed in on an elderly Newcastle supporter, all decked in his black and white colours. He was too old to be jumping about, but anxiety was clearly lined on his face. He looked about 80 and thus was definitely old enough to remember the Jackie Milburn years. He would have been a young man in 1932, when Newcastle won the Cup, and might even in his early days have recalled Hughie Gallacher. He would also have been a man who would have borne a disproportionate share of hardship and sorrow. When the full-time whistle went, he turned to a younger man (his son presumably) and smiled. His beloved team were once again at Wembley, a stadium they had not graced for a Cup Final for well over 20 years.

By the time that the Cup Final was played, Newcastle's League season had finished anonymously, the impression being given that nobody particularly cared whether they won or not. There had been one very good win over Chelsea giving the Geordie crowd grounds for optimism, but Arsenal were deserved League Champions. Those journalists who favoured Newcastle were careful to temper their optimism with phrases like 'on their day' and 'if Shearer turns up trumps'.

Indeed the parallels with 1974 were quite striking. On paper, Newcastle had little chance against a technically superior team, but they did have a charismatic goalscorer. Macdonald had spectacularly failed to deliver in 1974. Would Shearer manage to produce the goods this year? There was also the previous year's FA Cup Final to consider. Last year a north-east team also played a London team when near neighbours Middlesbrough took on Chelsea. Sadly Boro lost a goal within the first minute, then never recovered. Newcastle would have to watch the dangers of freezing on the day.

Sadly this was exactly what happened. Arsenal, unlike Chelsea the previous year, did not actually score in the first minute, but within five minutes of the start of the game they had threatened the Newcastle goal on two occasions, highlighting the weaknesses of the Newcastle team, weaknesses that had been apparent to the Toon Army for some time but had been hidden under the huge tarpaulins called self-deception and euphoric hysteria, as everyone told each other that they would come good when they had to.

Newspaper reports were particularly hard on men like Speed, Pistone, Howey and Ketsbaia, but the truth was that the whole team performed dysfunctionally, psyched out apparently by the seeming invincibility of Arsenal. It was as if they all believed the southern newspapers' tales of how good the Gunners were. The truth is that no team is invincible and every team can be beaten on the day. It requires dedication, hard work, commitment and self-belief, though. All these qualities manager Kenny Dalglish singularly failed to instill.

It was the acceptance of fate and the inability to fight back which distressed the Toon Army that day. They shouted and sang and generally enjoyed their day out in London on a very warm and pleasant day, but the buses and trains were silent, sombre places that Saturday night. Back home the city centre was a silent place that afternoon as everyone watched the TV and it stayed silent at night as well. Many of the TV watchers, knowing that Newcastle simply did not have it in them to fight back, had switched channels by the last quarter of an hour to watch the rather more exciting Scottish Cup Final in which Hearts beat off a late revival from Rangers.

The goals were simple. Halfway through the first half, the ponytailed Emmanuel Petit released the speedy Marc Overmars, who simply ignored the half-hearted challenge from Pistone and ran on to beat Shay Given. 'That goal has been coming for a while' said the commentators, and the Toon Army knew it. It was a wonder that it was only 1–0 at half-time, and it was at a similar stage of the second half when Arsenal killed off what little chance there was of a Geordie revival.

Shearer had hit the post and Dabizas had headed against the bar. Had either of them gone in things might just have been different, but one always had the impression that the Gunners could score whenever they wanted to. For the second goal, it was Nicolas Anelka who was released by Parlour to run through a non-existent Newcastle defence and score the goal that gave Arsenal the FA Cup for the seventh time.

It might have been different. Mention has been made of the times that Newcastle came close. Arsenal's second goal might have been offside. Gary Speed also shot past the post. Had these things turned out the other way, Newcastle might have won. But this cannot be allowed to disguise the fact that Arsenal were by far the better team and that they could have upped a gear at any time. Shearer disappointed and earned himself a booking with a reckless and needless first-half tackle on England colleague Tony Adams. Newcastle had a few other players who in no way enhanced their reputations that day.

It was a pity that this Final had not taken place a couple of years earlier when Newcastle, under Kevin Keegan, were far better and Arsenal had not yet evolved to be the mighty force that they were in 1998. For the massive Geordie fan base throughout the world it was a major source of sadness, not that they were defeated, but that they were so comprehensively outclassed. But it was good to be back at Wembley again. That at least was a step forward.

41

Date: 22 May 1999

MANCHESTER UNITED

Match: FA Cup Final   **Venue: Wembley**

Score: 0–2   **Attendance: 79,101**

Newcastle United:	Manchester United:
Harper	Schmeichel
Griffin	G. Neville
Domi	P. Neville
Dabizas	May
Charvet	Keane*
Solano*	Johnsen
Lee	Beckham
Hamann**	Scholes**
Shearer	Cole***
Ketsbaia***	Solskjaer
Speed	Giggs
Maric*	Sheringham*
Ferguson**	Stam**
Glass***	Yorke***

Referee: P. Jones, Loughborough

It would be safe to say that unless you are a devotee of Manchester United, you tend not to like them. There are reasons for this in that Manchester United are phenomenally rich and phenomenally successful. Feelings towards Manchester United tend to be coloured by jealousy. Yet they were not always so successful. Their history has included a year in the Second Division in the 1970s and a long painful time in the 1980s when they seemed forever to be doomed to be second best to Liverpool. They also, for a while at that time (and it was no coincidence), seemed to be cursed with a dreadful support who regularly ransacked towns they visited in a way reminiscent of the hordes of Attila the Hun.

Against that they have had two great managers in Matt Busby and Alex Ferguson who have lifted them to great heights. They have had many great players like Billy Meredith, Jimmy Delaney, Johnny Carey, Bobby Charlton, Denis Law and George Best, and they are a team that is seldom far from the headlines in world football. They survived the dreadful Munich air disaster in 1958 to become the first English team to lift the European Cup 10 years later. 1999, however, was destined to be their greatest season of them all.

It was the fortune of that other United to face this mighty team in the 1999 FA Cup Final. Comparisons between the two sides highlighted the stark contrast between what wise stewardship and management of a club can do. Both start from the same sort of base. Manchester United had had their low points as well but had bounced back. Newcastle United, for most of the latter part of the 20th century, had been sunk in the mire, victims of short-sighted organisation and feckless management. It was plainly obvious to every Magpie that Newcastle United could have been, indeed should have been, what Manchester United were. Both came from a large industrial city with a huge latent support, and in Newcastle's case there was not even the rivalry of a Manchester City. But this situation could be changed – Kevin Keegan had almost done it a year or two ago, Kenny Dalglish had reached the FA Cup Final of 1998 – and the Final of 1999 provided another opportunity.

Newcastle's form in season 1998–99 under manager Ruud Gullit, who had taken over from Dalglish the previous year, had been see-sawing in the League, ranging from the brilliant to the mediocre to the downright dreadful in a way that supporters found hard to comprehend, but there had been some fine performances in the FA Cup. Avoiding a potential slip-up at Crystal Palace, that bogey team and bogey ground of 90 years ago, in the third round, they then dealt adequately with Bradford City and needed a replay to get the better of Blackburn Rovers before turning on a sparkling display against Everton in the quarter-final, which impressed commentators and began to nurture the impression that 1999 might at last be the year for Newcastle United.

The semi-finals paired Newcastle with Tottenham Hotspur, another team who were finding it hard to live up to the expectations of their supporters. The game was played at Old Trafford on Sunday 11 April, and the vast TV audience saw a close-fought but none-too-brilliant 90 minutes. Semi-finals rarely are great games, but this one came alive for the Geordie nation in extra-time when Sol Campbell unnecessarily handled in the penalty box and Alan Shearer scored from the spot. It was Shearer again who scored the clincher as time was running out, and what a strike it was. He picked up a pass from Silvio Maric and hammered the ball first time from outside the penalty area straight into the net. It was the trademark goal of a great striker.

Newcastle were now back at Wembley. They had been there the year before when they had notoriously frozen on the day against Arsenal. It would not be Arsenal this year, however, because they had lost out to Manchester United in their replayed semi-final, and so 22 May was to be a battle of the two Uniteds. Could this be the year in which Alan Shearer would do it? Could he do a Jackie Milburn and win the trophy for his adoring fans? Or would he end up like Supermac in 1974 and repeat his performance of the previous year, in which he was unable to produce the goods on the big occasion?

A lot depended on manager Ruud Gullit. He had been a brilliant player in his time, but question marks were often raised about his man-management skills. Those who watched the team every week often questioned his sometimes erratic and unpredictable team selection, and there did seem to be a problem in his attitude to certain players, notably Alan Shearer. There was nothing new about this on Tyneside, where fallings out – sometimes spectacular ones – had been the trademark of the club for many decades. It would all be different if only they could win something. Personality clashes could then be forgiven and forgotten.

There was something that could come back and haunt Newcastle that day, and that was Andy Cole. Cole had been a great striker with Newcastle in 1993–94 with 41 goals, something that even beat the record of Hughie Gallacher in 1927. Press headlines about 'Coles for Goals!' and 'Coles to Newcastle' became a cliché. But then suddenly, and for no apparent reason, at a time when Newcastle were going well in the Premiership, Kevin Keegan transferred him to rivals Manchester United. This happened in early January 1995, and even in the long and lamentable history of Newcastle United, was there ever such a crazy decision?

The truth behind this preposterous transfer will probably never be known, but it was certain that Newcastle paid in full for it, failing to land the Premiership in the most painful of circumstances in 1996 and 1997, and even this year, when Manchester United came to St James' Park in March, having the mortification of watching Cole score twice for his new employers. Was this going to happen at Wembley?

Two weeks before Wembley, Manchester United had clinched their fifth Premier League in seven seasons. It had been close enough this season but there was little doubt about which was the best team in England at this time. They also had a very important date with Bayern Munich in the Final of the European Champions League in Barcelona on the Wednesday immediately after the FA Cup Final and they were on course for what would have been a unique treble. Newcastle, on the other hand, had finished 13th in the Premiership, well clear of any relegation problems but behind teams like Middlesbrough, Leicester City and Derby County, whom they would have expected to beat. Form clearly favoured Manchester United, but Newcastle did not lack their ever-optimistic and ever-forgiving support, who filled their half of Wembley and outshouted their Manchester counterparts.

Unfortunately, that was all that Newcastle won that day. Those who feared that their team might freeze on the day, as they had against Arsenal the year before, would have their fears confirmed. Newcastle started brightly enough but the first incident of note was an injury to Roy Keane following a clash with Gary Speed. Keane, complaining bitterly, had to go off and was replaced, surprisingly, by Teddy Sheringham as Ferguson rearranged his whole team. Sheringham had barely found his bearings when he scored. It was a lovely, sweeping move involving Cole and Scholes splitting open the Newcastle defence for Sheringham to race in and sweep the ball past Harper.

Little more then 10 minutes had passed and a substitute had scored for Manchester United! To use the phrase 'the heads went down' does not begin to cover the devastation felt at the Newcastle end and among the hundreds of thousands watching them in Newcastle itself and elsewhere among sympathisers throughout the world. The sinking feeling that the game was already lost began to take over.

Newcastle's midfield now failed to function with Nolberto Solano and Rob Lee fading badly after an early bright start. Temuri Ketsbaia gave the impression that he might just manage something for the team, and there was always Alan Shearer, but the Manchester United defence made sure that the ball seldom got near him. There were one or two half chances for Newcastle, but Manchester had more. Half-time was reached with Newcastle still in the game and with an outside chance, but quite clearly second best on the day.

Gullit then decided to take a desperate measure. He took off Dietmar Hamann, who was by no means the worst of Newcastle's players that day, and replaced him with Duncan Ferguson. This looked like the last cast of the die, and it was. Ferguson ('Drunken Duncan' he was unkindly called) had talent but was unreliable, had a criminal record and had seldom convinced Geordie supporters (or those of any other team that he played for in either Scotland or England) that he was a winner. This move failed spectacularly, as it was always likely to.

Newcastle's fate was sealed in the 53rd minute when Paul Scholes scored. It came about after a basic error by Nikos Dabizas, which conceded possession to Solskjaer who then found Sheringham. Sheringham slipped the ball to Scholes, the job was done and the Geordie fans might as well have switched off their television sets and gone to watch a cricket match or taken the dog for a walk.

Once again, after the damage was done, there was a little rally but Manchester United, with the two Nevilles absolutely immense in defence, had things well under control. The full-time whistle came and Newcastle were once again shattered, the bridesmaid but not the bride. The scenes of devastation among the support can hardly have been enjoyed by any football fan, but the pain of losing has seldom been longer-lasting or as intense in any place other than Newcastle.

Manchester United were a great side and deserved the treble that they went on to win the following Wednesday, but gloom had once again descended on the Tyne.

Date: 19 September 1999

42

SHEFFIELD WEDNESDAY

Match: Premier League

Venue: St James' Park

Score: 8–0

Attendance: 36,618

Newcastle United:	Sheffield Wednesday:
Harper	Pressman
Barton	Newsome
Domi*	Nolan
Goma	Walker
Hughes	Emerson
Solano	Sonner
Speed	Rudi*
Lee	Donnelly**
Shearer	DeBilde
Ketsbaia**	Booth***
Dyer***	Alexandersson
Glass*	Haslam*
McClen**	Sibon**
Robinson***	Carbone***

Referee: N. Barry, Scunthorpe

Rarely had Newcastle started a season as badly as they did in 1999. Still reeling from the psychological blow of losing the FA Cup Final of the previous May (and the year before as well) with the knowledge that they had frozen on the day, it was hard to motivate the players or the supporters. Six games had been lost in the League with only a draw against Wimbledon to show for their efforts.

It was hardly surprising that manager Ruud Gullit had quit towards the end of August claiming, improbably, that he was fed up with the permanent scrutiny of his private life. The truth was that he had not kept Alan Shearer on side and had thus alienated a great deal of the support and 'lost the dressing room' as the saying went. One can get away with doing crazy things like dropping the talisman if one keeps winning, but he was clearly failing to do this. Gullit's major mistake was keeping Shearer on the bench one rainy night when the team lost to Sunderland – always a difficult defeat for Magpies to take, but in this case, there was one fairly obvious scapegoat. Gullit, therefore, departed the scene on 28 August, doing very little to dispel the common perception that Newcastle was a graveyard for managers.

Shearer, for his part, was not entirely blameless in all this. He had now, for two years in a row, 'done a Macdonald' at Wembley in the FA Cup Final and failed to produce the goods when he was confidently expected to do so. He might also, some players and supporters felt, have done a little more to help Gullit instead of being perceived as the leader of the rebels. It is surely incumbent on senior players to take a little responsibility here. He found himself in September 1999 still very popular on Tyneside and in the country generally (he was playing well for England, having scored a hat-trick against admittedly poor opposition in Luxembourg on 4 September) but with a little still to prove to his devoted Newcastle admirers as he approached his 30th birthday.

As manager Newcastle made the perhaps surprising choice of Bobby Robson, a man who, everyone felt, had seen better days. He was 66, a year over the normal retiring age for the general population, and was surely wealthy enough not to need to work. He was a respected senior statesman of the game. But he was a Durham lad, loved Newcastle United, although he had never had the opportunity to play for them, and also loved football, which he had in his blood. The offer of the job of managing Newcastle United was just too much for him, and his appointment was greeted with much enthusiasm by the fans, even though one would have expected that they would by now have wearied of the clichés whenever a new manager was appointed. 'Taking Newcastle back to greatness', 'restoring some pride to a football mad area' and 'bringing back the glory days' were the usual yawn-inducing mantras and litanies that Geordies were fed almost, it appeared, on an annual basis. And was the word 'messiah' heard again?

Robson took up his post during the international break. His first game in charge was at Stamford Bridge, and Newcastle had cause to feel aggrieved at a narrow 1–0 defeat to Chelsea, whose goal came via the penalty spot. A better result came in midweek when the team went to CSKA Sofia in Bulgaria in the UEFA Cup and won 2–0. It meant that all eyes would be turned on St James' Park on the following Sunday for Robson's first home game in charge when Sheffield Wednesday came calling.

Sheffield Wednesday were old foes of Newcastle United. A team of tremendous pedigree in the old days, Wednesday had fallen a little from grace as Lancashire teams had gradually taken over from Yorkshire ones throughout the 20th century, but as recently as 1993 they had been involved in two heartbreaking Cup Finals against Arsenal, and in 1991 they had actually won the League Cup. They had a good ground and a great support, but their start to the 1999–2000 season had been exactly the same as that of Newcastle, with only one draw, against Bradford City, to their credit, and already there were strident calls from the less patient among their support for the head of Danny Wilson, the beleaguered manager. Things were about to get an awful lot worse for poor Danny and for Wednesday.

The ground was full, the atmosphere was upbeat, Bobby Robson was given the cheer that newly arrived managers usually get and the game was under way. It was immediately obvious that there was a new urgency to the team, with everyone trying to impress and do well for the new manager, who no doubt had said in the dressing room that he was starting with a clean sheet as far as players were concerned and that whatever had happened in the past stayed in the past.

Wednesday started well too, and might have gone ahead in the first 10 minutes when Andy Booth scored but was flagged for offside. This would be Sheffield Wednesday's only good moment of the day as Newcastle then took charge, 'knocking Wednesday into Thursday' in the words of a Gallowgate End comedian. Poor Andy Booth of Sheffield Wednesday was subsequently carried off after a clash of heads with Alain Goma, but that was of less concern for the Wednesday fans than what was happening on the pitch.

First of all Kieron Dyer crossed for Aaron Hughes to direct a header past goalkeeper Pressman, but then the Alan Shearer show really began. First a well-directed flick from a Nolberto Solano cross, then a conversion of a penalty after Emerson Thome handled in the area (more objective observers than the rabid Tynesiders might well have given Wednesday the benefit of the doubt because it appeared that the ball played the man rather than that the man played the ball), and then just before half-time Shearer was on the spot to score another predatory goal following some more good work from the excellent Dyer. Shearer had thus scored a hat-trick before half-time. He was making a habit of this – he had done likewise against Luxembourg for England, but this performance was far better as Sheffield Wednesday were at least full-time professionals, as distinct from the school teachers and bankers of part-time Luxembourg. It was his first hat-trick for two years for Newcastle, and how he and his fans were enjoying it!

The teams walked off at half-time to strains of *Walking In the Robson Wonderland*, and it was as if it were all a dream. There was almost the feeling that it was too good to be true and that sooner or later we would all wake up to mother telling us it was time to go to school. This could not be the same Newcastle team, could it, which had brought such sneering and ridicule on the city only a few weeks ago?

It was true, however, and the slaughter of the bewildered Sheffield men continued throughout the second half as another four goals were scored to the delight of the fans, the chagrin of the few Sheffield supporters, some of whom had attempted to escape at half-time, and the utter amazement of the radio and television commentators. Dyer scored from close range after some neat interchanging passes a minute or two after half-time, and then Newcastle seemed to take their foot off the pedal. Whether it was a genuine reluctance to further humiliate their fellow professionals, because they had temporarily run out of steam, or whether Wednesday were making a spirited attempt to bring some sanity to the proceedings did not matter to the now ecstatic Geordie faithful, who continued in their praises of Bobby Robson and wondered why he had not been brought to St James' Park before.

Within the last quarter of an hour the goals started again. Solano, one of the many players who was doing his cause no harm that day, took a corner kick which found the head of Gary Speed, who rose virtually unchallenged to head home. A few minutes after that, goalkeeper Pressman made a hash of a punch out and the ball came to Alan Shearer, who hammered home to make it 7–0 before, with time running out, Haslam brought down substitute Paul Robinson in the box. Shearer obliged from the spot to go 'nap', as the saying used to be for a man who scored five goals.

Mr Barry's whistle came as a relief to Sheffield Wednesday and was greeted with prolonged cheers from the Magpie faithful, who could hardly believe what their eyes had seen. It was the second-biggest victory in the Premier League (Manchester United gave the luckless Ipswich 9–0 in the 1994–95 season) and Newcastle's second-biggest victory of all time after the 13–0 thrashing of Newport in the days of Len Shackleton immediately after World War Two. Alan Shearer's five goals, although by no means unprecedented, put him in the 'unusual' category. He personally had never scored more than three.

That Sunday night the Toon went mad. In the immediate euphoria of victory, given the traditional Geordie penchant to believe that world domination is just round the corner, foolish things were said about Bobby Robson. Alan Shearer himself, well aware of the innate gullibility of the Newcastle support, was careful to douse the excessive enthusiasm by warning supporters of the dangers of getting carried away.

Fine performance though it was, one had to bear in mind that it was just one game against a team that would be relegated that season. Had Liverpool or Manchester United been put to the sword in this sort of fashion or, more tellingly, if Newcastle could keep on playing like this even when away from home, it would have been a different matter. And would they ever see Shearer scoring five goals, a hat-trick or even at all in a game that mattered, like an FA Cup Final? But no one could grudge the Toon Army, so often defeated, dispirited, demoralised and depressed in recent times, their moment of joy. It was a great day for them, and one wonders what Ruud Gullit made of it all.

43

Date: 24 October 2004

MANCHESTER CITY

Match: Premier League **Venue: St James' Park**

Score: 4–3 **Attendance: 52,316**

Newcastle United:	Manchester City:
Given	James
Carr*	Mills
Elliott	Distin
O'Brien	Dunne
Bernard	Thatcher
Jenas	Wright-Phillips
Butt	Bosvelt
Bowyer	McManaman
Robert**	Sibierski
Shearer	Macken**
Bellamy***	Anelka*
Hughes*	Fowler*
Milner**	Flood**
Ameobi***	

Referee: S. Dunn, Gloucestershire

It is often said of a game of football that it 'had everything'. This can never be literally true, but sometimes a game can contain quite a lot. This was one of them. In fact, all the exciting stuff was contained in the second half, for the first 45 minutes, although not without bite, were devoid of any real excitement. At the end of the game, the fans were left gasping for breath. Seven goals, some of which were superb, penalty-kicks, bookings, a team twice losing the lead and then holding out to win, one manager going berserk at the referee – all this and a great deal of what is commonly called 'previous', not least in the case of the Manchester City player roundly booed as the teams were read out because his name was Thatcher.

In the first place, City were now managed by Kevin Keegan. He had twice arrived at St James' Park to be called 'the messiah' and had twice left the Geordies feeling unfulfilled. He was not finished yet either. As Arnold Schwarzenegger might have put it for him, 'I'll be back'. This time, among another few bizarre statements, he told everyone that referee Mr Dunn should not expect a Christmas card from him. This must really have put a dampener on Mr Dunn's festivities.

It was Newcastle's manager, however, on whom most attention centred. This was the ever-controversial Graeme Souness. He had not been the Newcastle manager for long, but even his enemies would have to say that he was doing quite well, with wins over his old team Blackburn Rovers, Southampton and West Bromwich Albion and draws against Birmingham City and Charlton Athletic. Progress in the League Cup had been a somewhat scratchy victory over Norwich City, but a victory nevertheless. There had recently, however, been a rather spectacular fall-out with Craig Bellamy.

Bellamy, a fast, talented Welshman with an ability to score goals, had a reputation for speaking his mind. He had this week done just that. He had scored against Charlton Athletic at the Valley the previous Saturday, but then was substituted in the second half. No player likes being taken off when he feels he is doing well, but Bellamy made his feelings rather too obvious as foul-mouthed obscenities were clearly uttered.

Souness was possibly just too new in his job to take the action that he would have taken later in his time at Newcastle, grudging apologies were uttered and Bellamy was included in the team to play Manchester City. The whole matter, however, became a matter of national conversation and people began to wonder if Souness and Bellamy were not perhaps two of a kind and that an irresistible force was fast approaching an immoveable object. But speculation would have to wait until this game was over.

Manchester City had, in the past few decades, suffered from the inevitable comparisons with the other Manchester team, United. There was, it often appeared, a chip on the shoulder and they were as desperate for some kind of sustained success as Newcastle were. Like Newcastle, frustration was the order of the day. Their League Cup win over Newcastle in 1976 had been their last success. 1998 had even seen them playing in the third tier of English football, and there had been no major day out to Wembley since they had lost the FA Cup Final of 1981. Newcastle United and Manchester City meeting each other was akin, one felt, to old enemies waking up in hospital and seeing each other in the next bed suffering from the same incurable disease – in this case, generations of feckless management.

It was a pleasant Sunday. The game was played on the Sunday not because of the demands of television, but rather because Newcastle had been playing in Europe the previous midweek, beating the Greek side Panionios on the Thursday with a late Shearer penalty. Frankly, they looked jaded in the first half – a 45 minutes in which very little happened. A few booed Bellamy for his verbal indiscretions at Souness, who was still unbeaten since he joined the club, others discussed the problem and expressed the hope that the two could get along, because the club quite clearly needed both. Half-time came without anyone having any reason to get excited.

Keegan had been given a curious reception from the Geordie crowd. He was still loved for his mighty deeds of yesteryear, but he was also now the manager of the opposition. It was not the wholehearted traditional booing of the type normally associated with former players returning with another club, but nor was it a 'nice to see you, again, Kevin!' greeting from a magnanimous Newcastle crowd.

The second half was a totally different matter from the first. Within a quarter of an hour Newcastle were two up, both goals coming from set pieces. The first was a clever free-kick from Laurent Robert, Newcastle's talented French midfielder, after Nicky Butt had been fouled by Bosvelt. Robert seemed to lose his footing as he took the free-kick, but it was still good enough to beat a Manchester City wall that looked as if it had been built by a cowboy builder.

That was in the 48th minute, and 10 minutes later Stephen Carr was brought down by goalkeeper David James, and a penalty-kick was awarded to the disgust, one presumes, of Mr Keegan. Alan Shearer seldom missed penalties and Newcastle were now two up with Geordie fans, euphoric and naïve as always, convinced that in Souness they had the answer to all the problems.

Anyone who has ever watched Newcastle, however, really should know that assumptions are dangerous things to make about the team. Newcastle defenders should certainly never buy a dog in case they threw away its lead. It was a good goal that brought City back into the game when a long ball from Mills found the excellent Shaun Wright-Phillips, who skipped past a rash tackle from Elliot, charged in on goal and beat Given. City now had their tails up, and by halfway through the second half they were level after Jamie Fowler, who had come on as a substitute for Nicholas Anelka, was tackled by Nicky Butt and referee Dunn pointed to the spot. It was a dubious penalty, but Fowler himself took it and scored.

The game was now beginning to really warm up, and Newcastle regained the advantage a minute or two later when Robbie Elliott headed on a Robert free kick. He did not seem to have got a clean header on to the ball, which scraped the inside of the post and almost apologetically entered the net. Those who felt, however, that Newcastle's defence would learn a lesson and not concede another goal that could have been prevented were doomed to disappointment when a throw-in was not defended adequately and the ball came to Shaun Wright-Phillips, who was thus enabled to score his second goal of the game and send the Geordie fans once again into one of their attacks of depression that were no easier to deal with no matter how often they occurred.

Over 10 minutes remained, and with both teams going hell for leather anything could happen with neither team defending well and the talented players in both teams giving the impression that they could create another goal at any time. How fitting it was that the man of the moment, Craig Bellamy, should have the last laugh. It was a fine goal, just at the end of regulation time, when he steered home a good cross from Bernard. The whole ground erupted, but immediately after that there were anxious looks around the ground at clocks and watches to see whether the Newcastle defence had the time to throw it all away again.

Then, in injury time, Souness did something which was either conciliatory or provocative depending on one's point of view. It is good tactics to make a substitution late in the game when one is in the lead to use up time and to take the sting out of the frenzied opposition attacks, but Souness decided to take off Bellamy. He was either saying 'I will substitute you if I want, no matter what you have just done' or he was giving Bellamy a chance to milk the applause that came his way as he trotted off waving to the fans, some of whom had been none too enamoured of him an hour previously. Certainly Bellamy seemed to enjoy the moment, and the whole stadium went into raptures when the final whistle went a minute or two later to herald the end of one of the most entertaining and enjoyable games seen for a long time at St James' Park.

What the main characters said at the end was illuminating. Keegan moaned about the standard of refereeing, even though the Manchester City penalty looked to neutral journalists to be soft; Souness made a joke about how this was not good for a man like himself who had undergone heart surgery in the past and went out of his way to say good things about Bellamy's commitment; and Bellamy issued a statement about the future orientation of his life, which seemed to include toeing the line with Souness and Newcastle.

It was not likely to last, however, with two such volatile characters. By January there had been another falling out and Bellamy was on his way on loan to Celtic, where he was welcomed with open arms by the support because Souness had once managed Rangers. The praises were sung of Bellamy by the green and white fans:

'Like me and you
He hates Souness too,
Oh, Craig Bellamy!'

Bellamy won a Scottish Cup medal with them in 2005 before returning to play for a variety of clubs in England, including Manchester City.

Newcastle continued their mediocrity, although they reached the semi-final of the FA Cup, losing to Manchester United, after which Mr Bellamy saw fit to send a few gloating text messages – something that did little for any hope he might have had of returning to play for Newcastle United.

Newcastle finished 14th in the Premier League, and in spite of their limited success in Cup competitions (they also reached the last eight of the UEFA Cup), mediocrity remained the order of the day. It was a mediocrity illuminated by a few good performances, such as this one.

Date: 16 March 2005

44

OLYMPIAKOS

Match: UEFA CUP fourth round, second leg   **Venue: St James' Park**

Score: 4–0   **Attendance: 32,163**

Newcastle United:	Olympiakos:
Given	Nikopolidis
Carr*	Movrogenidis
Taylor	Vallas
O'Brien	Anatolakis
Hughes	Pantos
Jenas	Maric
Bowyer	Stoltidis*
Butt	Kafes
Robert**	Djordjevic**
Dyer***	Giovanni***
Shearer	Castillo
Ramage*	Taralidis*
N'Zogbia**	Okkas**
Milner***	Filipakos***

Referee: K. Plautz, Austria

Not for the first time in their lives Newcastle fans were beginning to believe that a good team was now in place on Tyneside. League form, admittedly, had not been too great in the autumn and the winter, but now that spring was here it seemed that the team was hitting form just at the right time in their quest for two trophies – the UEFA Cup and the FA Cup. Seven games in a row had been won, ensuring progress in Europe and including a win over the mighty Liverpool in the Premier League. There had also been two immensely satisfying wins over London opposition in Chelsea and Tottenham Hotspur in the FA Cup, and a semi-final date against Manchester United beckoned.

A great deal of this success was due to the controversial character of the manager, Graeme Souness. It would be fair to say that Souness did not enjoy universal popularity – Craig Bellamy, for example, was now playing in Scotland for Celtic as a direct result of a personality clash with his manager, and Souness had taken some time to win over the Toon Army, who had suddenly turned all nostalgic for Bobby Robson – but he was a winner. His collection of winners' medals from his Liverpool days would prove that, as would his managerial success with Rangers, but he had also had his failures.

And there was Alan Shearer, the man who would have given anything to win something for Newcastle. Not since the days of Jackie Milburn had there been such a symbiotic relationship between fans and one player as there was with Alan Shearer. As in the case of Milburn, Shearer was 'one of ours', and it showed in the way that he played the game. Clichés like 'wearing his heart on his sleeve' were frequently spouted, but that did not seem to quite cover the commitment that Shearer showed to the club and the frustrations that he shared with the fans.

There was also a great love for Irish goalkeeper Shay Given. The Donegal man had played for the club since 1997 and had never let the club or the fans down. He was one of those players with whom the crowd had an empathy, and the affection was mutual. He went out of his way to talk to fans, realising that they were the lifeblood of the game, particularly in a city like Newcastle where the performances of the team sometimes had a perhaps unhealthy influence on the general well-being of its citizens.

Other players the fans were less convinced about. Kieron Dyer had his moments, both good and bad, Nicky Butt had been a tremendous player for Manchester United but had perhaps come to Newcastle too late in his career and Lee Bowyer, although no one could fault his effort on the field, had been involved in rather too many unsavoury incidents in the past with other clubs to be totally loved by the Magpie faithful. But there could be little doubt that things were now seeming to take a turn for the better at Newcastle United, and a few fans were beginning to dare to hope that there might yet be a chance of a much-coveted piece of silverware arriving at St James' Park.

The UEFA Cup did not look totally impossible. Of the teams that were left, there was no one with an unbeatable look about them. Neighbours Middlesbrough were also in this tournament – in fact, the two north-east clubs were the only two British teams left – but Boro had slipped up rather badly the week before by going down 3–2 to Sporting Lisbon at home. Only a determined late rally gave them any cause for optimism after a fragile defence had conceded three goals in the early part of the second half. Newcastle were approaching this second leg having won the first game 3–1 in Greece against Olympiakos, a team who were good but by no means great. It was rather surprising that only 32,163 appeared that night at St James' Park, but there were reasons for this. TV provided a counter-attraction, the prices were exorbitant and there was the feeling that Newcastle had done the hard part abroad – a dangerous thing to believe but possibly true on this occasion, even though Newcastle had a few injuries.

Olympiakos, 3–1 down, had little to lose, and, knowing that attack was their only chance of victory, were relying on an early goal to silence the crowd. They started well, knocking the ball about to each other, but without managing to score the crucial goal. It was actually Kieron Dyer who scored the vital goal. Dyer was a very versatile player. He was very fast and could play in midfield or on the right wing, but tonight injuries and team tactics determined that he was to play up front alongside Alan Shearer. It was a remarkable goal. Robert took a free-kick, but it was not adequately cleared and the ball came to Bowyer, who flicked it on to Dyer. Kieron was badly positioned and facing the wrong way, but, proving that good players can do most things, he simply back-heeled the ball into the net.

This goal effectively killed the tie and just on half-time Shearer, who had had bad luck on a couple of previous occasions, was on the spot to hammer home a Dyer cross after some fine work on the right wing. The team thus left the field to the resounding cheers of the Geordie faithful, who were now more and more convinced that this could be the long-awaited year for the club.

The second half provided more food for optimism as Lee Bowyer scored at his second attempt after the goalkeeper had parried his header to Jenas, who returned the ball to him to finish off. Then St James' Park went into overdrive following a classic goal from their hero, Alan Shearer, who latched onto a Jenas pass, rounded the goalkeeper and scored.

This completed the scoring, although Newcastle could have scored a great deal more if they had needed to. The remainder of the game was spent with Newcastle showboating, entertaining the fans and generally enjoying themselves, while the fans, for their part, now reckoning that the team had won eight games on the trot (and that had not happened very often before!), cheered and called out the names of the players and even Souness, now, for all his abrasiveness and ruthlessness, accepted freely, openly and publicly for the first time by the Geordie crowd.

It was as well that the Toon Army did not know what was coming to them. It was a classic piece of self-destruction, all within 15 days in April. It all began on 2 April with a home game against Aston Villa, a game of comparatively little significance but one which was to send the Geordies into a downward spiral so rapidly and totally as to almost defy comprehension. In this fairly meaningless fixture Aston Villa had just gone 3–0 up, but that was no justification for the crazy things that happened next. For no apparent reason and with play raging all about them, Lee Bowyer and Kieron Dyer came to blows. As everyone gasped in amazement other players, notably Aston Villa's Gareth Barry, tried to separate them, but referee Barry Knight had little option but to send them packing for violent conduct. The reasons were hard to fathom. A girl? Gambling debts? Sheer thuggery? A previous incident on the training ground? All these were trotted out by 'someone who knew', but the effects on Newcastle were catastrophic. Newcastle finished the game with eight men as Steven Taylor also got a red card that day.

With Tyneside and indeed the whole football world still reeling over this, Newcastle then lined up against Sporting Lisbon in the UEFA Cup quarter-final five days later. A 1–0 victory was hailed as a good result, with Dyer being replaced by Bowyer in the second half. After all, the park was not big enough for both of them! So far, so good. A victory was still possible, the fans thought. The crucial away goal had not been conceded, and an early goal in Lisbon would mean that the Portuguese would have to score three to win.

However, the following week, with both Dyer and Bowyer on the park in Lisbon and Dyer scoring the first, apparently defining, goal, Newcastle then obeyed the apparently immutable law that they must cave in to the face of determined opposition. In front of Lisbon fans, who had been muted when they were behind but then became more and more animated before eventually turning fanatical, Newcastle collapsed to lose four second-half goals to Sporting Lisbon in a way which baffled the 3,000 travelling support and the thousands more watching on television back home.

After that, everyone – directors, management team, players and supporters – all went to the Millennium Stadium in Cardiff for the semi-final against Manchester United expecting a hiding. They duly got it. They were two goals down at half-time, including one crucially lost on the half-time whistle, then there was flicker of a possibility when Ameobi pulled one back after Manchester United had gone three in front before a final late sickener. The fans were sullen and angry, blaming Nicky Butt for most of it as if he had been psyched out by his former teammates, and wondering, not for the first time, why a city the size of Newcastle simply cannot have a good football team when a month previously everything had looked so rosy.

The tragedy of Newcastle has always been that there are times when they can touch success, but for one reason or other they fail to do so. In this case, it was quite clearly because of internal matters that had not been resolved and the demoralising effect that this has on the rest of the team. But there was another dynamic as well, and this was the feeling that Newcastle were, somehow, not meant to win trophies, that they were not allowed to do so. Self-belief has for a long time been lacking. It is only when it returns that success will become possible.

For a while the game against Olympiakos furnished that self-belief, but for a supporter there are times when one is almost afraid to get excited about the Toon because there exists the lurking feeling of pessimism based on the past 50 years that, sooner or later, the team will 'blow up'. Such thoughts kept entering exultant minds in the midst of all the rejoicing at the railway stations the night of the Olympiakos game.

Date: 23 October 2005

SUNDERLAND

Match: Premier League

Venue: St James' Park

Score: 3–2

Attendance: 52,302

Newcastle United:	Sunderland:
Given	Davis
Carr	Nosworthy
Boumsong	Breen*
Taylor	Caldwell
Ramage	Hoyte
Solano**	Lawrence
Emre***	Miller
Parker	Whitehead
N'Zogbia	Welsh**
Shearer	Gray***
Ameobi*	Elliott
Chopra*	Stubbs*
Clark**	Arca**
Faye***	Le Tallac***

Referee: R. Styles, Hampshire

Newcastle and Sunderland derbies have always had an atmosphere of their own. Newcastle United have in some ways suffered from being the only team in the city, and one often feels that they might have prospered at certain key points of their history if there had been a Newcastle City or a Newcastle Rovers as well. But there is Sunderland little more than 10 miles away, a team, like Newcastle, whose performances and achievements have been a lot less than what might have been expected given the extent and passion of their support.

Tyne–Wear derbies have sometimes been dangerous. In the early years of the 20th century overcrowding caused serious problems, leading on at least one occasion to the abandonment of a game, and in recent decades there has been more than a little violence from the young (and sometimes not quite so young) and intellectually challenged of both cities. There is ill-disguised relief from the police forces of both cities when the teams are in separate divisions.

The supreme irony of all this passionate and primeval rivalry is that the two teams are frequently competing merely for that grossly overused phrase, 'bragging rights'. Such things are important when one meets members of the 'enemy' at schools and places of work, but it would be nice one day to see the two great institutions of the North East playing to be the champions of England rather than to be the temporary top dogs of the somewhat success-starved area of the country which is, frankly, of little concern to anyone else.

Be that as it may, this particular derby of Sunday 23 October 2005, with its early kick-off, had more than the normal importance to Newcastle and in particular to Newcastle's manager, Graeme Souness. Things were simply not happening for the Geordies that season. Only two games had been won out of nine played. There had been a great deal of hard luck, but there are limits as to how much 'bad luck' the supporters will put up with, and there was a groundswell of opinion that was demanding the sacking of the manager. There had always been a faction who did not like the assertive Scotsman, but the faction had now grown, particularly after the previous week's defeat at Wigan as Wigan were one of those teams that Newcastle fans felt they should not be defeated by.

It was not that Souness had not entered the transfer market. In particular he had spent £3.8 million on Emre Belezoglu, the Turkish international, but injury had limited his appearances and Newcastle fans were beginning to wonder if the money had been well spent. He had appeared as a substitute in the previous week's unfortunate encounter at Wigan, but he was given a start for the arrival of Sunderland. It would be as good a time as any to prove himself worthy of his huge transfer fee.

There was also the even higher profile and more valuable Michael Owen, formerly of Liverpool and Real Madrid. As with Emre, injury was a problem and once again the phrase 'bad luck' was used. But then again, one often makes one's own luck, and Souness seemed to be cursed with the lack of it, as good money seemed to be spent on men who had the unfortunate tendency to get injured, or perhaps to have a pre-existing injury that had lain undetected.

Sunderland were in a far worse state than Newcastle, with only one win and one draw to their credit in the League campaign. The win had been a very satisfactory one over the third team in the area, Middlesbrough, but that hardly made up for the other disasters. Sunderland manager Mick McCarthy was under just as much pressure as Souness was. The two of them were old adversaries, having crossed swords in their playing days in Glasgow when McCarthy was with Celtic and Souness with Rangers.

That there was a great deal at stake in this game was seen within the first minute when referee Rob Styles had cause to brandish a yellow card at Dean Whitehead for a foul on Emre, which looked like a fairly cynical attempt to put Emre out of the game. The crowd, already passionate, now turned hysterical, and the players responded, not, thankfully, in a violent or brutal way, but with an equally firm determination to play their hearts out for the team. It was almost like the old days, said one veteran fan, when the game was played not for money and bonuses, but for the sheer desire to win, and they shared the same thirst for victory that the fans had.

It turned out to be a great game with the fans in perpetual excitement and the radio and TV commentators running out of adjectives to describe the action. The ground was full, with the Mackems in the top section of the John Hall Stand giving almost as good as they got in terms of encouragement of their team. In a seven-minute spell just before half-time, each side scored twice, Newcastle scoring first on both occasions only for Sunderland to equalise.

It was the much undervalued Shola Ameobi, only playing for the team because of injuries, who put Newcastle ahead. In the 33rd minute Emre took a corner and Ameobi outjumped his marker Stephen Caldwell to put the home side ahead. St James' Park erupted at this, as one would have expected, but scarcely had the flush of triumph subsided when Sunderland equalised with a fine strike by Liam Lawrence, who picked up a pass from Gary Breen and hammered home a low shot from well outside the penalty area, which gave Shay Given little chance. The effect was quite dramatic. Apart from the triumphant cries of the red and white clad at the top of the away end, the Newcastle crowd was stilled and sat down in morbid introspection.

Two minutes later, the roles were reversed when Ameobi scored again. It was another header, this time with a goal that used to be described as a 'three-card trick'. A cross from Carr went all the way across to N'Zogbia on the opposite wing, who sent the ball back into the penalty area for Ameobi to rise like a bird and score again. Then, incredibly, Sunderland scored again with another great strike but this time from Irish international Stephen Elliott, who curled a great shot into the top left-hand corner of the net.

The half-time whistle came almost as a relief after all that, and the players trooped off to the cheers of the crowd, some of whom were actually sufficiently nonpartisan to admit that it had been a great game of football and that both teams had done themselves proud. Apart from the four goals there had been countless close things at both ends, and the quality of the passing had been uniformly excellent. The commentators were at a loss to explain why both teams were at the bottom of the League, but the question answered itself – two goals had been scored by each team, but, by the same token, two goals had been lost. Titles are seldom won by teams who concede two goals before half-time.

The second half was hardly an anticlimax after this, but it failed to live up to what had happened before in terms of goals scored. There was only one more goal, but it was a great one and one which went a long way to answering the questions of the sceptics who could not work out why Emre had been signed. Twenty minutes of the second half had elapsed in which Sunderland had looked slightly more likely to score than Newcastle, but then the Geordies won a free-kick. It was not really in what one would have called shooting range, being at least 10 yards outside the penalty area. One wondered whether it was worth Sunderland's bother forming a wall, but the ground was a sea of acclamation when Emre's free-kick gave Davis no chance off his left-hand post to put Newcastle ahead for the third time in the game.

The game continued at a furious pace, and only the hardest-hearted of Newcastle supporters would deny that Sunderland deserved at least something out of the game. Given had at least two splendid saves, and once he was beaten by a Elliott lob which then hit the bar. Then, in the game's only really controversial moment, it seemed that Sunderland were unlucky to be denied a penalty within the last quarter of an hour when Lawrence seemed to be tripped by N'Zogbia, but Rob Styles, a generally highly regarded referee, said no.

Full-time came with both sides still pressing for the goal that would make such a difference. When Rob Styles pointed to the pavilion Sunderland's men were seen to collapse in distress, whereas Souness greeted all his men and backroom staff with hugs and handshakes. It was reckoned to have been one of the best derbies of the North East for many years, with that undefinable quality called luck seeming to be on Newcastle's side at last after so much misfortune this season. McCarthy rather unfairly blamed the pressure of the crowd for the referee's failure to award the penalty-kick that might have made the difference, but Souness said that it was a great advertisement for the football played in the North East.

It was a shame that such a good game had to be marred by pathetic scenes of violence outside the ground, on the way to the station and throughout the whole area as fights broke out among fans who had been watching the game on the television. It seemed in some ways that this typified the self-destructive tendency of the region in that they had to spoil what had been a great game of football with insane internecine strife. Why couldn't they just enjoy the football?

The other thing that puzzled the outsider was why the two great teams, well supported and with strong players, could not do better. As it turned out, this was one of the few bright spots in the season of both clubs and neither manager, Souness nor McCarthy, saw the season out, both facing the bullet early in 2006. Newcastle's dismal form after the turn of the year saw the departure of Souness as yet another man who was supposed to bring glory to Tyneside bit the dust, and St James' Park continued its reputation as being a graveyard for managers.

46

Date: 4 February 2006

PORTSMOUTH

Match: Premier League

Score: 2–0

Venue: St James' Park

Attendance: 51,627

Newcastle United:	Portsmouth:
Given	Kiely
Ramage	Griffin*
Boumsong	Primus
Bramble	O'Brien
Babayaro	Taylor
Solano*	Routledge**
Parker**	Davis***
Emre***	Mendes
N'Zogbia	O'Neil
Shearer	D'Alessandro
Ameobi	Mwaruwari
Dyer*	Pamarot*
Clark**	Todorov**
Bowyer***	Diao***

Referee: M. Halsley, Lancashire

A few Newcastle supporters have had the privilege of seeing both Jackie Milburn and Alan Shearer. Milburn's era was in the 1950s, Shearer's almost exactly 50 years later. They would have been the lucky ones to have seen both.

There were similarities between Milburn and Shearer. They could both score with their feet and their heads, they were both quicksilver fast, they both played for England with distinction (although, in Milburn's case, not as often as his fans would have liked, nor as often as he should have), and they were both local boys who knew what it meant to be a Newcastle supporter with all the pain that that would entail. They both suffered under managers who did not like them. They were both cult heroes and meant a huge amount to a great deal of people.

There was, however, one crucial difference, and Shearer was all too painfully aware of it. Shearer had not won anything with the club. He had won the English Premier League with Blackburn Rovers in 1995 but nothing as yet for Newcastle, having singularly failed to produce the goods in the two dreadful FA Cup Finals of 1998 and 1999 when so much had been expected of him. Like Malcolm

Macdonald of 1974 he had been found wanting when the club and history demanded that he produced. Milburn, on the other hand, had three FA Cup medals, in 1951, 1952 and 1955, and scored in two of them.

Arguments would rage about who was the better. Such arguments are pointless because they played in different circumstances and in different times. What is certain is that each would have approved of the other if they had seen each other play, and for Shearer it was certainly a great thrill to find himself mentioned even in the same breath as 'Wor Jackie' Milburn.

Alan Shearer had grown up in the 1970s and 1980s hearing from his father and men of his father's age about how good a player Milburn had been in contrast to the lesser men who had attempted to fill his boots since he had retired. It had hurt the Geordies to see men like Beardsley, Waddle, Gascoigne and Cole, who might just have become the new Milburn, depart south to richer clubs, seduced by grasping agents, promises of large cheques and allowed to go by spineless and pusillanimous management. Shearer had gone to Blackburn Rovers but had pined for home, and although the transfer fee was huge and barely comprehensible to simple-minded supporters Shearer had made it clear that this was the only club he really wanted to play for. On at least two occasions he had turned down Manchester United.

As 2005 gave way to 2006, however, both Alan Shearer and Newcastle themselves were in a certain degree of chaos and crisis. This was hardly for the first time in recent decades, but the problem seemed to be that goals were beginning to dry up for Shearer. By the turn of the year Shearer had scored only four League goals and one League Cup goal, and supporters were beginning to doubt the wisdom of Shearer's decision to continue playing. He had previously said he would retire in summer 2005 before changing his mind. Retirement now looked as if it might have been a good idea.

Shearer, aged 35, was certainly beginning to struggle as younger, fitter defenders got to the ball before he did, but this was not the only problem at St James' Park. The team had started the season with three defeats and two draws before eventually winning a game on 18 September, and although things had improved since then, consistent winning form was a long way off. In particular there was a tendency to surrender pitifully to teams like Manchester United, Chelsea and Liverpool in a way that supporters found unacceptable. Newcastle, after all, had a fan base that was second to none – and certainly had more supporters than Chelsea or Liverpool – so why could they not compete?

Much of the criticism centred on manager Graeme Souness. A tough, abrasive Scotsman with a great playing record and a degree of success as a manager in Scotland with Rangers (admittedly at a time when Celtic were going through a prolonged crisis), he had never been a great winner as a manager in England and had a far more tenuous rapport with the Geordie faithful in Newcastle than Sir Bobby Robson had. Robson's failures could be tolerated; the fans were less prepared to wait for success to come from Souness, who had effectively driven away some good players, like Craig Bellamy, from the club.

Nevertheless, it seemed strange that the axe should have fallen on Souness when it did on 2 February 2006. Newcastle, although failing to inspire in the Premiership, were still in the FA Cup. They had beaten moderate opposition in Mansfield and Cheltenham, unimpressively in both cases, and Southampton at home in the next round did not look in any way impossible, but a sad Premiership defeat at Manchester City on Wednesday 1 February was the catalyst for Souness's departure and the temporary appointment of Glenn Roeder. Roeder had been a good player, a tall, stylish and elegant centre-half, for the club in the past, and was still well liked by the fans.

Souness and Shearer had had a great mutual admiration. In fact, it was said that it had been Souness who had encouraged Shearer to stay on for the extra year, and now that Souness had gone it was speculated whether Roeder might drop Shearer for the game against Portsmouth on Saturday. Certainly it would have been hard to justify Shearer's inclusion on the grounds of recent form.

There was another dynamic at work here as well. Shearer had scored in the defeat of Mansfield in the FA Cup third-round tie on the first Saturday in January. This had brought his tally up to 200, the same number as Milburn had scored in official matches. Since 7 January Shearer had been trying hard to beat the record that would have meant so much to him and to all of Tyneside. He was still the most likely character to score for the club, and Roeder did not want to rock the boat when in temporary charge. Shearer stayed.

As often happens with a regime change, there was an irrational burst of enthusiasm for the game against Portsmouth. Portsmouth, another team with a great tradition but a miserable present, were in a worse position than Newcastle. Their heyday had been round about the same time as that of Newcastle in the late 1940s and early 1950s. Currently under the managership of that sometimes controversial character Harry Redknapp, they were already out of both Cup competitions and were flirting with relegation, having won only four Premier League games. They were a team that Newcastle would in normal circumstances have expected to beat. But these were far from normal circumstances on Tyneside.

The game started poorly, with both sides struggling to get any sort of rhythm to their play, and misplaced passes and the ball going out of play being a common phenomenon. Gradually Newcastle, playing towards the Sir John Hall Stand, with their supporters giving them every encouragement, began to gain some sort of ascendancy with the wing play of Nolberto Solano and Charles N'Zogbia looking particularly impressive. About five minutes before half-time they went ahead.

Solano made space down the right wing and delivered an impeccable ball to Shearer, but his effort was well saved by the inspired Dean Kiely in the Portsmouth goal before Charles N'Zogbia hammered home the rebound. It was a good goal and well applauded by the faithful. Newcastle finished the half well ahead. The goal had been a good one, the only regret being that it had not been Shearer who scored it.

It was now high time that this particular monkey was off everyone's back. The press had kept it up, wondering before every game whether or not this was to be the day that Shearer scored his 201st goal to beat Milburn's record, and the supporters were sick of it. The other players must have wondered what was more important – Shearer beating the record or the team winning games, and Shearer himself must have had nightmares about it all, even to the extent of wondering whether he had made the right decision in not retiring when the going was good in summer 2005.

About 20 minutes into the second half, it finally happened for Alan Shearer. A long ball upfield from Shay Given found Shola Ameobi. The crafty Nigerian beat two men then, with everyone except Shearer expecting him to do something else, he back-heeled the ball into the path of Shearer, who needed no second bidding to hammer home in spite of a strong challenge from ex-Magpie Andy O'Brien.

He then held up his hand to the Gallowgate End (where he used to stand as a lad) in characteristic, even iconic, celebration of his goal. It was a trademark goal – many of the 201 had been like that – and now that he had scored it he and the Newcastle team began to relax and play better football, finishing the game with a well-deserved 2–0 victory to ease relegation worries.

For the first time for a long time Newcastle fans were happy with their team and they could now toast their hero's success. Shearer would only play another few games after that and finished his career after a win against Sunderland near the end of the season. Newcastle finished the season strongly, earning a more than respectable seventh place in the League and thus a berth in the UEFA Cup the following season. Glenn Roeder was allowed to keep the job and Alan Shearer became a BBC pundit, although his name would forever be linked to Newcastle United.

The match against Portsmouth on 4 February 2006 remained a great event in the life of Alan Shearer, and he had a humbling experience the following day when he received a telephone call of congratulations from a lady called Laura Milburn, the widow of the great Jackie.

Date: 26 September 2009

IPSWICH TOWN

Match: Championship

Venue: Portman Road, Ipswich

Score: 4–0

Attendance: 27,059

Ipswich Town:	Newcastle United:
Wright	Harper
Rosenior	S. Taylor***
Bruce*	Khizanishvili
Balkestein	Coloccini**
Delaney**	Jose Enrique
Walters	Smith
Trotter	Nolan
Colback	Butt
Leadbitter	R. Taylor
Edwards	Carroll
Priskin***	Ranger*
Smith*	Harewood*
Peters**	Lovenkrands**
Counago***	Donaldson***

Referee: M. Jones, Cheshire

Sir Bobby Robson died on 31 July 2009. He was a great man, much respected and loved, and remarkably for a man who had been in football for so long, he had very few enemies. He had played for Fulham in two spells and West Bromwich Albion, and had managed Ipswich Town and Newcastle United, as well as several foreign teams, and, of course, England. He had taken England to the semi-final of the 1990 World Cup and had played for the country 20 times between 1957 and 1962. Had he been a little younger, there would seem to be little doubt that he would have graced the England team that won the World Cup in 1966.

Robson had been battling cancer for some time, and his dignified struggle had impressed everyone just as much as his playing career had done. He was quite happy to appear in public and was a constant inspiration to countless others who were suffering from the same condition. Even those who knew little about football knew that Sir Bobby Robson was a battler.

As well as being an ex-manager of Newcastle United, Bobby had grown up in County Durham and had been very much a Newcastle supporter in the immediate post-war years when he had seen

Len Shackleton, Jackie Milburn and Bobby Mitchell – men fit enough to win a place in any team in any era. Robson would have done anything to play for the club, but, as has sadly happened with many other local boys, Newcastle's management failed to notice him and he moved to play for Fulham. Even after he had established himself with Fulham, more imaginative management at St James' Park might have enticed him home, but it was West Bromwich Albion who enjoyed his talents in the 1960s.

The outpouring of grief at his death was sincere and sustained, and when Newcastle were due to play Ipswich Town on 26 September 2009 at Portman Road both teams asked for and were given permission to wear special commemorative strips for the occasion. At half-time the North Stand was renamed the Sir Bobby Robson Stand in a ceremony featuring his widow, Lady Elsie.

Robson had been a more successful manager for Ipswich than he had been for Newcastle. He was fortunate in that he was given 13 years at Portman Road, which allowed him to build a team that won the FA Cup in 1978 and the UEFA Cup in 1981. He was with Newcastle from 1999 until 2004, and although the performances of the team were respectable he failed to bring home the elusive piece of silverware that would have made such a difference to the life and culture of the city. Eventually Robson had to go, having failed, like everyone else, to satisfy the impatient demands of the fans. Newcastle is the last resting place for many managing careers.

Robson was the national team manager between 1982 and 1990, seeing the squad through two World Cup Finals, in Argentina in 1986 and Italy in 1990, losing only on a penalty shoot-out in the 1990 semi-final. Even when the press turned on him (as they invariably do with all England managers) he retained his dignity. His gentlemanly demeanour saw him famously describing Diego Maradona's cheating 'Hand of God' goal in 1986 as the action of a 'rascal' when stronger words were used elsewhere, and possibly by Robson himself in private. He was a diplomat and statesman, and he deserved the success he achieved abroad with teams like Porto and PSV Eindhoven.

This particular game was played at 5.30pm on 26 September and was shown on television. It was about a great deal more than Sir Bobby Robson. Newcastle had in 2009 suffered the ignominy of relegation from the Premier League. That was bad enough, but there was a lot more going on at boardroom level that distressed the ever-loyal supporters – particularly when the club was offered for sale and no one seemed to want to buy it. Newcastle, for so long a byword for political infighting and under-performance on the field (and the two things are surely connected) was sinking now to the level of ridicule. However, under the caretaker management of Chris Hughton, an unpretentious character who had had a moderate career as a player with Tottenham Hotspur and Eire, a respectable start had been made to the season.

The same could not be said of the struggling Ipswich. They were now managed by Roy Keane. Roy had never been the darling of the Newcastle Gallowgate in his days as a player with Manchester United, and there was the recent Sunderland connection, because he had been manager at the Stadium of Light for a brief and disastrous spell during the previous season. He did seem to have the unfortunate ability to upset people wherever he went, but there could be no doubt that he had been a tremendous player for Manchester United and the Republic of Ireland. The sheer fact that he was Roy Keane meant that there was no lack of incentive for the Toon Army to beat Ipswich.

It was a fine, balmy autumn night in Suffolk for the Toon Army, who travelled down in large numbers. Respects were paid to Sir Bobby and the game began in the trim, compact Portman Road ground, which will never be one of the great stadia of England, although it is functional and has done a good job for the aspirations of the East Anglian side. Ipswich were attacking the stand that would after half-time become known officially as the Sir Bobby Robson Stand, but it was Newcastle who started the brightest and caused many Ipswich fans to wonder why they had been relegated the previous season.

Captain Nicky Butt was inspirational and well supported in midfield by Alan Smith and Kevin Nolan, while upfront was Andy Carroll, a young man of tremendous potential and another youngster with the unusual name of Nile Ranger. This game was to be all about Nolan, however. A few minutes after getting a yellow card for a rather pointless foul, the former Bolton Wanderers man put

Newcastle ahead. Ryan Taylor took a free-kick on the right after he had been fouled and sent over a perfect cross for the unchallenged Kevin Nolan to nip in at the near post and head home from close range. This was on the half-hour mark, and in another few minutes the game was over. Nolan scored again a couple of minutes later, and this goal was sheer class. He picked up a pass from the industrious Andy Carroll, cut inside and hammered home to beat the goalkeeper by shooting across him. If the Geordie fans had been pleased with his first goal, they were absolutely ecstatic about the second, and rightly so. This was good stuff.

A couple of minutes after that, it was 3–0. This time a Ryan Taylor free-kick was hammered sweetly through a static, demoralised and catatonic Ipswich defence, who must have been yearning now for the half-time whistle. They were lucky not to be further down because Newcastle's two front men, neither of whom had scored in this game, tried to muscle in on the act and Ranger in particular showed what a massive physical presence he could be. Half-time came with no further scoring as Newcastle fans went wild with delight – they had not had such a day for a long time – and the Ipswich fans sank into the depression that comes when one just knows at half-time that there will be no revival and that there is no way back into the game.

The ceremony for the renaming of the stand took place and due reverence was paid to Lady Elsie and her two sons. The crowd then began to sing the Frank Sinatra song that was apparently one of Bobby's favourites, *My Way*. He had done things his way, and it was somehow appropriate that Bobby's long and unusual career was marked in this way.

The slaughter continued in the second half. Remarkably, only one more goal was scored, but it was a very good one involving some great teamwork. It began with the Georgian Zurab Khizanishvili, making his first-team debut for Newcastle after service with Dundee and Blackburn Rovers. He beat two men down the flank before sending in a good pass to Ryan Taylor. Taylor saw that Ranger was unmarked and sent a high ball to him. Ranger however, unable to score himself, headed across goal so that Kevin Nolan could once again hit the back of the net. This was after only five minutes of the second half.

There was no further scoring, with Newcastle totally dominant but lacking the desire or the need to further humiliate their fellow professionals. The Newcastle fans cheered, applauded, and sang *The Blaydon Races* and other less pleasant stuff about Roy Keane and his private life. The Ipswich fans, by contrast, were stunned into silence, and although a few of them half-heartedly sang vacuous inanities about 'We never sacked Bobby Robson', there was little doubt that this was Newcastle's day.

It would be a highly significant day in the season for Newcastle. In the first place, it gave a solidity to the management team and it was no accident that Chris Hughton was given the full manager's job a month later. This had been a festering sore for some time. The Alan Shearer rumours would not go away, and various other improbable names were thrown about, but, as Shearer himself said, Chris was doing a good job, and it was only fair that he was given a go at the most difficult job in English football. In addition to that, this game also laid down the marker that Newcastle meant business. Although they had been relegated the year before in that awful season of turmoil, new players were emerging and they were far too good a team for the Championship. Immediate promotion was now on the cards.

Due respect had been paid to Sir Bobby. He had been a dignified elder statesman of the game, and his Indian summer of managing the Toon, after taking on the job at the age of 66, had been a marvellous time of his life. It remained a pity that he had not won anything with the club that he loved, but he would have been delighted at the new Newcastle United that he saw emerging that day at Ipswich.

48

Date: 20 December 2009

MIDDLESBROUGH

Match: Championship   **Venue: St James' Park**

Score: 2–0   **Attendance: 49,644**

Newcastle United:	Middlesbrough:
Harper	Jones
Colocinni	Hoyte
Jose Enrique	Pogatetz
Simpson	Williams
Taylor	McMahon
Nolan	Wheater
Guthrie	O'Neil
Gutierrez	Arca**
Harewood**	Osbourne
Smith*	Lita***
Ameobi***	Kitson*
Ranger**	Bent*
Butt*	Yeates**
Pancrate***	Franks***

Referee: K. Friend, Leicestershire

The Geordies were in rare good humour as they set out for this Sunday game against their neighbours, Middlesbrough. Both teams had been relegated from the Premier League during the previous year, and Newcastle continued to suffer severe and unresolved problems at boardroom level, but under manager Chris Hughton spectacular progress had been made in the Championship, and Newcastle were now seven points clear of their nearest challengers, West Brom.

The Toon Army were aware that the game would provide a stiff test. Local derbies always do, although it would have to be said that Middlesbrough had stuttered of late after a bright start. Gareth Southgate had been sacked (unfairly, some said) and replaced by former Celtic manager Gordon Strachan, an abrasive, cheeky little Scotsman who was no stranger to success as a player. He had learned his trade under Alex Ferguson at Aberdeen before moving to England to play for Manchester United and Leeds United, but his record in management in English football with Coventry and Southampton was open to debate. On the other hand, as manager of Celtic he had won the SPL three seasons out of four. He would have a difficult job to do, as attendances at the Riverside Stadium were dipping at an alarming rate, and a constant theme of complaint from the Boro fans was the lack of commitment from some of the players. Curiously, in all his appearances at St James' Park as player and manager, Strachan had never won a game in Newcastle.

Christmas was approaching, and the weather was seasonal. The view from the top of the high Milburn and Sir John Hall stands afforded an excellent view of the snow-capped skyline of Newcastle on a bright but cold day. Boro fans travelling the short distance to the game had found road conditions difficult, with severe problems on the A19 as Teesside had been particularly badly hit by the bad weather. The city of Newcastle itself, however, while by no means clear of snow, had no major traffic problems and a Championship record attendance of 49,644 appeared – an attendance that was all the more indicative of the fanaticism of the North East, given the bad weather and the fact that the game was live on BBC One with a lunchtime kick-off.

A sign of the times was evident before the start when soldiers of the British Army marched round the playing area to the music of a pipe band. They were the Royal Northumberland Fusiliers, who had seen action in Afghanistan and were invited to watch the game as guests of the club. They were warmly greeted by most of the crowd, well aware of the difficult job they were called upon to do in the Afghanistan war, to which Prime Minister Gordon Brown was now committing more and more troops, even though the casualty list kept growing. Having done their march round the ground, the soldiers took up their places at the front of the Milburn Stand to watch the game and support the Toon.

The large crowd were in good voice, the Boro supporters particularly so. Some of their chants were amusing, others simply obscene and one or two particularly hurtful and wounding to the Geordie psyche like 'Have you ever seen a Geordie with a Cup?' and 'There's only one Mike Ashley!' There was, as always, an extra bite to the chanting, as this was a derby day and the only one that the Geordies were likely to have this season, for the Mackems of Sunderland were still in the Premier League.

Phrases like 'great atmosphere' and 'cauldron of excitement' had seldom been used in the context of St James' Park in recent times, but this game was different. It was a derby. Both teams had suffered the trauma of relegation, and both sets of supporters felt that they were worthy of better. Seeing the vast crowd and the sheer enthusiasm of the fans on this midwinter day, one would have found it difficult to disagree with their expectation of higher things.

Newcastle had disappointed slightly in their previous game at Barnsley, a 2–2 draw, and Hughton made no fewer than four changes in personnel. He had clearly got this right, because the goals both came with the active cooperation of those who had been restored to the side. Andy Carroll was suspended, and Marlon Harewood and Shola Ameobi were the forward pairing. Danny Simpson was brought back in defence and the veteran Nicky Butt relegated to the bench.

The under-soil heating had clearly done a great job in the severe wintry conditions overnight. There were a few traces of snow on the pitch and at the side, but the surface looked good. Newcastle started off kicking towards the Sir John Hall Stand, but it was Boro who started better, giving the lie to the idea that their players lacked heart and commitment to the club. Yet it was a game, typical of derby fixtures, perhaps, where the desire to do well in front of a passionate crowd leads to edginess and a few mistakes with misplaced passes and an inability to control difficult balls.

Quarter of an hour had gone when Newcastle went ahead. Danny Guthrie, having a good game, took a free-kick about 25 yards from goal. He might have opted to take a shot, but instead directed a long ball to the far post to find Ameobi. The Boro defenders would claim bitterly in their prolonged protests to referee Kevin Friend that Ameobi then fouled McMahon as he went up for the ball, whereas pro-Newcastle reports use words like 'out-muscled'. In any case the ball came to Marlon Harewood, who had the easiest of tasks to put his side one in front.

Ten minutes later a similar scenario developed when Newcastle won a free-kick in almost exactly the same spot. This time the ball cannoned into the wall and rebounded to Alan Smith, whose shot went narrowly past. At the other end, a scramble saw Newcastle goalkeeper Steve Harper emerge victorious with the ball after it had seemed that Boro had a good chance to draw level.

Half-time came with Newcastle still on top but Boro far from out of it, with only their worrying lack of firepower in the forward line preventing them from being level. Alan Smith came out for the second half but had clearly been carrying an injury and was fairly soon replaced by the evergreen Nicky Butt. It being a derby, no quarter was sought or given, and some of the tackles were fierce. A couple of Boro players were booked and Danny Simpson was added to their number with a rather silly and late challenge on Boro captain, O'Neil.

It was the other Danny, however, Danny Guthrie, who played a large part in sealing the game when he sent an inch-perfect cross to find the head of Shola Ameobi, who leaped high to defeat the Boro defence. It was a classic goal and perhaps a token of the play which ensured that the Toon would now spend Christmas 10 points ahead of their nearest challengers.

It was nice to see Ameobi doing so well for Newcastle. The Nigerian had now been with the club for almost a decade, and his career had had several peaks and troughs with injuries and his relationship with the various managers under whom he had served. But there was little doubt that today he was the man of the match in the eyes of most Newcastle supporters.

Ameobi's fine goal happened in the 60th minute and the heads of the Boro players and supporters went down as Newcastle took command. Ranger and Pancrate, who had been omitted from the starting line-up, were given a game as the clock was run down. Boro did have a couple of occasions when they managed to send dangerous balls into the Newcastle area, but the Geordie defence was usually able to deal with any threat, and the longer the game went on the more it began to appear that this was indeed a very competent Newcastle side. They would take some shifting from their course. The huge Geordie crowd saw their team finish the game well on top, and although Chris Hughton would warn about the dangers of complacency, it would be a fine Christmas on Tyneside.

It was all the more disturbing, therefore, to see the less acceptable side of Geordie behaviour after the game. In scenes reminiscent of the bad old days of the 1970s, which we all hoped had gone forever, the outnumbered Boro fans were subjected to a dreadful torrent of abuse and intimidation as they made their way to the station, with chunks of ice being thrown at them by the more intellectually challenged members of the Newcastle support. If it wasn't for the rapid deployment of policemen in strength, things might have become more serious.

There is little doubt that some of the Boro fans would also have excelled themselves in the battle to win the title of the 'Thickest Thugs in the North East', but this is little excuse for the Newcastle supporters. The point had been made on the field; the team had won 2–0, and there was no rational reason for such behaviour. As a veteran Boro fan said 'What's wrong with shaking hands and saying "Well done" or "Tough luck"?'

Apart from this sad behaviour from those who wore Newcastle colours but who could hardly be called 'supporters' in any sense of the word, there was a lot to be happy about this Yuletide. The team were succeeding and were clearly well on their way to restoring themselves to where they should have been all along – the Premier League. Fine young players were developing, and the unpretentious style of management employed by Chris Hughton was a lesson to other more flamboyant but less reliable men. The future looked bright for the rest of the season – but how would they do in the Premier League?

As the 'noughties' came to an end, the future for Newcastle was unclear. A hundred years had passed since Newcastle had first won the FA Cup, and more than 100 years had elapsed since the great days of three League Championships. Would the Geordies ever see these days return? Or were Newcastle United forever destined to remain the little team with the large support?

Date: 6 March 2010

49
BARNSLEY

Match: Championship **Venue: St James' Park**

Score: 6–1 **Attendance 44,464**

Newcastle United:	Barnsley:
Harper	Steele
Coloccini	Hassell
Jose Enrique*	Foster
Williamson	Dickinson
Simpson	Shotton
Nolan***	Colace
Guthrie	Filipe Teixeira
Gutierrez	Hallfredsson**
Pancrate	De Silva*
Lovenkrands	Doyle
Carroll**	Gray***
Best*	Preece*
Kadar**	Macken**
Taylor***	Bogdanovic***

Referee: G. Hegley, Hertfordshire

There was a quiet confidence in the step of the Geordies as they made their way to St James' Park on the fine spring day of 6 March 2010. The winter had been a bad one as far as the weather went, but Newcastle were still points clear in the Championship, having achieved something that had never been a great feature of Newcastle's footballing history – consistency.

There were several flies in the ointment. The club had already exited from the FA Cup – it was now 55 years since they had last won it – something that sat ill with older supporters and those who knew the history of the club. There was still considerable doubt about what was happening or going to happen at boardroom level, and there was uncertainty about how the club would perform in the far more demanding milieu of the Premier League, but all these things were secondary considerations. The important thing was that the team were doing well, and a fine crowd of 44,464 – streets ahead of anyone else in the Championship and many teams in the Premier League – assembled to see the latest chapter in what they hoped would be Newcastle's march to winning the Championship.

There was cause for optimism. Other than a strange, unaccountable reverse at the hands of Derby County, form in February had been good and the unpretentious manager Chris Hughton was doing a great deal to make the Magpies forget the horrors of what had happened the year before. Hughton had been given the managerial job, though he had not arrived to the fanfare of trumpets and no one had ever thought of him as any kind of 'messiah'. He had worked hard and brought on a few good players. Newcastle were several points clear at the top, and to gain an automatic promotion spot all they had to do was keep winning, in particular against teams like Barnsley, who were respectable, middle of the table, but no more than that.

It was technically a spring day but it was still cold enough for some to wonder when the winter was finally going to disappear. Newcastle started off playing to the Gallowgate End and in a dullish first half had one or two attempts on goal before the moment that changed it all. A minute or two were left in the first half. Peter Lovenkrands was charging in on goal and Barnsley's goalkeeper, Luke Steele, came out to challenge him. Steele went to ground and tried to clear the ball with his feet, and Lovenkrands stumbled and fell. The referee awarded a penalty-kick.

Even the hardest-hearted of Newcastle fans would have to admit that this was less than a clear-cut penalty-kick. The incident was replayed countless times and the contact seemed to be pretty minimal, but Mr Hegley, who was not far away from the incident, seemed in no doubt and a penalty-kick was given. What made matters worse and in fact changed the course of the game was the need for Mr Hegley to send off the Barnsley goalkeeper on what is loosely called the 'last man' rule, or more properly the 'denying an obvious goalscoring opportunity' rule. This rule, which appeared in the 1990s, often seems to be a little too draconian. Surely the award of a penalty-kick is enough, and there is a certain amount of evidence to suggest that referees will find any sort of excuse not to inflict the ultimate penalty on a player. A yellow card would surely suffice.

Be that as it may, poor Luke Steele had to go, and David Preece of Barnsley was drafted into the goal to face Lovenkrands's penalty. Lovenkrands made no mistake in shooting, and Newcastle left the field a goal and a man ahead while Barnsley nursed a sense of injustice, shared by neutrals, not so much at that particular decision as at Law 12, which tended to indicate that in this case the law is indeed an ass.

Lovenkrands had had a difficult, unsettled time at St James' Park with all sorts of personal problems to sort out as well as a little indifferent form, but he was now looking good, and it was apt that he then scored the second goal after the restart. It was a delightful goal involving three men – captain Stephen Foster, then Andy Carroll, before Lovenkrands scored with his head. It was his 12th goal of the season, and it put Newcastle two up. It was at that point that we knew that there would be no comeback from a defeated and dispirited Barnsley side.

Three minutes after that the Newcastle crowd went into overdrive as Danny Guthrie shot from outside the box and the ball beat deputy goalkeeper David Preece with the aid of a deflection. A real goalkeeper might have done better, but it is always difficult to deal with deflections, and certainly there was very little that any goalkeeper on earth could have done with the fourth goal, which will be talked about (along with its aftermath celebration) for a long time on Tyneside.

It was scored by Jonas Gutierrez, or Jonas as the back of his shirt says. Gutierrez was an Argentinian who had joined Newcastle United at the start of the previous season. He had the misfortune to miss a large part of that season through injury after an impressive start, and it is arguable whether his loss played a large part in the relegation of Newcastle at the end of the season. He had struggled to regain his place and his form had never been the best in the Premiership, yet it was always felt that he had potential. He had won the Primera Division Argentina in 2005 with Velez Sarsfield, then had gone to Spain to play for Real Mallorca, where he had earned the name 'Spiderman' after he put on a red Spiderman mask to celebrate goals. Newcastle fans were beginning to wonder whether they would ever see him doing the same for Newcastle.

He scored a wonderful goal against Peterborough in November with a lovely mazy run, but his goal against Barnsley was absolutely breathtaking as he charged across the field from the left, parallel with the goal, and crashed home a wonderful strike off the bar. It was one of those goals where there is a moment's pause as everyone takes in what has happened before the stadium erupts in a sea of acclaim, and yes, the fans did see the Spiderman mask, which he had secreted on his person just on the off-chance of scoring a goal. He had promised that he would do this but he could hardly have anticipated that it would have been a goal of this quality.

The one-way traffic continued. There was a moment of laughter when Barnsley brought on a substitute by the name of Jonathan Macken. Some people with imperfect hearing thought that the PA man described him as Jonathan 'Mackem', but the poor man made no difference.

Newcastle's fifth goal, in the 69th minute, was a strange one. It was a free-kick from some considerable distance, taken by Danny Guthrie. It was one of those strange free-kicks that seemed to deceive everyone and simply drifted into the net. As the Barnsley defence blamed each other, it became apparent that no Newcastle player had managed to touch the ball and therefore it was Guthrie's second long-range goal of the game.

Two minutes later and it was 6–0. This time it was skipper Kevin Nolan who scored, picking up a flicked header from Andy Carroll, rounding the goalkeeper and popping the ball into the net before running across and punching a corner flag in celebration. It was different from putting on a Spiderman mask, but the goal was no less celebrated by the Newcastle faithful, who could not believe what they were seeing. It was a long time since they had last seen a Newcastle side playing like that, an even better performance than the defeat of Cardiff City a month previously.

The goal tally could have been more as more chances were created, and Lovenkrands was unfortunate not to have his hat-trick when his header from Jonas Gutierrez's cross hit the inside of a post, and he was also in a good position to score if Fabrice Pancrate had passed to him rather than trying to score himself.

Such things were forgiven by the Geordie faithful, some of whom were even prepared to be magnanimous and cheer Barnsley's late consolation goal when substitute Bogdanovich took advantage of some hesitation between Simpson and Coloccini to score a good goal. It was really a rather bad goal for the Newcastle defence to lose, but at this stage of the game and of the season it hardly mattered.

Newcastle finished the game now eight points clear of their nearest challengers, Notts Forest, with 12 games of the season left. Even the most pessimistic of Newcastle fans, inured to heartbreak, had now to feel a shaft of sunlight appearing, as they trudged to their cars, buses and trains. Promotion and the Championship were now there for Newcastle to grasp – or to throw away.

Barnsley's manager Mark Robins would claim, not without justification, that but for the red card it would have been a different game. Yet that ignores the fact that Newcastle were clearly the better team even in the first half when it was 11 versus 11. It would also have been difficult to imagine any team in the Championship and even several in the Premier League able to cope with the Toon on that performance.

The euphoria continued in the city for days afterwards, and supporters were now already contemplating life once again in the Premier League where they should have been all along. It was also felt that it was time that Chris Hughton was getting the credit that he deserved. He had picked up the side at a time when they were on their knees with the crushing disappointment of relegation and a distinct doubt about what the future was likely to be with the ongoing uncertainty of the ownership of the club. But 'ownership' of Newcastle United is not really in doubt. There were over 40,000 of the owners there. The fans are the real owners or trustees of the club, and how they enjoyed themselves that day!

50

Date: 29 March 2010

NOTTINGHAM FOREST

Match: Championship **Venue: St James' Park**

Score: 2–0 **Attendance: 45,987**

Newcastle United:	Nottingham Forest:
Harper	Camp
Simpson	Perch
Coloccini	Wilson
Williamson	Morgan
Jose Enrique	Gunter
Routledge	Anderson
Guthrie	Moussi
Nolan	Cohen
Gutierrez	Tyson*
Lovenkrands**	Majewski**
Carroll*	Blackstock***
Ameobi*	McCleary*
Barton**	Earnshaw**
	McGoldrick***

Referee: A. Wiley, Staffordshire

The clocks had changed the day before, and one would have anticipated a fine spring evening on Monday 29 March. Not a bit of it! The weather was foul with heavy, driving rain, on occasion looking more like sleet and snow than rain, and although wiser counsel would have urged Geordies to stay at home or go to the pub to watch the game on Sky, an astonishing crowd of 45,987 turned up to the ground. Newcastle, with a good run of form behind them, were closing in on one of the automatic promotion spots, and they were up against the team that was third – Nottingham Forest.

Forest's Brian Clough-driven European glory days were clearly long behind them, but they and their supporters (and they had a sizeable travelling support with them) clearly felt that the Premier League was their natural habitat as well, and they too had had a good season, already guaranteed a Play-off spot. Like most teams, however, they would prefer to avoid those nail-biting occasions, however romanticised and lucrative they had been made by the TV companies. Their manager was a tough-spoken little Scotsman called Billy Davies, who had played for and managed Motherwell, then had managed Preston and Derby County before coming to Notts Forest in 2008. In his previous jobs he had been no stranger to the triumphs and disasters of Play-offs and was keen to avoid them.

Newcastle's manager, Chris Hughton, had earned consistent praise from inside and outside the Toon for his low-key approach to managing the club and the atmosphere of stability that he had brought to an organisation that craved peace and quiet after all the turmoil of the last decade and more. There were some fine players that Hughton had moulded together – Andy Carroll and his lookalike (from the top of the stands, at any rate) Jonas Gutierrez, Peter Lovenkrands, Danny Guthrie and in recent weeks Wayne Routledge, a man who had joined the club in the January window from Queen's Park Rangers.

But Newcastle would not be Newcastle if the self-destruct button had not been pressed at some point. This had happened a few days previously when details emerged of a training ground spat between Andy Carroll and defender Steve Taylor. It then became clear that it was a little more than the average difference of opinion. Taylor's jaw had been broken and he was out for the rest of the season. This was hardly Carroll's first involvement in unpleasant incidents – he was no stranger to the strong arm of the law – and speculation grew that strong action might be taken against him. Whatever strong action was taken by manager Chris Hughton remained behind closed doors and Carroll, a free-scoring forward, retained his place in the team for the Doncaster Rovers game and scored the only goal, his 16th of the season. Some newspapers, notably the national heavies the *Guardian* and the *Daily Telegraph*, criticised Hughton for his failure to axe Carroll, but in the Toon itself it was generally perceived that the important thing was to win the Championship. Other things assumed less importance.

The word 'pragmatic' was used by many journalists to describe this. There seems little doubt that had Carroll been a less influential player, he might well have found himself facing a lengthy club suspension or perhaps even the boot, but Hughton, with the backing certainly of the fans and presumably the club establishment, decided that Carroll should be retained and that the feelings of Taylor should be sidelined. Taylor, perhaps predictably and understandably, immediately expressed a desire to leave the club. Whatever one's take on this issue, it remains a collector's item to showcase Newcastle's ability to attract the wrong sort of headlines.

Unbeaten at home this season, Newcastle started off playing towards the Gallowgate End in heavy rain. From the start it was a fine game. Sometimes, in circumstances when there is a great deal at stake, the standard of football suffers. Not here. Forest played open football as well, and although Newcastle were the better team in the first half, one would not have been totally astonished to see Forest score first.

Nolan missed a chance for Newcastle in the early stages, but the controversial moment of the first half came when Peter Lovenkrands went down in the box following a tackle by Forest defender James Perch. It looked like a penalty, but referee Mr Wiley (a man whose fitness had been questioned earlier in the season by Sir Alex Ferguson) said it was not, and TV replays of the incident would later indicate that it was a good tackle by Perch and a good decision by Mr Wiley.

That was of less significance in the long run, however, because the ball then ran to Andy Carroll, who, for some unaccountable reason and with over 40,000 Geordies shouting at him to pull the trigger, overplayed the ball, tried to get himself in a better position, thereby allowing more defenders to get back in position, and the chance was lost. If ever anyone needed an example of the old footballing maxim 'shoot first time' this was it.

Both teams went in at half time feeling that they had done themselves justice, and also both of them were aware that a goalless draw would not be the end of the world as far as their chances of playing in next season's Premier League were concerned. Forest felt that they too might have had a penalty when Radoslav Majewski was challenged by Mike Williamson.

Forest's best chance came at the start of the second half when, following a good move, Nathan Tyson got a clear header, but he could only direct the ball weakly to the hands of Steve Harper.

Soon after that, Andy Carroll, who had taken a knock in the first half, decided that he could not go on and was substituted by Shola Ameobi. It would be fair to say that the Nigerian, who had been with the club for well over a decade and was now approaching the veteran stage, had infuriated and delighted the fans in turn, but he remained a popular figure on Tyneside and this particular night he would show his fans just what he could do. It was his first appearance since 9 February, and the great cheer that greeted his appearance was an indication of just how popular the African was with the Geordie crowd.

His presence made an immediate difference to the team, and gradually Newcastle took a grip on what had been an even contest so far. Danny Guthrie, Kevin Nolan and particularly Wayne Routledge came into their own as Newcastle won more and more of the 50–50 balls in midfield and pressed forward for the goal that would make such a huge difference to the rain-soaked fans who had kept up their noise from the start.

Ameobi won a free-kick on the edge of the box, but Guthrie put the ball over the bar. The determined Newcastle kept pressing and it was Ameobi himself who put Newcastle ahead, and a fine goal it was. It was in the 70th minute, and although there was a touch of luck when a Forest clearance hit a defender on the heel and the ball rebounded to Nolan, there was nothing fortuitous about Nolan's pass to Ameobi on the left, nor Ameobi's brilliant manoeuvring of himself into position or his angled shot from the 18-yard line, which beat goalkeeper Lee Camp. It was his first goal since Boxing Day, but seldom had he scored a better or a more valuable goal for his club.

Newcastle were now very much in the ascendancy, and the excellent Camp was called upon to make several more saves as the rampant Geordies now pressed home their advantage. Routledge and Nolan both had chances, and as the game reached its closing stages it looked as if Newcastle would win the game 1–0 with the common and cliched addendum 'more comfortably than the scoreline would suggest'.

Not a person in the crowd, nor any of the vast TV audience could have predicted who was to score the next goal. The board had gone up indicating a minimum of four extra minutes to be played, and almost immediately after that came the glory day of Jose Enrique. The young Spaniard, such a ferocious tackler that he earned the nickname 'El Toro' or 'the bull', had been with Newcastle since 2007. He had taken a while to adapt to Newcastle – hardly surprising in the turmoil that prevailed there – but this season had shown a definite improvement with a willingness to move forward and join the attack on occasion. This was just one such occasion.

The goal followed a short corner, possibly designed to use up time rather than with any attacking intention, but the ball came to Ameobi, who back-heeled it to Jose Enrique inside the penalty area. Jose Enrique then waltzed past a man, found himself in a good position and shot home to put Newcastle 2–0 up. It was the first-ever goal of his footballing career, and he clearly considered it to be worth a booking, taking his shirt off to show to his female admirers his chest before he disappeared under a huge rugby scrum of delighted Newcastle supporters, who saw that promotion to the Premiership was now within touching distance. He later told NUTV that he couldn't breathe under there but didn't care!

The game finished soon after that, and the city celebrated as if promotion was already won. In truth, there was a certain way to go yet, but it did not seem as if there was going to be much to stop Newcastle from regaining their rightful place in the top tier of English football. Chris Hughton was rightly delighted with what had happened and said that the celebration of the goal was an indication of the tremendous team spirit that the team had. Not for the first time that season, the fans of Newcastle United were beginning to sense that payback time for the sufferings of the past few seasons was approaching.

It would be a very happy Easter for the Toon. Newcastle beat bottom-placed Peterborough on the Saturday, and by the time that they lined up to play Sheffield United on the night of Easter Monday they knew that they were already in next year's Premier League, because Notts Forest had only drawn. It was thus carnival night at St James' Park even before the game started, but they gilded the lily by beating Sheffield United as well to give the city one of its happiest nights for a very long time.